13·95

Modern drama in theory and practice    Volume 3

Expressionism and epic theatre

2004

By the same author

*The Elements of Drama*
*The Dark Comedy*
*The Dramatic Experience*
*Shakespeare's Stagecraft*
*Chekhov in Performance*
*The Challenge of the Theatre*
*Drama, Stage and Audience*
*The Shakespeare Revolution*

# Modern drama in theory and practice

VOLUME 3

## Expressionism and epic theatre

J.L.STYAN

*Franklyn Bliss Snyder Professor of English Literature and Professor of Theatre*
*Northwestern University, Emeritus*

CAMBRIDGE
UNIVERSITY PRESS

Published by the Press Syndicate of the University of Cambridge
The Pitt Building, Trumpington Street, Cambridge CB2 1RP
40 West 20th Street, New York, NY 10011-4211, USA
10 Stamford Road, Oakleigh, Melbourne, 3166, Australia

© Cambridge University Press 1981

First published 1981
First paperback edition 1983
Reprinted 1985, 1986, 1988, 1990, 1991, 1993

Printed in Malta by Interprint Ltd

*Library of Congress Cataloguing in Publication Data*

Styan, J. L.
Modern drama in theory and practice.

Includes bibliographies and index.
CONTENTS: 1. Realism – 2. Symbolism, surrealism,
and the absurd. – 3. Expressionism and epic theatre.
1. Drama – History – 20th century. 2. Theatre –
History – 20th century. I. Title.
PN1861. S76   809.2   79 – 15947
ISBN 0 521 22737 2 volume 1 hardback
ISBN 0 521 29628 5 volume 1 paperback
ISBN 0 521 22738 0 volume 2 hardback
ISBN 0 521 29629 3 volume 2 paperback
ISBN 0 521 22739 9 volume 3 hardback
ISBN 0 521 29630 7 volume 3 paperback
ISBN 0 521 23068 3 set of 3 volumes, hardback

# Contents

*The dates are usually those of the production*

# Illustrations

# Acknowledgements

The author and publisher gratefully acknowledge the permission of the following to reproduce their illustrations in this book: National Film Archive, Stills Library/Atlas Films International, London (1); The archives of the Max Reinhardt Research and Memorial Institute, Salzburg (2, 3, 4 and 19); Drottingholms Teatermuseum, Stockholm (5 and 6); Nordiska Museet, Stockholm (7); Schauspielhaus, Zurich —photo W. E. Baur (8); Beata Bergström, Stockholm (9); Hamlyn Group Picture Library, ©SPADEM, Paris, 1980 (10); Historisches Museum der Stadt Wien, © SPADEM, Paris, 1980 (11); photos, Denis Calandra, Department of Theatre, University of S. Florida, reprinted from *Theatre Quarterly*, VI, 21, 1976 (12 and 13); Theatermuseum des Instituts für Theaterwissenschaft der Universität Koln (14, 15, 32 and 33); from Macgowan and Jones, *Continental Stagecraft*, Benn Brothers, 1923 (16 and 20); Ullstein, West Berlin (17 and 37); Society for Cultural Relations with the USSR, London (21); Trustees of the British Museum (22 and 23); Norris Houghton, from *Return Engagement* (24); Louis Sheaffer Collection (25); Collection, The Museum of Modern Art, New York (27 and 34); New York Public Library (26, 28, 29 and 30); Raymond Mitchenson and Joe Mander Theatre Collection, London (18 and 31); Bildarchiv Preussischer Kulturbesitz (35, 36, 38 and 39); Hildegard Steinmitz, Munich (40); Günter Englert, Frankfurt (42); Chelsea Theater Center New York. Photo Amnon Ben Norris (41); from *Theatre Arts Monthly*, 1938 (43); Dominic, London (44); Roger Mayne, Dorset (45) and Chris Davies, London (46).

# *Preface*

It is a principle increasingly accepted that the manner of playwriting is inseparable from the kind of theatre it is written for. The new attempt of this study is to look at some of the important plays of modern times, not as isolated literary works, but in relation to their production and performance. The intention is to trace some of the interactions between playwright and performing artist (this term to include all who are involved in production: actors and directors, lighting and scenic designers), and the subject of the study is, in the widest sense, the bearing of theory on practice, and of practice on theory. Like any art form, drama is sometimes aroused by fitful rebellion, but it always builds upon the testing of ideas on an audience and the total theatre experience of the past.

The story of the theatre is one of rebellion and reaction, with new forms challenging the old, and old forms in turn providing the basis for the new. But the labels we use, realism, symbolism, and so on, too easily blanket the details of dramatic and stage history. These details are not often found in the laws of playwriting or in the manifestoes of fashionable movements, but remain to be extracted from the day-to-day dealings of the stage. We must judge less by intentions than by results, aware that theory and practice are more often in conflict than in accord: in John Gassner's words, we must recognize 'the breach between ambition and attainment'. It is necessary to turn to the promptbook and the acting edition, the *Regiebuch* and the *Modellbuch*, to notices and criticism, interviews and memoirs, as well as to the text of the play itself, to know what happened.

To adapt a concept of the art historian, E. H. Gombrich, drama originates in our reactions to the world, and not in the world itself. By this argument, the changes which an audience perceives on the stage between, say, the grim naturalism of a *Lower Depths* and the violent fantasies of Edward Bond, are changes in itself. The abiding secret of dramatic interpretation lies in its 'style', the *way of seeing* of writer, player or spectator, and style is the one ingredient, it must be supposed, which a play and its performance should ideally have in common, since it is the *sine qua non* of dramatic communication. Moreover, if an artist's perception of reality is conditioned by the age he lives in and by the medium he works with, an understanding of style will supply some of the clues to both. This study, therefore, concerned as it is with the limitations and possibilities of drama since Büchner and Wagner, Zola and Ibsen, may afford an insight into ourselves and our modes of perception.

The threads of many different styles, however, are interwoven within a single play in performance. This is especially true of this century, which can draw upon a multitude of conventions from the 'imaginary museum'. In practice, it is impossible to find a play of, say, naked realism or pure symbolism, and the best playwrights are constantly resourceful: Ibsen is a realist and a symbolist, Strindberg embraces both naturalism and expressionism, in writing a symbolist drama Pirandello becomes a progenitor of the absurd, Weiss arranges Artaudian cruelty within a Brechtian epic frame and so on. Theatre artists are similarly elastic: Meyerhold, the originator of constructivism, produced the outstanding *Inspector General*, Jouvet showed himself master of Molière as well as of *La Machine infernale*, Barrault produced a fine *Phèdre* and was also superbly sensitive to Chekhov.

A final explanation. In order to follow a clearer path through a jungle of detail, *Modern Drama* is presented as three extended essays on realism, symbolism and expressionism, with developments in the last two into surrealism, absurdism and epic theatre. Discussions focus upon those landmark productions of modern times in order to be as specific as possible. In one way, it may seem unfortunate that these essays appear separately, artificially dividing the total theatrical scene; yet, in tracing the several competing structures of signals and responses between stage and audience, it is remarkable what continuities are revealed. At all events, my hope is to provide another aid towards a properly stage-centred dramatic criticism, using performance equally with theory as the basis for a history of the stage.

I am grateful to a Fellowship from the National Endowment for the Humanities of the United States, as well as to Northwestern University, for giving me the opportunity to write this study. I also owe a great debt to the British Library, the Colindale Newspaper Library, the Victoria and Albert Museum and the British Theatre Centre, as well as to the Ford Curtis Theatre Collection of the Hillman Library of the University of Pittsburgh and to the Library of Northwestern University. Robert Schneideman of Northwestern University, Leonard Powlick of Wilkes-Barre University and John and Barbara Cavanagh of Mottisfont Abbey have been of material assistance to me. Grateful acknowledgement is made to Edward Braun and Methuen and Co. Ltd., for permission to quote from *Meyerhold on Theatre*. The staff of Cambridge University Press have been of great help from beginning to end. A larger kind of debt is owed to the scholarship of countless fine students of the modern drama, and to the creative work of an even greater number of theatre artists.

J. L. S.

# 1 Expressionism in the theatre

In the view of the art critic Herbert Read, expressionism is 'one of the basic modes of perceiving and representing the world around us'. Asked what he expected of expressionism in the theatre, the ordinary playgoer is likely to be vague. In realism, he might say, actors sit about on chairs and talk about the weather, but in expressionism they stand on them and shout about the world. The reason is not far to seek. Of all the dramatic modes of this century, none has proved more accommodating, but the one element common to all expressionistic plays is a rigorous anti-realism. Expressionism began as a form of windy neo-romanticism and grew to be a hard-headed, dialectical kind of realism. Certainly it is today associated, as it will be in this book, with more than the youthful German drama of the 1910s that gave it birth, and even current epic theatre has retained strong formal links with the very expressionism against which it rebelled. Today, the term is generally applied after the fact, and is often better defined by the play to which it is applied than by the critic who applies it. Nevertheless, in its basic techniques it has been an enduring thread of great strength and vitality in the story of modern drama, binding such giants as Strindberg and O'Neill, Brecht and O'Casey.

The term was first applied to painting. It was thought to have been coined by the French painter Julien-Auguste Hervé in 1901, but John Willett has since found it in use half-a-century before then. In the 1900s it was a useful word to distinguish early impressionist painting from the more energetic individualism of Van Gogh and Matisse, each of whom refused to render exactly what he saw, in order, Van Gogh said, 'to express himself with force'. Where the impressionist tried to paint external reality, the expressionist insisted on conveying his private experience, his inner idea or vision, of what he saw. The expressionist flatly rejected any realistic style as being obvious imitation: he was not interested in objective reality, and he refused to be wedded to surface detail. Beyond this, expressionism in painting had no aesthetic philosophy as had naturalism and symbolism in literature. The new expressionist was defiantly subjective, imposing his own intense, and often eccentric, view of the world on what he painted. In the theatre, such subjectivity can keep an audience critically alert, but if it is too private, the reason may reject it entirely.

As so often, a useful general term is shared by other art forms. 'Expressionism' was soon applied to music, architecture, poetry (typically to imagistic, lyric verse — parts of Eliot's poem 'The Waste Land' might stand as an example) and fiction (we may think of Joyce's *Ulysses* with its 'Nighttown' episode, or the nightmarish stories of Kafka), but it was especially at home with the drama. 'Impressionism' had been a suitable term to apply to the novel where it described a technique which conveyed the author's own selective sense of reality, but it could not be usefully applied to the more objective elements of drama. Now the stage had a term which could identify any play or production that departed from realism and showed life in a highly personal, idiosyncratic manner, the form of the play 'expressing' its content, and it was particularly applicable to the perfervid movement which gripped the German theatre in the 1910s and early 1920s.

Only afterwards were the characteristics of expressionism recognized in forerunners like Büchner, Strindberg and Wedekind, and these were claimed as the new masters. The style spread sporadically through Europe, appearing in the work of the brothers Čapek in Czechoslovakia, Lenormand in France and O'Casey in Ireland. In America, its enthusiastic adoption by O'Neill also encouraged experiments by Rice, Wilder, Williams and Miller. It resulted in a few outstanding German films, among them Robert Wiene's *The Cabinet of Dr. Caligari* (1919) and Fritz Lang's *Metropolis* (1926); both of these films are worth seeing if only for the record of early expressionist styles they preserve. Through the greater skills of Kaiser and Toller, the movement became more disciplined, and it flourished anew with a radical variation in the plays of Bertolt Brecht, whose 'epic' manner in turn touched the quasi-absurdist drama of the Swiss playwrights Frisch and Dürrenmatt. The lively

conventions of expressionism have now become part
upon which the contemporary dramatist can draw.

   Ideologically, expressionism in the German thea.__ was at
first a drama of protest, reacting against the pre-war authority of
the family and community, the rigid lines of the social order and
eventually the industrialization of society and the mechanization of
life. It was a violent drama of youth against age, freedom against
authority. Following Nietzsche, it glorified the individual and idealized the creative personality. On top of this, the advent of Freudian
and Jungian psychology in the first quarter of the century constituted a challenge to the playwright to disclose and reproduce his secret
and hidden states of mind. Then the impact of the First World War
and its mass slaughter of men in the trenches began to undermine
the personal and subjective content of the new expressionism, and
hastened the introduction of a more sophisticated concern for man

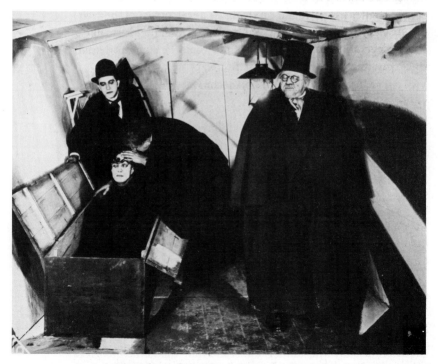

1. *The Cabinet of Dr Caligari*, Germany, 1919. Film directed by
Robert Wiene.

and society; at which point, expressionist drama assumed a politically radical and Marxist temper.

An early example of a play which in 1922 caused a furore in the expressionist theatre was Arnolt Bronnen's *Vatermord (Parricide)*, which he had written as early as 1915. In this play, the new rebellion is expressed by having a young man make love to his mother and stab his father. Here was a crude dramatization of Freudian thinking, but, as the author explained, he was not attempting to write what could be *seen*, only what he *felt* — nothing objective, all subjective. Needless to say, that explanation in no way lessened the sensation intended and the shock taken. 'Man screams from the depths of his soul', wrote Hermann Bahr in *Expressionismus* (1916); 'the whole age becomes one single, piercing shriek. Art screams too, into the deep darkness, screams for help, for the spirit' (translated R. S. Furness). Thus in its early stages expressionist drama was a dramatization of the subconscious, a kind of scripted dream, with the consequent loss of character motivation and rational plot development of the well-made play. This loss, however, did not necessarily imply a surrealistic formlessness: a play's true, inner unity could be supplied by the single vision of the dreamer himself.

Particular characteristics and techniques became associated with the early expressionist play:

1. *Its atmosphere* was often vividly dreamlike and nightmarish. This mood was aided by shadowy, unrealistic lighting and visual distortions in the set. A characteristic use of pause and silence, carefully placed in counterpoint with speech and held for an abnormal length of time, also contributed to the dream effect.

2. *Settings* avoided reproducing the detail of naturalistic drama, and created only those starkly simplified images the theme of the play called for. The décor was often made up of bizarre shapes and sensational colours.

3. *The plot and structure* of the play tended to be disjointed and broken into episodes, incidents and tableaux, each making a point of its own. Instead of the dramatic conflict of the well-made play, the emphasis was on a sequence of dramatic statements made by the dreamer, usually the author himself. From this structure grew Brecht's epic theatre, also a drama of episodes and demonstrations, although these were arranged to stimulate the intelligence of the

audience, and not to appeal to the emotions as in expressionist drama.

4. *Characters* lost their individuality and were merely identified by nameless designations, like 'The Man', 'The Father', 'The Son', 'The Workman', 'The Engineer', and so on. Such characters were stereotypes and caricatures rather than individual personalities, and represented social groups rather than particular people. In their impersonality, they could appear grotesque and unreal, and the mask was reintroduced to the stage as a 'primary symbol' of the theatre: 'It is unchangeable, inescapable', wrote Yvan Goll; 'it is Fate.'

5. *The dialogue*, unlike conversation, was poetical, febrile, rhapsodic. At one time it might take the form of a long lyrical monologue, and at another, of staccato telegraphese — made up of phrases of one or two words or expletives. The lines made no attempt to obey the laws of Pirandello's 'spoken action', in which the words directed the actor's movement and gesture, but they tried instead to evoke sympathetic feeling directly.

6. *The style of acting* was a deliberate departure from the realism of Stanislavsky. Moreover, in avoiding the detail of human behaviour, a player might appear to be overacting, and adopting the broad, mechanical movements of a puppet. All of this lent a sense of burlesque to the image of life presented on the stage, a quality which was suitable for certain kinds of comedy, like Gogol's *The Inspector General*, but which had soon to be modified for more solemn material.

Paul Kornfeld (1889–1942), the Czech dramatist who later became Reinhardt's *dramaturg*, assumed the role of spokesman for the movement, and the 'Epilogue to the Actor' which in 1913 he appended to his play *Die Verführung (The Seduction)*, may be read as the manifesto of expressionist acting. Kornfeld coined the term '*Seelendrama*', 'drama of the soul', believing that realistic character psychology was miserably earthbound, and that 'the soul pertained to Heaven'. The actor should therefore play accordingly:

> Let him dare to stretch his arms out wide and with a sense of soaring speak as he has never spoken in life; let him not be an imitator or seek his models in a world alien to the actor. In short, let him not be ashamed of the fact that he is acting.

Let him not deny the theatre or try to feign reality (translated Joseph M. Bernstein).

A real human being was too complicated a creature, had too many memories, Kornfeld argued, to be able to 'externalize' himself; by contrast, the expressionist actor was free to pick out 'the essential attributes of reality', and to be 'nothing but a representative of thought, feeling or fate'.

The actor was not the only one to enjoy a new freedom from the restrictions of realism. Since so much of the subjective impulse behind an expressionist play was left unspoken and unseen, the director and his scenic and lighting designers were afforded opportunities for creative experiment they had not known in the production of realistic drama. A period of unusual flowering in the theatre arts followed in the 1920s, and the German theatre alone produced a unique generation of directors of international standing, among them Reinhardt, Jessner, Piscator, Feuchtwanger, as well as Brecht himself. The ingenuity of these men in turn encouraged an exceptional interchange between playwright and theatre artist in this period.

However, the movement in German expressionist drama as originally conceived died soon after it was born. So idealistic and sentimental a treatment of life could not long survive in a theatre which, since Goethe and Schiller, had traditionally played a serious social role. But certain external elements of expressionism lived on in the work of greater writers who acquired a more purposeful philosophy of the stage. With new discipline in the work of Reinhardt, Piscator and Brecht, the German theatre struggled to become an instrument for social change. Epic theatre, as we shall see, removed the emotional appeal of expressionism, and told a more sober story.

The reversal was felt in Brecht's first play, *Baal* (1918). Although this remained Dionysiac and to a degree poetic, it deliberately undercut the idea of the youthful poet as the martyr among materialists, and appeared to be a parody of Hanns Johst's play *Der Einsame* (*The Lonely One*), written only the year before on the romantic subject of the dissipated nineteenth-century writer Christian Dietrich Grabbe. Brecht's second play, *Trommeln in der Nacht* (*Drums in the Night*, 1922), went even further, and undermined the idealism of revolution. So it was that the expressionist movement was quickly stripped of its sentimentality and, under a different banner, became the leading anti-romantic force in the modern theatre. If something of the scandalous subject-matter remained, the frenzied, strident tone, the easy mysticism and the almost religious fervour of the early German expressionists were not heard again. In any case, their anti-establishment attitude could not long have withstood the authoritarian rule of the Nazis.

## 2 *Forerunners of expressionism: Büchner*

*Danton's Death* (1902), *Woyzeck* (1913)

The German expressionists had not exactly invented a new form of drama, because they were working in the shadow of three great predecessors. Lyrical plays of social criticism, satire and protest which fell well outside the naturalistic movement existed before the 1910s in the work of Büchner, Wedekind and Strindberg. All three had conceived forms of expressionism before its time of fruition, with all three achieving full recognition for their innovations rather late. This is especially true of Büchner, who has in recent years been claimed as a model by a wide variety of playwrights from the surrealistic to the politically realistic and documentary.

Georg Büchner (1813–37) died of typhoid fever at the age of twenty-three, without having seen any of his plays produced, and long before any modern movement in the theatre had been conceived. But his brief years of playwriting anticipated so many techniques of modern expressionism that it has been a commonplace to name him at the first modern playwright. Since the first production of *Dantons Tod* (*Danton's Death*) was not seen until 1902, and that of his masterpiece *Woyzeck* until 1913, it is right to place him squarely at the beginning of the expressionist movement, when his work, like Wedekind's, was fortunate to catch the interest of Max Reinhardt, the German master of the theatre in the early years of the century.

The question remains why it took a hundred years for others to follow
Büchner's initiative and take up his experiments, and part of the
answer lies in the fact that these would have been as startling in
the nineteenth century as they were in the twentieth.

   In all his playwriting, Büchner tried to find new ways of
expressing his fatalistic perception of society and events, and of
substantiating his view that 'the individual is no more than foam on
a wave'. He was an active reformist and a member of *Das junge
Deutschland*, the 'Young Germany' movement, and in 1833 he was the
author of an early communist manifesto in *The Hessian Peasants'
Messenger*. Moreover, the brutal repressive measures of the authorities left him totally disillusioned. Therefore, for his first literary
subject, he chose the unhappy story of the French revolutionary
leader, Georges Danton, who became the victim of his own revolution at the hands of Robespierre. Danton, with a disgust like
Büchner's own, died recognizing that the people for whom he had
fought were little better off than before any blood had been spilled.
Büchner wrote *Danton's Death* in five weeks in 1835, when it was
published in a cautiously amended version with a subtitle supplied
by the publisher, 'Dramatic Pictures from the Reign of Terror'; the
original was not published until 1850.

   *Danton's Death* is an amazingly accomplished first play. As the
French Revolution fails, so the Reign of Terror succeeds. The 'incor-
ruptible' Robespierre, the apparent pattern of virtue, has become the
head of the notorious Committee for Public Safety, which was first
created to defend the principles of the Revolution. Robespierre
grows viciously puritanical, and orders more and more executions.
Danton, who had successfully raised the armies of the Revolution,
has become bitter about politics, and his services to the country are
forgotten. The opposite of the austere Robespierre, Danton is pictured
as a remorseful sensualist sickened by the bloodshed he has witnessed, and wishing that the Revolution could be humanized. He
seems to long for oblivion:

> I'm making eyes at death. How charming to coquette with
> her from a distance, through a quizz-glass! (translated
> Geoffrey Dunlop)

For Danton, political action is futile, and he allows himself to be denounced, condemned and executed. Neither of the principal characters is without virtue, neither without vice; and so the play ends ambiguously. Its sheer pessimism was no doubt another reason why it did not get a production until the twentieth century.

The ambiguity is managed by generally cutting from Danton to Robespierre and back again, so that the form of the play resembles a debate between those who hold opposite views — we should recognize such a form today as 'dialectical'. The episodic nature of the play's construction anticipates the techniques of the cinema, and echoes Shakespeare's method of swift changes of scene and mood. Act I, scene 2 in *Danton's Death*, indeed, seems to borrow from the scene in *Julius Caesar* in which the citizens of Rome attack Cinna the poet, the tone dropping from high rhetoric to street invective as an impersonal crowd torments a 'Young Man' who is merely blowing his nose:

> VOICES. Look at him! He's got a handkerchief! That's an
>   aristo! Up with him — over to the lantern — up!
> SECOND CITIZEN. Why can't he use his fingers? Hang him up!
> (*A lantern is let down.*)
> YOUNG MAN. Gentlemen!
> CITIZEN. 'Gentlemen' — what? There aren't any. You're the
>   last. Up he goes!
> *Some sing*:   Those that rot below the ground
>         Slowly by the worms are found;
>         Better far to swing on high
>         Than a lazy death to die.

In this way the incident is coarsely lyricized by songs which anticipate Brecht's ballads, and the whole is ingeniously framed by an irrelevant quarrel between a man and his wife, enough to touch in the Parisian atmosphere of common life which continues uninterrupted through the atrocities. Later scenes in street or prison are enriched by the presence of characters chosen to add local colour: a ballad singer, a soldier and his whore, a lady and her gallant, as well as gaolers, carters, grisettes and executioners.

The style of the dialogue does not maintain classical consistency, but ranges boldly from the vernacular to a vigorous cynicism laced with gritty imagery:

— Robespierre needs the Revolution for a class-room, to
give lectures on morals. The guillotine's his teaching-
desk.
— Praying-hassock!
— He'll end by lying on it instead of kneeling.

At the climax of Danton's death, the play bears the marks of the
romantic drama which is its literary and historical context, and yet
its spirit remains surprisingly modern. At bottom it is dispassionate,
and distanced by a tone that Carl Mueller believes to belong to the
self-conscious theatre of non-illusion, as when Danton remarks,
'We are always on the stage, even though we are finally stabbed in
earnest.' The word for this game with audience current today is
'metatheatre'.

The performance of *Danton's Death* in 1902 was only for a single
matinee at the Neue Freie Volksbühne in Berlin, and it did not have
a fair test until 1913 in Munich. There the revolve of the Residenz
Theater suited the rapid sequence of the play's scenes, and captured
the rhythm of the whole. Max Reinhardt's celebrated Berlin productions were at the Deutsches Theater in 1916 and the Grosses
Schauspielhaus in 1921, with Ernst Stern as his designer and
Alexander Moissi as Danton. Reinhardt's productions were heavy
with the use of light and shadow, and his penchant for crowd scenes
rather blurred the roles of the protagonists, Danton and Robespierre.
Where Büchner's Parisians supply a simple period background, in
Reinhardt's hands they became a revolutionary force in themselves,
and with actors judiciously placed in the auditorium, the crowds
seemed to expand to include the audience itself. No audience objected
to such treatment, and Reinhardt's skill as a director ensured that
Büchner's reputation as a classic German playwright was per-
manently established.

Through the 1920s, *Danton's Death* became a popular choice
as a play for politically inclined audiences, although the more revolutionary productions smothered Danton's ambiguity in order to
enhance Robespierre's arguments. Reinhardt continued to make
spectacular use of the French citizenry, and even inserted passages
from the more obvious and romantic *Danton* of Romain Rolland.
Needless to say, the revolutionary motif was played down in

Germany after the accession of Hitler in 1933, and again in the desperate years following the end of the Second World War in 1945. The characteristic spirit of the play did not return until the angry decade of the 1960s.

Reinhardt's production visited New York in 1927, but as the performance was in German, the director of the play was more the object of admiration than its author. A moody production of the play was presented by Orson Welles's Mercury Theatre in 1939, a production which failed for lack of support from the Communist Party, who saw in Robespierre and Danton an unwelcome parallel with Stalin and Trotsky. At the New Theatre, London in 1971, the National Theatre company produced the play with Christopher Plummer as Danton and Charles Kay as Robespierre. Patrick Robinson's set consisted of a number of museum cases, some of which displayed the effigies of aristocrats, and Jonathan Miller's direction denied the play its force by requiring the actors to behave chillingly like puppets with white faces and monotonous voices. Not only in London, but also in Milan, with Giorgio Strehler directing, techniques of production of which Büchner knew nothing have been applied to the challenging material of this play, and on occasion over-stylization has distracted attention from its human detail.

Possibly because of its allegorical nature, less interest has been shown in Büchner's comic folk-tale *Leonce und Lena*, written in 1836 and published in 1850. The light-hearted story is of the jaded and pessimistic Prince Leonce of Popo, who must endure a marriage of convenience with his opposite, the optimistic Princess Lena of Pipi, neither party having seen the other. However, they meet each other by accident, and fall in love and marry without having discovered each other's identity. Together they choose to build a Utopia to replace the old system. This romantic theme is undercut by harsh poetry, and in the guise of a deceptive folk-story Büchner is able to introduce politics into his play.

In recent years an imaginative production of *Leonce und Lena* has come from the Bulandra Theatre in Bucharest, where it was directed by Liviu Ciulei. This production toured Europe and was seen at the Edinburgh Festival in 1974. Ciulei also revived his production with American actors for the Arena Theatre in Washington,

DC in 1975, its first professional production in America. The stage was set with draped metal scaffolding, arranged to recall a *commedia dell'arte* scene to match a *commedia* element in the text, and the performance was presented in the burlesque style known as 'high camp'. The content of the play was somewhat obscured by clowning devices, including comic chase scenes, the mocking repetition of chosen lines and many modish exchanges with the audience. Such ingenious tricks suggest that the director considers the play to be too simple to be interesting without them.

Büchner's most extraordinary achievement was the unfinished *Woyzeck*. This unique play was written in 1836, and discovered, deciphered and published in 1879, its first editor reviving the faded manuscript with chemicals. It consisted of about twenty-seven unnumbered and unsorted scenes, with almost as many variant fragments, and editors and directors have been shuffling them like a pack of cards ever since. The play's expressionistic episodes are far less logical than those in *Danton's Death*, and so the author's original order will probably never be know.

The material of the play was based upon the true and sordid case of a regimental barber in Leipzig who stabbed his mistress in a fit of jealousy and was sentenced to death. The critical question whether Woyzeck was sane or insane provided Büchner with the idea of a dialectical play, and permitted him to pursue more subtly his pessimistic philosophy of determinism. *Woyzeck* became the brutal tale of a simple soldier, a Chaplinesque creature of pathetic dignity and sensibility, but since he was also inarticulate, he was a kind of early 'anti-hero'. Mocked and tormented on all sides, Woyzeck is driven to cut his wife's throat before he himself dies.

Woyzeck's world is peopled by soldiers and trollops, apprentices and children, policemen and peasants, all using the language of the streets and singing ballads. Each of the episodes in the play is a demonstration of how some force, social, religious or military, affects Woyzeck's actions — a plan that would have appealed to the naturalists later in the century, since the play shows how the central character is the victim of a society over which he has no control. Indeed, life is a torment for poor Woyzeck. He is beaten and humiliated by his rival the Drum Major, used for dietary experiments by the regimental doctor, and considered to be a fine joke as a cuckold by his commanding officer the Captain.

In one scene, at a fair, animals are dressed like grotesque people, suggesting that man is only an animal too. A monkey dressed like an officer walks on his hind legs and fires a pistol, and a donkey dressed as a professor of philosophy urinates before the assembled crowd. When the Doctor asserts that man at least has the power of free will, Woyzeck is ironically unable to control his bladder, and urinates against a wall. As in *Danton's Death*, the dialogue is shot through with racy obscenities which were totally unconventional on the German stage, and it is possible that Brecht took this dramatic feature for his own plays.

In another scene, Woyzeck stands at the window of an inn watching the Drum Major dance past with his wife, Marie:

> WOYZECK *clasps his hands.* Turn, turn – round, round. Go on. God, will you blow the sun out? Let it all run together and turn – all together – round, round, round, all in filth together. Men and women – humans and beasts. They do it in glaring day: they do it on your hands like flies do (translated Geoffrey Dunlop).

Finding that Marie is unfaithful to him, Woyzeck believes all men and women to be consumed by lust. So the utter purposelessness of his life becomes more and more obvious through an apparently casual sequence of episodes, until he is driven to murder. After he has killed his wife, he tries to wash the blood from his hands in a pond, into which he falls and is drowned – an ironic touch which underlines the cynical, ambiguous theme of the whole play.

The 'open' structure of Büchner's plays is his most striking and serviceable innovation. 'Parataxis', the juxtaposing of dramatic elements without an apparent link, was Shakespeare's imaginative method of scene arrangement, and it has become one of the film director's greatest resources after Eisenstein. It enabled Büchner to place his central characters in a montage of people and events, and by this method he could suggest his character's historical background and the fragmentation of his perception. The device is used so extensively in *Woyzeck* that it must account for much of the difficulty the scholars have had in arranging the scenes of the play in a satisfactory order. In this play in particular, the Aristotelian causal sequence is completely replaced by a series of dramatic incidents, each having some psychological or symbolic importance in itself. A scene might tell some of the story, but it could equally well bring out a theme or motif and comment upon it. Thus, in what seems to be an irrelevant episode towards the end of the play, an Old Woman tells a tale of a poor orphan who finds the moon to be a piece of wood, the sun a dried-up flower, the stars nothing more than dead flies, and the earth itself a chamber-pot turned upside down. This is a scene of direct symbolism, here intended, it may be supposed, to extend the mood of disillusion and loneliness represented by Woyzeck himself. This kind of rapid, serial presentation of scenes became one of the outstanding marks of modern expressionism on the stage.

The first production of *Woyzeck* was in 1913 at the Residenz Theater, Munich, where again the revolve served the play's structure well, and Albert Steinrück successfully brought the soldier Woyzeck to life. The audience was surprised that the play was so stageworthy, and, taking Büchner for some new author of the avant-garde, it exultantly hissed its disapproval in the expected way – a response taken to be the best compliment the play could have received.

Reinhardt's production at the Deutsches Theater, Berlin, in 1921, designed by John Heartfield and Franz Dworsky, with Eugen Klöpfer in the title part, again had the advantage of a revolve. It was played in a nightmarish and claustrophobic setting of black curtains, with a few props to suggest a change of scene as needed. Most important, this production managed to keep a good deal of naturalistic detail among the larger symbolism of character and event, and the critic Julius Hart made a note of the contrast with the performance at Munich:

> There was in Steinrück's performance a dangerous and threatening force, a rebellion and revolution, and the red flags waved. Eugen Klöpfer's suffering Job, groaning in misery and flailed by despair, seems to me to grasp more penetratingly and intimately Georg Büchner's man, who is rooted, finally, only in love and pity, and for whom even a French Revolution does not mean liberation and deliverance (translated David G. Richards).

The contrast was between a pre-war and a post-war mood. For Reinhardt's post-war production, the emphasis was on the play's submerged sense of suffering, and not on its political element. The enduring humanity of the play for the twentieth century was confirmed by its becoming the source for Alban Berg's misnamed opera *Wozzeck* in 1925, and being listed among the likely subjects chosen by Artaud in his first manifesto for a theatre of cruelty in 1938.

In recent years, the unfinished and fragmentary nature of the *Woyzeck* text has encouraged a freely experimental approach to the expressionistic production of the play. Each director assumes a licence to arrange Büchner's building blocks differently to meet his own perception of the play's theme. He works out a new montage of scenes, tries new juxtapositions, and so creates new meanings from the same material. This directorial licence has also been encouraged by the play's non-Aristotelian characteristics. Woyzeck himself is central only as the apparent source of the play's vision, and, with the large number of characters around him, there is no conventional character development. Nor is the 'plot' itself more than sketchy, and it does nothing to bind the parts of the play together. Thus a new director of *Woyzeck* has the choice of several possible points of departure. For example, Woyzeck's flat statement of his own identity

> I am Friedrich . . . Johann . . . Franz Woyzeck, private.
> Fusilier, Second Regiment, Second Battalion, Fourth Company. Born on the Day of the Annunciation. . .

may suggest the cold surface appearance beneath which the army, society and the soldier's personal life are stewing, as the rest of the play could show. Or the choric parable of the poor orphan spoken by the Old Woman to Marie and the children may be used to prefigure the madness which Woyzeck encounters in the play, and her speech could stand at the beginning of the action rather than at the end. Or the curtain could rise on the scene of Woyzeck in the fields with his friend Andres, the scene in which the audience is given a vision of terror:

> This place is cursed. See that light streaking across the grass . . . Listen, Andres. Something's running. (*Stamps on the earth.*) Hollow! All hollow. A passage. Shaking. Listen! Something is moving underneath us. Can you hear? Underneath, moving with us . . . There's a fire running from earth

to heaven, and a sound with it like trumpets blaring ...
Silent! All silent again, as if the world was dead!

Such speech may also suggest that the action which follows is all in
Woyzeck's head tormenting him, and arranged to torment us accordingly.

The growth of Büchner's work in the esteem of playwrights
and directors is one of the special developments in the theatre of the
1920s. He attracted Ernst Toller by the timely timelessness of his
subjects and their treatment, which seemed to solve the tiresome
problem of reaching the public effectively with a political theme.
Büchner also attracted Brecht by providing him with a model for a
chronicle play: *Danton* and *Woyzeck* demonstrated that the narrative
element necessary to a history play did not have to fit into a well-
made mould, but could be presented first from one point of view,
then from another — dialectically. Brecht's debt to Büchner also
included the use of the ballad on the stage, a device which Brecht
wanted not only to make direct statements as by a chorus, but also
to distance the realistic material in the action. Büchner's use of
nameless figures to fill in the play's social background also served
Brecht, as did the sensational effect of the vernacular in the dialogue of the characters. Above all, Büchner's interest in the methods
of Shakespeare and Elizabethan stagecraft led Brecht himself towards
a productive study of Shakespeare's plays — a kindness that was
worth a hundred expressionist experiments.

---

# 3   *Forerunners of expressionism: Wedekind*

---

*Spring's Awakening* (1906), *The Lulu Plays* (1898, 1905)
Another enthusiastic follower of Georg Büchner was Frank
Wedekind (1864—1918). The tentative efforts of the young German
expressionists do not seem quite so revolutionary when set beside
the earlier work of the notorious Wedekind, who had been breaking
taboos and anticipating the outrageous stage effects of expressionism

some twenty years before. His playwriting, uneven though it was, daringly attacked the shams of bourgeois society and provocatively introduced hitherto unthinkable subjects to the stage. The chief of these was sex, and like Brecht and Genêt after him, he also made heroes of criminals and glamorized his prostitutes. Most important for our story, Wedekind's work was especially attractive to the young.

In about 1886, Wedekind had been introduced by Gerhart Hauptmann to Büchner's recently appreciated plays, and in his introduction to his translation of *The Lulu Plays*, Carl Mueller suggests that it was Büchner who furnished Wedekind with the stylistic devices he was looking for. These devices included ways to counteract realism, and consisted of 'fragmented dialogue, frenetic, episodic scenes, a distortion of natural phenomena to arrive at the true centre, and the disarmingly modern technique of isolation as seen in the tendency of characters to talk past rather than at one another'. On top of this, Wedekind's sexual obsessions supplied him with a theatrical imagery all his own.

Wedekind's first attempt at playwriting had dealt with the adolescent dreams of repressed young girls in a boarding school. The following year, *Frühlings Erwachen (Spring's Awakening, 1891)*, his first play in print, expressed the adolescent wonder and fear of sex in both girls and boys. Not unexpectedly, the stage history of this play has been one of constant battle with the censor. It was consequently not produced until 1906, when it was put on in a cut version in the Berlin Kammerspiele by Max Reinhardt, with the author himself playing the part of the Masked Man who appears in the last scene. This production ran for a record 321 performances, and after that Wedekind could not be ignored. The play was a reasonably honest and unsentimental treatment of puberty, to which it added a plea for toleration and for a recognition of the truths of nature. But for the audience of the time, the content of the play was too highly charged, and was considered unquestionably obscene. Although there is not a prurient line in it, Wedekind's reputation as a pornographer had begun, and because of the accusation of obscenity, the immediate influence of *Spring's Awakening* was limited. In the long term, however, it can be seen to have foreshadowed the better characteristics of the expressionist drama to come.

*Spring's Awakening* is the story of three children. One of them, Moritz, shoots himself in the head because of his failure at school and his ignorance and anxiety about his bodily functions. His friend Melchior gets fourteen-year-old Wendla pregnant, with the result that Melchior is sent to reform school and Wendla dies from the abortion forced on her by her mother. The cause of the girl's death is given as 'anaemia'. Thus does the mutual attraction of an adolescent boy and girl come to a tragic end when faced with an inflexible social code, represented by the pettiness and prudery of the parents and teachers who make up the adult world of the play. This account may suggest a strongly realistic technique in the play, but the final scene at Wendla's graveside is all fantasy. Moritz appears as a headless ghost and tries to persuade Melchior to take his own life as he did. At this point, an unknown Masked Man enters to symbolize the life force and to advise Melchior to continue the struggle. At the fall of the curtain, the forlorn little ghost of Moritz remains alone by the forlorn little grave of Wendla.

2. Wedekind, *Spring's Awakening*, 1891. Production by Max Reinhardt at the Kammerspiele, Berlin 1906. The graveyard scene, with Frank Wedekind as the Masked Man.

The play was an uncompromising attack on the values of bourgeois family life and morality, and especially its hypocrisy towards youthful sexuality. It is built of short episodes which constitute a loosely narrative structure. The dialogue is a consciously developed rhetoric, with the tender, lyrical speech of the children strictly contrasted with the stiff, declamatory speech of the older generation. The teachers have names like 'Gutgrinder', 'Bonebreaker', 'Tonguetwister', 'Flyswatter' and 'Thickstick', and at one point play out a scene of sheer farce that suits the unreality of their names. Such simplified characters can be played only in an impersonal and mechanical manner, anticipating a puppet-like style that would become a commonplace of expressionist performance. Wedekind was accustomed to directing his own plays, and so was in a good position to try out the effects he wanted.

The outburst of furious indignation provoked by *Spring's Awakening* was aggravated by its plan to have the audience sympathize with the moving scenes of the children, and then see themselves depicted on the stage as pompous fools. However, it was this scheme which invited imitation by other playwrights. For example, *Der*

3. Wedekind, *Spring's Awakening*, 1891. Production by Max Reinhardt at the Kammerspiele, Berlin, 1906. The schoolroom scene.

*junge Mensch: Ein ekstatisches Szenarium (The Young Man: An Ecstatic Scenario*, 1916) by Hanns Johst (1890– ) is a sugary dramatic elegy to the beautiful people who die young, and it ends with another graveyard scene in which the dead hero of the title rises from the grave as the spirit of rebirth; as such, he triumphantly leaps the cemetery wall and embarrassingly makes as if into the auditorium. When *Spring's Awakening* was made into a film, it also spawned a number of maudlin films on the subject of adolescent sex. The compassionate side of Wedekind's theme was easily forgotten.

In London, it is pleasant to record that the Stage Society presented *Spring's Awakening* as early as 1910, if only in a private performance. The Royal Court staged a cut version in 1963, and the Bremen Theatre Company played it in German at the Aldwych in 1967. It had its first uncensored production in English by the National Theatre at the Old Vic in 1974, when it was translated by Edward Bond and directed unsentimentally by Bill Bryden. The play successfully retained its original pathos and charm, but the impact of its sensational subject could not be re-created after so long a lapse of time.

In the so-called 'Lulu' plays, Wedekind's advocacy of sexual freedom became explicit. The plays are *Erdgeist (Earth Spirit)*, published in 1895 and first produced in Leipzig by Carl Heine in 1898 with Leonie Taliansky as Lulu and Wedekind himself as Dr Schön, and *Die Büchse der Pandora (Pandora's Box)*, published in 1902 and first produced in Vienna by Karl Kraus and directed by Albert Heine in a private performance in 1905 with the bewitching eighteen-year-old Tilly Newes as Lulu. The two plays together made up *ein Monstretragödie*, 'a monster tragedy', as the subtitle had it.

Wedekind's thesis on sex and the cult of the senses has been generally found shallow and indulgent, although it admittedly includes warnings of the disaster which awaits its acolytes. Wedekind had met Strindberg in 1894, and the plays also introduce Wedekind's first Strindbergian woman in the shape of the cunning, lustful and desirable Lulu, set in a context of cynical social satire which at times borders on the absurd. As for the male sex, it is explicitly referred to as a 'zoo' and 'a menagerie at feeding time', which may be the level at which life in these plays is conceived.

Nevertheless, there are at least two ingredients in these plays which make them acutely modern. One is the extraordinary set of devices Wedekind employed in order to control the tone of the performance. The other must be the actual character of Lulu, a figure of simultaneous attraction and repulsion, a creature whose strength and independence are ambivalently balanced by the evident moral justice working to bring about her death. According to her

4. Wedekind, *Earth Spirit*, 1895. Production by Frank Wedekind at the *Deutsches Theater*, Berlin, 1912, with Tilly Wedekind as Lulu and Frank Wedekind as Schön.

autobiography, Tilly Newes herself believed she was the type for the part, which she considered to be 'young, naive, and yet erotic'. She was 'a creature of instinct with a lively intelligence, but led by her inclinations. Not refined, but beyond the realm of good and evil.' To these intriguing ambiguities she added that the author wanted a madonna in the part, not a devourer of men.

*Earth Spirit* is a demonstration of lust — the 'earth spirit' is identified with the sexual impulse. The play quickly introduces the diabolical Lulu, the incarnation of animal sexuality as the primal force. In one way she is innocence itself, since she acts without malice aforethought; but in doing so she destroys others. She seems to behave like a chameleon, being called variously Nelly, Mignon, Eve as well as Lulu, as her different lovers see her. She wins her lovers in a variety of ways, and Wedekind has her repeatedly change costume to suggest the different roles she plays as a woman ('She learned the art of quick-change while still a child'). Her first husband dies of a stroke, her second cuts his own throat, and she murders her third after making love to his son — she puts a glass of champagne to her dying husband's lips and cries, 'The only man I ever loved!' In addition to her husbands, she also has a procession of preposterous lovers: a lesbian countess, an old lecher who could be her father, a trapeze artist, a schoolboy and several others. She glories in her sexuality.

In three acts the scene of *Pandora's Box* changes from a magnificent hall in German Renaissance style, to the white stucco of a spacious Louis XV room in France, to, finally, a shabby attic room in London, with the rain pouring down outside. These set changes trace Lulu's decline. Her lesbian lover, the Countess Geschwitz, helps Lulu escape from prison, but not before the Countess has infected her with cholera, so that Lulu emerges as a 'bag of gnawed bones'. Lulu is now Pandora, all things to all men, which is demonstrated in a depraved party in Paris in act ii, and in the dirty garret where she works as a ragged prostitute in act iii. There we meet her clients, one of whom is none other than Jack the Ripper (originally played by Wedekind himself). Lulu and the Countess accordingly meet their expected end, a bloody one, in a scene that for one critic held all the horror of the Last Judgment. Before the first performance of *Pandora* in Vienna, Karl Kraus announced that 'in this narrow world, the source of joy must turn into a Pandora's box'. And the young Alban Berg was in that first audience, evidently impressed enough to compose his opera *Lulu* years later.

Wedekind reworked his Lulu plays several times, always expanding the central part. The text abounds in what later became known as alienation effects, and it is interesting to note that Brecht himself became one of Wedekind's admirers. His characters are larger-than-life, more caricatures than characters, and farcical clowning is introduced to drench the action constantly in icy humour. At times, as in act IV of *Earth Spirit*, the play takes on the appearance of late nineteenth-century bedroom farce, with four or more lovers hiding from one another at the same time. The acting convention is also that of the period, with an added air of burlesque: characters 'sink to their knees', or 'rush across the stage', or 'throw themselves down'. Like Strindberg, Wedekind was skirting the boundaries of naturalism, but mixing the bizarre with the realism and dipping into nightmare for no apparent reason. The actor Friedrich Kayssler told him, 'You have throttled the naturalistic monster of probability and brought the element of play back to the theatre' (translated Nicholas Hern). Wedekind's outrageous cynicism, however, was very far from the fervent tone struck by the young expressionists who climbed on his shoulders. Yet after these unusual techniques, the Lulu plays betray their severe limitations. For all their effects of undercutting, their subject, human sexuality, emerges each time as the tragic trap from which there is no escape except in death, and as a satirist Wedekind is finally unable to transcend his obsession with his material.

With his wife Tilly Newes, Wedekind formed an actors' company and toured Germany performing in his own plays; according to Brecht, he was a powerful actor full of suppressed energy. His plays presented a rare challenge to the new directors who were looking for non-realistic material at the turn of the century. Reinhardt produced *Earth Spirit* at his Kleines Theater in Berlin in 1902, with Gertrude Eysoldt as another impressive Lulu, and Reinhardt's support was important to Wedekind's continuing development as a force in the German theatre. Jessner also brought his skills to reviving the plays, and made *Earth Spirit* into a film in 1922. G. W. Pabst made the notorious film *Pandora* in 1929, with Louise Brooks as Lulu, and a questionable tradition of heartless vamps was carried on by Marlene Dietrich as Lola in *Der blaue Engel* (*The Blue Angel*) in 1930.

Echoing Wedekind to some extent, the comedies of Carl Sternheim (1878–1942) also contributed to the theatrical undermining of bourgeois respectability in both content and technique. Sternheim gave his plays the ironic title *From the Heroic Life of the Middle Class*, and made his characters into grotesque types who already speak the characteristically staccato 'telegraphese' of the expressionists to come. *Die Hose* (*Knickers*, 1909) tells the risqué tale of one Theobald Maske, a clerk whose pretty wife loses her *Unterhosen* in the street just as the Emperor is passing. Ironically, the incident becomes celebrated overnight, and consequently the lady much in demand. Theobald, the prototype of the materialistic bourgeois, is able to attract lascivious admirers to his house and turn the occasion to a profit. So the play remorselessly ridicules both the grasping husband and the rest of society. Sternheim followed *Knickers* with sequels depicting the selfish tribe of Maske, *Der Snob* (1913) dealing with his mercenary son, and *1913* (1915) dealing with his mercenary granddaughter. Prophetically, these plays reveal a shockingly opportunist world on the brink of disaster.

---

# 4 · *Forerunners of expressionism: Strindberg and the dream play*

---

*A Dream Play* (1902, prod. 1907), *The Ghost Sonata* (1907)

Strindberg was the most frequently performed modern dramatist in the German theatre just before the First World War. R. S. Furness has calculated that between 1913 and 1915 no less than twenty-four of Strindberg's plays received 1,035 performances in Germany. James Agate said that Strindberg 'regarded the world as an asylum and peopled it accordingly', and perhaps he had captured the spirit of the times. Young German playwrights saw his work as pointing the way they should take, and found his personal discontent with society to their taste. It was the enthusiasm with which this group of writers followed Strindberg's lead that justifies the claim that he is the father of expressionism. Nevertheless, since it proved so hard to find a good way to produce his dream plays, we may wonder how his influence in matters of form and style spread as far as it did.

The first of his purely expressionistic works, the trilogy *To Damascus*, was written in 1898. It exhibited the primary characteristic of Strindbergian expressionism, that of splitting a single personality into several characters, each representing a facet of the whole and together illustrating the conflicts in the mind. All the images and action in *To Damascus* are seen through the eyes of 'The Unknown' (sometimes translated as 'The Stranger'), who represents the author himself. This character shares his poverty and his guilt with 'The Lady', who represents the author's wife or wives. The Unknown thinks he recognizes himself in a Beggar and in Caesar, a madman, while other characters, a Doctor, a Confessor and

5. Strindberg, *To Damascus*, at the Royal Dramatic Theatre, Stockholm, 1900. Scene vi, in a ravine, with design by Carl Grabow. August Palme as the Stranger, and Harriet Bosse as the Lady.

the Lady's pious Mother, remind him of his guilt. So characters are not used in the usual way as figures who are part of a story. They are agents who together stand for a condition of mankind. A whole new mode of drama was in the making.

The Biblical title of the play refers to Saul's journey to Damascus and to his conversion to Christianity, but the play is otherwise auto-biographical, darkly translating to the stage Strindberg's unhappi-ness of the so-called 'Inferno' period which followed his divorce from his first wife in 1891. The structure of the play is as artificial as the characterization. Part I is made up of many scenes arranged in a mathematically symmetrical way, with those of the first half recur-ring in reverse order in the second half, the central and climactic scene to and from which the others lead being one of maximum delirium. After the crisis, which includes a confession of sin, the Unknown revisits the scenes of his earlier life, and the Lady finally leads him to a church where he is to hear 'new songs'. The same characters appear in parts II and III, but the drama grows increasingly subjective, and is notable chiefly for a scene in part II in which the elegant guests at a grand banquet given in honour of the Unknown are transformed into hideous beggars and prostitutes. The surrealist film-maker Luis Buñuel saw society in similar terms.

The first production of *To Damascus* was at the Royal Dramatic Theatre, Stockholm in 1900, directed by Emil Grandinson with August Palme as the Unknown and Harriet Bosse as the Lady. The performance dissatisfied Strindberg with its sentimental treatment of the central character, whom he had envisaged as a more vital creature. It also stretched the resources of the stage to the limits. For the many scene changes, an inner proscenium was built so that a series of backcloths could be quickly changed in the dark without closing the curtains. Both the location and even the properties were painted on these backcloths. Such early problems of characterization and setting were a hint of difficulties to come. The complete trilogy has been only rarely performed, although part I has been attempted occasionally. When Olaf Molander directed it in Stockholm in 1937, with Lars Hanson playing the Unknown more congenially, Gunnar Ollén considered Molander to have 'contributed to radical changes in the interpretation of Strindberg on the Swedish stage'.

Strindberg said that *A Dream Play* (1902) was his favourite, and it is this play which may be said to have prompted in part the expressionist revolution in European dramatic writing and practice. *A Dream Play* was less obviously symmetrical than *To Damascus*, although both plays end where they begin. But the later play works more certainly and improves considerably upon the new form, since it follows the pattern of a morality play. It traces the journey of the Daughter of Indra, the god of Hindu mythology, from the time when she descends from heaven to visit earth, 'the darkest and the heaviest of the spheres that swing in space'. When she arrives at the Growing Castle, she finds it to be 'the abode of human misery'. Again, one consciousness, that of the dreamer, determines the fantasy, and again the character is split — here into four principals: the Officer, the Lawyer, the Quarantine Master and the Poet, each of whom the Daughter of Indra rejects. Again the structure of the play is episodic, the action vaguely moving among ruined castle walls somewhat reminiscent of Maeterlinck's. The place obeys only the laws of fantasy, and time refuses to follow the clock or the calendar, as when the Officer grows suddenly older. The dialogue is increasingly 'polyphonic', Strindberg's term for the way in which one character picks up the thought of another. He has thrown off every restriction of realism, and, as in a dream, the play indulges every phantom of his mind. Distorted or 'deformed' reality became the familiar mark of the new expressionism.

Indra's Daughter was written for the beautiful Harriet Bosse, with whom Strindberg was then living — her Oriental eyes seemed right for an Indian character. Like the childlike Eleanora of *Easter*, the part was conceived in a spirit of compassion, and although Indra's Daughter symbolizes Christ and womanhood both, she suffers as if she were human. An early title for the play was 'Prisoners', and Indra's Daughter has the repeated cry, 'Det är synd om människorna', a colloquial and untranslatable line whose meaning varies in tone between 'Mankind is to be pitied!' and 'What a pity about men!' The Officer is an optimist always waiting for his beloved. The Lawyer is an idealist who nevertheless cannot escape the world's evil by living only in the past. Through his art, the Poet aspires to heavenly insight. The Quarantine Master, wearing black-face, is there to decontaminate the victims of cholera. But in spite of all this unhappiness, the play has touches of ironic humour, as when the Officer is sent back to school and cannot say his two-times table. At the end, Indra's Daughter goes back to heaven, the Growing Castle of evil living goes up in flames, and a giant chrysanthemum on its roof bursts into bloom as a symbol of hope.

*A Dream Play* was considered unstageable, and a production was not attempted until 1907, when it was taken off after twelve performances. The heavy, conventional direction of Victor Castegren disappointed Strindberg. To present the many changes of scene, he had at first thought of using projected slides, but as a student of the Royal Dramatic Theatre school he had once watched a rehearsal of Bjørnson's *Maria Stuart* performed without costume or décor, and in Germany he had also seen Shakespeare produced in the Elizabethan manner without scene changes. He therefore knew that the stage could manage without all the trappings of scenery and costume if the lines were well spoken: good drama lived through the spoken word. Strindberg consequently came to believe that simplicity was the answer to the problems of putting on a dream play. Too much visual decoration and too many effects made the dream seem too slow and solid. In 1908 Strindberg wrote to August Falck, the actor and director who had produced the first *Miss Julie* in Sweden, a famous phrase : 'A table and two chairs! The ideal!'

The small stage of his new Intima Teatern encouraged such

6. Strindberg, *A Dream Play*, 1902. Production at the Intima Teatern, Stockholm, 1907. Design for the Growing Castle by Carl Grabow.

simplicity in production, and for a proposed production of *A Dream Play* there, Strindberg considered that a few symbolic properties — a couple of shells for the sea, cypresses to suggest Italy, a hymn board for a church — set against a single curtain or backcloth would be sufficient to start the imagination working. His final stage directions call for permanent wings with 'stylized representations of interiors, architecture and landscape'. They also provide for the same scenic elements to have several different uses: the gate outside a stage door becomes the Lawyer's railing and then a chancel rail in a church; the billboard outside a theatre becomes the Lawyer's bulletin board and then a hymn board. In all this Strindberg was moving in a more practical direction. Since the preface to *Miss Julie* in 1888, he had argued for economy in the scene, and in his *Notes to the Members of the Intimate Theatre* of 1908 and 1909, he urged the use of simple set pieces with lighting changes. This is essentially the method that would be adopted for a production of the play today. To try to present so many scenes in any realistic way would challenge the best efforts of the cinema.

Apart from the difficulties of clumsy scenery, productions of *A Dream Play* continued to be mishandled for other reasons. An appropriate tone and style for the play were particularly elusive. It was a sign that the form had become better accepted when Reinhardt brought his outstanding production of the play to the Stockholm Royal Dramatic Theatre in 1921, but even though he had previously attempted *The Dance of Death, The Pelican* and *The Ghost Sonata,* his production was excessively gloomy and sombre, with elaborate effects and chanted speeches. Artaud found the play's symbolism suitable for an experiment at the Théâtre Alfred Jarry, and in 1928 presented *Le Songe ou Jeu de rêves* to the accompaniment of shouting and fighting in the house, to which the police had to be called.

However, an important series of five productions by Olof Molander in Stockholm between 1935 and 1955 gave *A Dream Play* its first real taste of artistic success. By suggesting Stockholm itself in the setting, Molander dared to emphasize the realism in the play, and although his productions tended to be slow, he used a spotlight against a black background both to isolate an episode and to hasten a scene change. Unfortunately, he had the idea of exchanging Strindberg's chrysanthemum for a crucifix, with the predictable result that the play was turned into an object lesson in Christian faith. Molander also made up the Poet to look like Strindberg himself, an act of piety which misled the audience into thinking that the other major characters, far from being aspects of the same personality, were merely casual acquaintances of the author.

Ingmar Bergman had not been successful with a production of *A Dream Play* on Swedish television, but in 1970, in a small studio of the Royal Dramatic Theatre having a capacity of only 350, he cut the play to two hours and played it without décor against simple backcloths of black or white. When the play was treated as a chamber play in this way, it came to life. This was the production which Bergman brought to the Aldwych in 1971. London has not yet seen a full production of this play in English, but in Edinburgh in 1974, the Traverse Theatre under Michael Ockrent's direction successfully doubled nine actors to create forty characters. This was in line with the developing tradition of doubling to suggest the unsubstantial nature of the dream characters, and to establish the idea of a single identity for the 'dreamer'. Nevertheless, such a procedure increases the risk of making the already shadowy images of the play all but imperceptible, and of confusing an audience already in some confusion.

Strindberg founded his Intimate Theatre with August Falck in

7. The Intima Teatern, Stockholm, 1907. The stage and auditorium.

Stockholm in 1907. This move was prompted in part by developments in Germany, where Reinhardt had opened his Kleines Theater in Berlin in 1902, and followed it in 1906 with his Kammerspielhaus, also in Berlin. Because they needed none of the elaborate, large-scale structure of the regular playhouses, intimate theatres and chamber play theatres began to proliferate. Strindberg's Intimate Theatre was merely a rented warehouse with a seating capacity of 161. It was for this theatre that he wrote his five *Kammarspel* or chamber plays, four of which he had completed in anticipation of its opening: *The Storm, The Burned House, The Ghost Sonata* and *The Pelican*. (The fifth was *The Black Glove*, 1909.) Now he had a place of his own where he could get involved with production, experiment with his new kind of play and tackle the problems of staging. Strindberg seized the chance enthusiastically, and the Intimate Theatre presented twenty-four of his plays before it closed. His *Notes* and *Open Letters to the Members of the Intimate Theatre* usefully set out his ideas about producing a chamber play.

The chamber plays were intended to be simple in theme and presentation — Strindberg could finally abandon all the demands of the well-made play and the commercial theatre. At first he considered *Miss Julie* to be a chamber play in prototype, as is evident from the preface, in which he argues for 'a small stage and a small house' to encourage more subtle acting, vocal flexibility, continuity in staging and unity in the whole. But as his thinking developed, even the pattern for *Miss Julie* seemed too limiting, and he proposed an absolute freedom from the conventions of plot and character. Each new dramatic theme was to dictate its own shape and form. It was as a result of this proposal that Strindberg took up the then fashionable notion of a 'musical' form appropriate to the theme of the individual play and ensuring its unity and consistency of style. The concept of chamber music was to be transferred to drama, and themes would be repeated as in a fugue. *The Ghost Sonata*, indeed, was named after Strindberg's favourite Beethoven piano sonata in D minor.

In theory, the musical element would also promote the hypnotic effect upon the audience that Strindberg had advocated in the preface to *Miss Julie*. He complained that 'Many went to the bar even before the curtain rose and regarded the play as the entr'acte', and he

allowed no interval in a performance which would dispel the mood
he had created. Emotion and atmosphere were to dominate
the play and its presentation, but not in the old way of building suspense to a climax as a way of holding the attention of the audience.
Intensity of feeling would be sustained as in music, and character
and incident would be arranged by balance and echo, like leitmotifs.
This arrangement would risk losing the interest of the audience,
but there would be a greater concentration of dramatic elements
to hit the eye and ear, and any or all of the other arts could be
brought into the service of the drama. This emphasis on mood and
theme at the expense of plot and character seems like the formula
for a Chekhovian play, but the difference was that a chamber play
was not bound by the laws of the realistic theatre, and was free to
create totally unreal effects. This theorizing suited well with
Strindberg's intense spasms of near-automatic writing, times when
he actually thought of himself as a psychic medium interpreting the
world of the unconscious, and is linked with the religious mysticism
which obsessed him in his last years.

There was a full house for the opening night of the Intimate
Theatre. Although Strindberg was absent, his laurel-crowned bust
stood majestically in the foyer. Yet the first play presented, *The
Pelican*, succeeded only in emptying the seats, and the other chamber
plays that were produced there subsequently, including *The Ghost
Sonata*, had the same effect. All were considered decadent, that
timeless term of abuse in the arts.

Today, *The Ghost Sonata* (1907) is the most frequently revived
of the chamber plays of Strindberg, probably because it is consistently
dreamlike, and more rigorously expressionistic than the others. It is
also rich in sensational images that smack of a grotesque surrealism.
In his introduction to the plays, Evert Sprinchorn wrote that Strindberg had invented a new dramatic idiom, in which metaphors could
assume life :

> To say 'time hangs heavy' is one thing; to picture, as Dali
> does, a watch hanging heavily, is another. To say that the
> sweet young thing you once knew now looks like an old
> mummy is one thing; to have this woman imagine herself
> a mummy and comport herself like one, as Strindberg has
> her do, is another.

So it is with the death screen (originally suggested by the screen placed round a hospital bed when a patient has died), the vampire Cook, the poisonous hyacinths, and many other material images in the play. Such images, whether inanimate or not, acquire a symbolic life just from being juxtaposed in the dramatic illusion one with another, the supernatural with the real, the fantastic with the particular. Moreover, they may seem irrelevant to one another — until they are all assembled in· an affective sequence.

*The Ghost Sonata* opens on a typical suburban Stockholm street scene, as it might be in Östermalm. It is a bright Sunday morning and the church bells are ringing. Church organs are also heard, and the bell of a steamship. The scene is set outside an imposing house, and inside the shadowy occupants go about their business. If the pace is strange, as in a slow-motion picture, and the dialogue curiously oblique, it is a busy scene, and everything otherwise seems almost normal. Behind the façade of the house and the street, however, human misery is hidden. Outside the house a young man, the

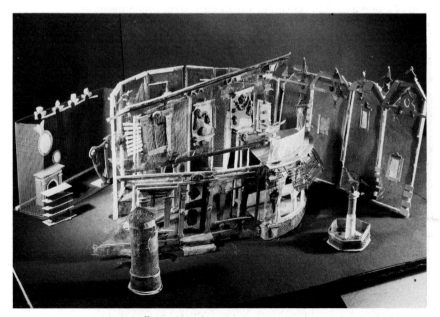

8. Strindberg, *The Ghost Sonata*, 1907. Production by Leonard Steckel at the Schauspielhaus, Zurich, 1952. Model of set for Act I.

Student, and a crippled old man in a wheelchair, Jacob Hummel, are looking through the windows. In the course of the scene Hummel persuades the Student to take an interest in his illegitimate daughter, the Young Lady, who will later appear as the Hyacinth Girl. So in this way we have a fleeting introduction to a few of the thirteen strange people who inhabit this place, and whose lives and destinies are tangled together.

The sense of eavesdropping on strangers living in a house on stage echoes the effect achieved in Maeterlinck's *The Intruder* (1890), and the next scene, that of the ghost supper, catches the terror of death felt in his companion play *Interior* (1894). But alongside the Maeterlinck, Strindberg's play is abrasive and ugly. The audience is brought a stage nearer the truth by being taken inside the house to observe its occupants more closely. It is a household presented with the bizarre imagination of the surrealist, mixing the real with the unreal. We see more clearly the white marble statue of a girl that was merely glimpsed in the first scene, and the Young Lady herself in the hyacinth room offstage. Hummel is now on crutches, and his former mistress, the mother of the girl, appears as a mummy kept in a closet and talking like a parrot. It is a household

9. Strindberg, *The Ghost Sonata*, 1907. Production by Ingmar Bergman at the Royal Dramatic Theatre, Stockholm, 1973. Act II, the ghost supper.

of self-deceivers, and in this scene 'they all sit silent in a circle', like a tableau of a hideous teaparty. No one is as he seems, and each is stripped of his pretences by Hummel. This he does with pleasure, until he who was formerly so confident is himself unmasked by the Mummy, and begins to talk also like a parrot. The old man was a death-bringer, a vampire, who now joins the living dead himself. 'The Ghost Supper' was to have been the original title of the play, and this gruesome scene is central to its conception.

For the last scene of the play, we pass with the Student into the naked heart of the house, to the bedroom of hyacinths, for a parody of a love scene. The stage seems like paradise, but the sensuous youth and fragile beauty of the Young Lady are in fact decaying: she is being bled dry by her parasitical Cook. Yet the Young Lady herself is exposed as another kind of vampire. Faced with the ugly truth about herself, she dies, and the death screen is placed around her. So the life-bringing sun floods in and the Student is released from her toils. The room vanishes, and Arnold Böcklin's painting 'The Island of the Dead' appears to the accompaniment of 'soft, sweet and melancholy' music, which is heard as if it is coming from the island.

The play has moved from outside to inside the house, from the past to the present, from the present to the future and from appearances to reality, suggesting the cycle of life and youth's inevitable tie with age. The progress is one of discovery and revelation as the drama probes more and more deeply. Martin Lamm thought that the play 'exceeds the possibilities of stage presentation in its attempt to depict simultaneously how people can show one personality to the world and live another with themselves' (translated H. G. Carlson). Certainly the action is compressed, the symbolism profuse and largely mysterious, the plot too tangential for an audience to follow. But this is not a play to be perceived with the logical mind, rather it is one to be savoured with the senses. It was praised by Artaud, no doubt because it explored that kind of theatre in which an audience could be emotionally overwhelmed.

*The Ghost Sonata* is a play that has yet to build its own stage tradition, like several of Shakespeare's. It had its first production at the Intimate Theatre in 1908 and was violently attacked by the reviewers, running for only fourteen performances. Not until 1916, when Reinhardt produced it at his Kammerspiele in Berlin with Paul Wegener as Hummel, and then brought this production to Stockholm in 1916 and 1917, did the play get good notices and begin to gather a reputation as an important piece in the history of the theatre. It was never very popular with the public, but the result of Reinhardt's work was that it received seven major productions in Europe in nearly as many years, with one by the Provincetown Players in New York at O'Neill's suggestion in 1924, and another (*'The Spook Sonata'*) by J. B. Fagan at the Oxford Playhouse in 1926, transferred next year to London's Globe Theatre. As the evening wore on, however, James Agate found it 'curiouser and curiouser', and this was the last professional stage production in English to date, although Stuart Burge directed it for BBC television in 1962, with Robert Helpmann as Hummel and Beatrix Lehmann as the Mummy. The visual flexibility of the television medium was able to reproduce the fleeting images of the play, and the production was well received.

The director who has given *The Ghost Sonata* most attention is Ingmar Bergman, who has to date produced it three times, in 1941, 1954 and 1973, each time drawing more power from it. Bergman considers the play to be the first absurdist drama, and the greatest play in Swedish. He has increasingly treated it as Strindberg's own dream, emphasizing its change from the partly realistic to the grotesque, and in the intervals projecting on a screen a huge photograph of Strindberg as an old man. This had the effect of reducing the role of the Student to one of the author's *alter ego*. Bergman also increased the continuity and unity of an otherwise fragmented play by judicious doubling. He wanted Hummel and the Student to be played by the same actor in order to emphasize the repetition of experience from one generation to the next, but this proved to be impossible. He did, however, have the Young Lady and the Mummy played by the same actess with striking effect, and even arranged for the actress to wear her hair and hold her hands and arms like the statue, lending more point to its presence.

The first scene was played as if the house was in the auditorium (where Bergman had imagined the attic to be in an earlier production of Ibsen's *The Wild Duck*). This had the effect of placing less importance on the visual setting and décor, and anything that needed to be seen was projected on two white concave screens placed upstage. In this way more was left to the spectator's imagination and there was a stronger focus on the actors. When mention was made of the collapse of the house, the actors froze, thereby greatly increasing the sense of terror, and at the same time generalizing the theme of corruption and decay. Lights were used for maximum suggestion: when Hummel told the guests at the ghost supper the truth about themselves, their heads sank on their chests and a brilliant white light marked the moment of their unmasking. A blue light drenching the hyacinth room at the beginning of the third scene changed slowly to a dull grey as the Young Lady mummified and died.

The symbolic death of the Young Lady was also conveyed by both the Cook and the Student. For her entrance the huge Cook was instructed to work her way out of the wall very slowly: 'first a hand, then a shoulder, finally a bottom'. The Student was no longer the compassionate onlooker, but as he realized that the girl was herself a vampire ('Why are the beautiful flowers so poisonous?'), he tore off her dress, dragged her to her knees and obscenely opened her legs. The sexuality in the concept of the hyacinth girl was thus made explicit, and the Student's last words of sympathy were given to the Colonel and the Mummy, her stepfather and her mother. The final effect in Bergman's treatment was one of a cold expressionistic criticism of the wretches who made up *The Ghost Sonata*. Egil Törnqvist has constructed an excellent account of Bergman's work on the play in *Theatre Quarterly* for September 1973.

Nevertheless, *The Ghost Sonata* may never fully succeed in production, if only because the nature of the experience which is the basis of the play is so subjective. The Student is not satisfactorily used as our representative on the stage or our agent of perception, and so the elements of the play, particularly the symbolism of the characters and the multitude of stage images, remain obstinately elusive, the links with reality too tenuous. Moreover, the motives of the many characters are never fully explained, their relationships remaining largely obscure and Strindberg's conceptions illogical and fragmentary. It is true that the audience at a dream play is not supposed to question the logic of the dream, but our trust in the dreamer, in this case the Student, puts a burden on the power of the actor to sustain the play's mood and justify our belief. The issue finally resolves itself into whether the confused content of a dream can be shaped into a manageable form for a play and accommodated to the needs of the stage and its audience. Nowhere in modern drama is the problem of evaluation more critical, since the submission of the audience must be justified by what happens.

Strindberg's loss of interest in external reality during his last years led him to write an expressionistic drama which made few demands on the conceptual thought of the audience, but through musical form, lyrical and incantatory language, mime and other visual suggestion, pause and silence, and the distortion of time and place, his appeal was to inner experience, unconscious feeling, akin to nightmare. That the new German writers seized upon the Strindberg of the last plays as their technical master may have been unfortunate, but his power of externalizing the warfare that went on inside his head provided a challenge to the young playwright that was unequalled. Sean O'Casey found Strindberg 'the greatest of them all', and made the tidy point that 'Ibsen can sit serenely in his Doll's House, while Strindberg is battling with his heaven and his hell.'

# 5  *Early expressionism in Germany*

*The Beggar* (1917), *Murderer, the Hope of Women* (1916)

The expressionist movement in the theatre was at first unusually confined to a single national culture. In one decade from 1912 to 1921, a handful of young men in their twenties and thirties set their stamp upon the modern German theatre with all the zest of political revolutionaries. Their plays may today seem crass and immature, but they are of great historical interest because they tried out a host of stage techniques, many of which are still in use. The content of these plays makes them unsuitable for revival, but they testify to the failure of social values in imperial Germany, and tell us a little about the crushing disaster wrought by the world war. Perversely, it was a time of enormous dramatic enthusiasm. In a characteristic address given in 1917, Kasimir Edschmid reported that the new expressionism was working in an atmosphere of continuous excitement. The work of the new artists was not merely descriptive, no mere photography, but was 'overcome by visions', searching for 'eternal significances' and 'new conceptions of the world' (translated Richard Samuel and R. Hinton Thomas).

The name Reinhard Sorge (1892–1916) is remembered for the publication of *Der Bettler* (*The Beggar*) in 1912, for although it was not produced until 1917, the year after its author was killed in the war, this play set the trend and remarkably embodied much of what was to come. It was intimidatingly subtitled 'A Dramatic Mission', and was semi-autobiographical. The Beggar of the title is Nietzsche's superhuman poet, a man who in his own eyes is yet humble enough to wish to devote his life to the enlightenment of the masses. This might strike us more as pride than humility.

Typically, all the characters are representative and nameless — the Poet, the Father, the Mother, and so on — and some also appear as phantoms, like 'the Apparition of the Man', 'the Voice of the Poet' and 'the Figure of the Girl'. The action is made up of a rapid sequence of scenes and incidents, the changes marked by differences in language, such as from prose to verse, as well as by the simple use of curtains and spotlights. The Poet appears and reappears throughout, first talking about his new work to a Friend in front of the curtain, and then, when the curtain is drawn, shown in a café among a crowd of newspaper readers and critics. Such representative groups of people appear regularly in the play, and behave like individual characters. This first group changes to a chorus of laughing prostitutes, which in turn disappears in darkness to reveal the Girl, who will be the Poet's only follower. Having made an ecstatic announcement of his plans for a better world, the Poet is replaced by another group, this time of woeful Airmen. The second act introduces the Poet's family, particularly the Father, who is a mad visionary who believes in the development of science and engineering. However, both the Father and the Mother are poisoned by the Poet as a necessary step towards his self-fulfilment, and at the end the Girl has conceived his child, an event which symbolizes hope for the future of mankind and is celebrated in a hymn of glory. We must also hope that this child does not choose to poison *its* parents when the time comes.

This silly play was inflated in style and painfully long, but it holds another interest for students of modern drama because it also possesses a 'metatheatrical' element: it is self-consciously a revolutionary play. The central figure of the Beggar-Poet, through whose eyes everything is viewed in what was to become the classic expressionistic manner, is actually in search of a new theatre for his work. He declares that he has written a play for the people, and not for the social and intellectual élite. *The Beggar* as a play, therefore, embodies a discussion rather than a statement of policy for expressionism, and was itself intended as a demonstration of how to do it. Even as it stands, therefore, the play is open-ended, and even if the Poet fails, the extraordinary influence of this play must indicate the success of the author.

Something of the colour symbolism of the French symbolists appears in the play. Sorge's stage directions call for a heavy use of red, signifying madness. A red curtain hangs as a backcloth. The carpet is red, the curtains are red, the cushions are red, the tablecloth is red. Sorge had also read his Strindberg for ways in which the subconscious mind could be realized on the stage. He achieves the dreamlike mood by having his nameless ones chant their lines rhythmically. A gauze diffuses the images on the stage, while focused lighting isolates first this, then that, part of the action. In the introduction to his useful collection of expressionist plays, Walter Sokel thinks that the spotlight which wanders from one group of characters to another serves to suggest the Poet's 'stream of consciousness', the wandering mind itself:

> When the latent substratum emerges, the centre of the stage
> is obscured while a particular corner — significantly sup-
> plied with couches or benches — is highlighted. When
> the mind shifts back to the surface plot, the corner sinks
> into darkness, while the centre is illuminated. The corner
> scenes, so puzzlingly unrelated to the main action centre-
> stage, can now be seen as only apparently unrelated. These
> scenes function as symbolically disguised commentary and
> reflection on the themes discussed in the centre, and in that
> lies their dreamlike quality (p. xv).

Here was a practical example of how the new lighting effects, which had been developed in the German theatre chiefly by Reinhardt, could be put to good use. Lighting could bind the themes of an expressionist play just as colours could, as if musically. It could relate each episode to the central intelligence, and balance one part of the play with another. So Sorge created a dramatic structure which had no need of the logic of cause and effect, and made no recourse to the elaborate apparatus of the well-made play.

The first production of *The Beggar* was in fact Reinhardt's for the *Gesellschaft des jungen Deutschland*, the Young Germany Society, at the Deutsches Theater, Berlin in 1917. Reinhardt was considered to have used an 'impressionistic' technique, with his spotlights picking out the white faces of the speakers against a black velvet curtain, their bodies appearing 'like chalk ghosts'. The English dramatist and critic Ashley Dukes, to whose enthusiasm J. M. Ritchie believes the British theatre owed its knowledge of German expressionism at this time, saw the play in Cologne in 1919 and recognized the originality of the staging. In *The Scene Is Changed* he wrote,

> The staging showed an understanding of the expressionist mind; across the proscenium hung a fine gauze, that now familiar device for preventing the diffusion of light on a subdivided scene ... The lighting moved from one part of [the] scene to another, leaving all the unlighted part invisible (p. 52).

But Dukes was finally impressed by what he felt to be a new poetic drama: 'It was the first expressionist drama, and perhaps the best because it never left the plane of poetry. The subject was modern yet timeless.'

Walter Hasenclever (1890—1940) was the first playwright of the new movement to have a play produced on the professional stage. This was in Dresden in 1916, and the play was the notorious *Der Sohn* (*The Son*). It was also produced by Reinhardt for Young Germany in Berlin in 1918. This piece of immaturity became a second cornerstone in the rebellion. It puts on the stage another son, a young man of twenty who has failed his examinations. Frustrated by an angry father, the Son is guided into the path of self-realization by a Friend – another key expressionist character borrowed from Sorge. The Friend promptly gives the Son a pistol with which to kill the Father. But we are spared an actual parricide because, when threatened with death, the unlucky man has a stroke at the last minute. Nevertheless, the revolutionary celebration of youth and happiness calls for universal parricide. Trying to kill one's father became obligatory for some of the new expressionist protagonists. Sorge seems to have started it, and, as we saw, Arnolt Bronnen (1895–1959) wrote a play actually entitled *Parricide*. Anton Wildgans (1881–1932) ended his *Dies Irae* (1918) with a similar confrontation, which in his case brought about the death of the Son and not the Father – perhaps an unintended comment on the whole charade.

Hasenclever's pacifist leanings showed themselves in his version of *Antigone* (1916), which Reinhardt distinguished with a production in the Grosses Schauspielhaus, Berlin, in 1920. Creon was modelled on the Kaiser, and Antigone symbolizes the love of mankind, the feeling her death is intended to promote. The play which introduced a technically more daring element, however, was Hasenclever's *Die Menschen* (*Humanity*, 1918). This is an expressionistic allegory about a man who is already dead, and he has a name – Alexander. He returns from the grave with his head in a sack, and lives a life of sin: drinking, gambling and whoring. He is finally convicted of being his own murderer from the past, and is sentenced to death. When Alexander is buried a second time, the actual murderer suffers remorse and is apparently redeemed by love. This story would be nothing were it not for the vigour Hasenclever brings to his text, which makes good use of mime punctuated by stark lines of two or three words apiece. *Humanity*, however, is an example of one of those plays whose stylistic virtuosity can deceive even a sophisticated audience into thinking it more profound than it is.

The Austrian expressionist painter Oskar Kokoschka (1886–1980) can also lay claim to precedence in the new movement, since his one-act play *Mörder Hoffnung der Frauen* (*Murderer, the Hope of Women*) was written as early as 1907. It was influenced by Strindberg's *The Dance of Death*, which had played in Vienna the year before, and it may also reflect the sex plays of Wedekind. In 1909 it was tried out in their school garden by the students of the Vienna Drama School, who borrowed some musicians (drums, cymbals, flute and clarinet) from a nearby café. The leading parts were played by Ilona Ritscher, a blonde Croatian girl with a hoarse voice and a face like a lion, and Ernst Reinhold, a red-headed Hungarian with

10. Herwarth Walden, ed., *Der Sturm* (*The Storm*), 14 July 1910. Title page showing text and illustrations for *Murderer, the Hope of Women* by Oskar Kokoschka.

blue eyes. Lit by flaming torches in the darkness, the effect was startling. The play was printed in Herwarth Walden's avant-garde paper *Der Sturm* in 1910, but it did not receive a professional production until 1916, when it was performed out-of-doors in Dresden.

11. Kokoschka, *Murderer, the Hope of Women*, 1907. Poster by the playwright.

Kokoschka's work is unique in its violent eroticism, and he made his name by offending the public. To emphasize his anti-social attitude, he shaved his head like a convict, and his theatre posters were intended not only to catch the eye, but also to shock the passer-by. *Murderer, the Hope of Women* was a grim battle of the sexes, set in a vaguely medieval and mythological period, and played by characters labelled 'Man' and 'Woman'. Each had a choric band of followers. The violent images of the play contain within themselves a paradoxically Christian symbolism: the scenes themselves correspond to the seven stations of the cross (an arrangement adopted later by Georg Kaiser for *From Morn to Midnight*), murder is heralded by a cock which crows three times, the Woman's body becomes a crucifix, and the crucifixion in the play represents a sexual climax.

The characters of the play speak in fierce, elliptical outbursts of feeling marked by symbolic colour and light changes. The Man is in blue armour, has a white face with a kerchief covering a wound, and is the leader of a savage crowd of men. The Woman has loose yellow hair and wears red clothes. As soon as these two meet, the Man orders his men to brand the Woman.

> THE MAN, *enraged.* My men, now brand her with my sign,
>    hot iron into her red flesh.
> MEN *carry out his order. First the* CHORUS, *with their lights,*
>    *struggle with her, then the* OLD MAN *with the iron; he rips*
>    *open her dress and brands her.*
> THE WOMAN, *crying out in terrible pain.* Beat back those men,
>    the devouring corpses.
> *She leaps at him with a knife and strikes a wound in his side*
> (translated Michael Hamburger).

So she is able to imprison him in a cage, round which she creeps 'like a panther' and whose bars she 'grips lasciviously' before prodding his wound and 'hissing maliciously, like an adder'. At the end, the Man recovers his strength and kills the Woman, an action intended to represent the murder of all women.

As can be seen, the dialogue is minimal, an invitation to the free expression of feeling and movement. Indeed, the actors in the first production were not given scripts, but a scenario of the action and a few necessary words and phrases. Just one rehearsal was held to choreograph patterns of wild movement and gesture, as for a primitive ballet, and to co-ordinate the words to be sung or intoned, as for an opera. The musical character of the play may be further suggested by the fact that it was made into an opera by Hindemith in 1920. The costumes and setting were sharply accentuated by primary colours, especially red, matching the verbal imagery and the dramatic ideas, and the naked parts of the actors' bodies were painted with veins and nerves. Needless to say, the opening performance was received by the middle-class audience with furious indignation, aggravated by the ironic cheers of some soldiers watching from outside the enclosure. When the Woman was branded, they turned the performance into a brawl.

*Der Brennende Dornbusch* (*The Burning Bush,* 1910) took the same theme, and had a Man and a Woman, each with a chorus, undergoing every torment until the two parties were cleansed of passion. This play was courteously afforded a production by Reinhardt in 1919, but nothing of Kokoschka had the impact of *Mörder,* which was performed by the dadaists as well as by Reinhardt, and was reprinted again and again. Kokoschka reached a peak with *Hiob* (*Job,* 1917, produced 1919), which depicted women as entirely evil. This was acted in great body-sized masks, with electric light coming from the eyes to give a strange effect in the darkness. The play introduces more and more surrealistic images. When Job's wife sleeps with a man who moves like a rubber snake to suggest that he is Satan, a cuckold's horns sprout on Job's crooked head, and the shadowy figures of the adulterous couple hang their underclothes on his horns whenever he rushes past their window. In such ways is the subconscious world realized theatrically, and in his discussion of the sources of the theatre of the absurd, Martin Esslin believed that this use of stage imagery made possible the appearance of Hamm's aged parents in ashcans in Beckett's *Endgame,* and the transformation of people into animals in Ionesco's *Rhinoceros* some forty years later.

With their windy emotions and explosive ideas, the enthusiasm behind such plays as these was exceeded only by the extravagance of their stagecraft. But the early expressionist experiments performed an extraordinary service in the story of modern drama by suggesting bold new ways of reaching a disillusioned public.

# 6  Expressionism in Germany: Kaiser and Toller

*From Morn to Midnight* (1917), *Masses and Man* (1921)

By two or three favoured plays which expressed the anguish of
war-torn Europe, two playwrights, Kaiser and Toller, were responsible for giving expressionism an international flavour. The former,
Georg Kaiser (1878–1945), introduced a larger purpose into a
movement which was too idiosyncratic. He was possibly the most
brilliant of the new German playwrights, and the best representative
of German expressionism, sustaining the passions of the movement
well after it had served its turn; Brecht never ceased to admire
him. He was a prolific and dedicated writer ('To write a play is to
think a thought through to the end'), writing about seventy plays in
his lifetime, and in one period of two years no fewer than ten, including his masterpieces *The Burghers of Calais, From Morn to Midnight*
and *Gas*. With the advent of Hitler in 1933, Kaiser's plays were
banned, and he fled to Switzerland in 1938 where he died in exile.
His last plays reflect his despair over lost causes and the folly of his
countrymen.

In 1903 Kaiser had broken with the symbolist poet Stefan
George on aesthetic grounds − an early protest against art for art's
sake. A work of art does not exist for itself, Kaiser argued; at bottom
it should be didactic in purpose, encouraging man to positive effort.
His Nietzschean manifesto of 1922, *Der kommende Mensch oder
Dichtung und Energie* (*The New Man, or Poetry and Energy*) constituted
an idealistic programme by which man could rise above his mach-
ine-age environment and return to the natural order of things. This
messianic programme was not a politician's platform for social reform, but a preacher's plea for *die Erneuerung des Menschen*, the re-
demption of the soul, and in character pacificist and humanitarian.
Kaiser's plays are *Denkespiele*, plays of ideas, and, like Shaw, he is less
interested in the conventional psychological conflict of character
than in a dialectical opposition of points of view. But when Kaiser

looked for a dramatic method, he turned, not to Shaw, but to Büchner.

*Die Bürger von Calais* (*The Burghers of Calais*, written in 1913 and produced in Frankfurt in 1917) may be Kaiser's best play. It is pacificist in intention, and embodies his 'new man'. The simple situation is that the English King will spare the besieged city of Calais if six hostages present themselves. On the one hand, the militarist Constable of France, Duguesclins, urges implacable resistance. On the other, the pacificist Eustache de Saint-Pierre argues that it would be madness to defend the city, with the consequent bloodshed and destruction. To make his point, Eustache takes his own life, although, ironically, the six are actually pardoned by a stroke of good luck. Nevertheless, his gesture illustrated the nature of pacificist self-sacrifice. At the end of the play, Eustache's coffin is placed upon the altar before which the King will kneel, and, symbolizing the victory of the spirit, Eustache's body rises up in an ethereal light like the Ascension of Christ.

Written just before, but produced just after, *The Burghers of Calais*, *Von Morgens bis Mitternachts* (*From Morn to Midnight*, 1916) made Kaiser's name everywhere in Germany, where it was first performed in the Munich Kammerspiele in 1917, directed by Otto Falckenberg. As a result of the advocacy of Ashley Dukes, who translated the play, it was produced by the Theatre Guild in New York in 1922, and at the Gate Theatre in London in 1925. The 1920 film by Karl Heinz Martin, with Ernst Deutsch in the leading part, left another record of the expressionist style of directing and acting, as Denis Calandra's article in *Theatre Quarterly*, 21 usefully indicates.

Kaiser had the idea for the play when he watched a poverty-stricken bank-teller handling a valuable letter of credit, and wondered why he did not take it and run. In the play he is called simply 'The Cashier', and he was to become the model for others of this type. He is at first a merely mechanical creature, but as a result of the momentary touch of the hand of a beautiful customer, he is suddenly sexually aroused. He miscounts and then hysterically stuffs 60,000 marks into his pockets. With this wild gesture he rebels against the dull routine of his work, and makes passionate advances to the lady. He wants to be free to live a life of thrills and achieve the ultimate experience, so he begins in a cyclodrome at a six-day cycle race, where he whips everyone into a frenzy by raising the prize money. He ends by spending a gaudy night in a Berlin cabaret, another satirical image of modern society. But his search for fulfilment fails and he suffers a revulsion of feeling. In a Salvation Army shelter, a racing cyclist, a prostitute, a father and a clerk all confess how they wasted their lives, and the Cashier realizes that they are telling his own story. He therefore tosses his stolen money into the crowd, but is appalled to see them fight for it like animals. Finally he falls in love with a Salvation Army lass, anxious to start a new life with her, but she betrays him to the police. When he is on the point of being arrested, he shoots himself in front of a crucifix.

*From Morn to Midnight* is a regeneration play, a morality play, made up of seven scenes or 'stations' (*Stationen*). The idea is borrowed from the stations of the cross, and the scenes trace the Cashier's progress through the day. Each scene is an expressionistic statement more stylized than the last. His life in the bank is that of a caged robot which moves in jerks to resemble a piece of machinery. On his way through a field covered in snow, he sees the figure of

12. Kaiser, *From Morn to Midnight*, 1916. Ernst Deutsch as the Cashier in the film. First scene: in his cage.

death formed by the snow in the branches of a tree like a giant skeleton. The scene at the races is like a madhouse, the promoters in identical silk hats behaving like automata. In the orgy of the cabaret, the beautiful girls he wants get drunk, fall asleep or turn out to be old and ugly; even the dancer has a wooden leg; and they all wear impersonal masks. At the end, the Cashier punctuates his speech with blasts on a trumpet, and as he shoots himself, 'all the light-bulbs explode' and he 'sinks with outstretched arms against the cross'. 'His death-rattle sounds like an Ecce — his final sighed expiration like a Homo.'

In London, Peter Godfrey opened his tiny Gate Theatre (actually a loft in Floral Street) with a production of this play, playing the Cashier himself. The production was so well received that it was transferred to the Regent Theatre, with Claude Rains as the Cashier, and was revived at the Gate several times in the years that followed. However, because the facilities at the Gate were limited, this production conditioned the British idea of expressionism ever after. The actors played without scenery against a black curtain, and even the trick of opening the play by drawing back the curtains

13. Kaiser, *From Morn to Midnight*, 1916. Ernst Deutsch as the Cashier in the film. Last scene: on the cross.

on a dark stage and then bringing up the lights came about because Godfrey had no cloth thick enough to hide a bright set with the curtains closed. As a result, expressionism was associated in London with bare stages and stark effects. In the unwitting words of James Agate,

> All expressionistic scenery has this two-fold appeal: it stimulates the eye by the little which it puts in, and the mind through all that it leaves out (*Red Letter Nights*, p. 135).

He was not to know that Kaiser would have preferred a more impressive visual treatment of his play.

Agate, like other London playgoers, did not approve of what Kaiser had to say, but was impressed by the way he said it:

> It is impossible to explain why four men waving silk hats with the co-ordinated rhythm of a lunatic ballet should be nearer to the truth of race meetings than a photographic representation of correct, stewardly behaviour. The fact remains that it is so. Possibly a point to be made here is that as soon as expressionism comes in at the door explanation in terms of words flies out of the window. For the thing has become abstract, like painting and music.

However, exciting stagecraft was not enough:

> The fact that a dramatist has found a magnificent way of saying something must not bluff one into the belief that the thing said is magnificent. I tried with might and main to see spiritual significance in Mr Kaiser's turgid bombinations, but all I could see, or rather hear, was a small cashier talking at enormous length through a very large hat (p. 136).

Since in dramatic criticism even turgid bombination is not inseparable from its visual context, Agate's comment, however generously intended, says nothing for the unity of the play.

A terrifying portrait of man in an industrial society appears in Kaiser's *Gas* trilogy, which shows human idealism defeated again and again by the progress of technology, a theme of utter pessimism. The three plays tell the story of an industrialist's family, and it begins with *Die Koralle* (*The Coral*, 1917), in which we meet a tyrannical capitalist named 'The Millionaire'. As a result of the deprivations of an unhappy childhood, he has sought and achieved great wealth and power, and he now salves his conscience by giving money to the poor. However, his own son and daughter turn against him, and so he tries to change places with his secretary, who had a happy childhood. Conveniently, the Millionaire and the Secretary are doubles, the latter identifiable only by the coral he wears on his watch-chain. Inconveniently, the exchange requires that the Millionaire kill his double. The idea of the *Doppelgänger*, the doubling or transference of human personality, is frequent in Kaiser's drama. In *The Coral*, the Millionaire is condemned to death for apparently murdering himself, but he gladly embraces his own execution because it signifies that he has achieved his object.

The Coral was hardly an inspiring treatment of its subject, but Kaiser took up the theme again in 1918, when *Gas I* was produced just after the Armistice. The scene is the Millionaire's factory, now identified as a gas works, the product supplying energy for modern industry. The protagonist in this play is the Millionaire's Son, aged sixty and running the factory as a profit-sharing business.

14. Kaiser, *Gas II*, 1920. Production at the Neue Theater, Frankfurt am Main, 1920. Design by Reinhold Schön.

Having in mind a perfect society, he has socialized the factory. However, led by the Engineer, a technician without human feelings, and inspired only by material self-interest, the workers defeat the Son's best efforts to have them go back to a natural life on the land. They demand that the works stay open, and in this they have the support of the army and big business, represented by a group of men dressed in identical dark suits. 'Here you are rulers!' cries the Engineer; 'follow the Millionaire's Son and you'll be peasants!'

*Gas II* (1920) is the most stylized play of the three and reflected the post-war mood most closely. A generation has passed, war has broken out and the factory is now producing a *poison* gas which eats away the flesh. The Millionaire's Grandson is now one of the workers, advocating the brotherhood of man and passive resistance to the war. The Engineer has now become a fanatic who moves like a piece of machinery. But, like his father, the Grandson is also rejected, and in his despair smashes a bottle of the poison gas inside the factory. Simultaneously, the place is bombarded, and a scene of terrible carnage follows: the skeletons of those attacked by the gas lie beneath gravestone-like slabs of concrete from the ruins of the building. It is the Day of Judgment. In this most pessimistic of Kaiser's plays, the message is that civilization will finally be its own destroyer.

In these plays are seen the characteristics associated with German expressionism in its mature phase:

1. *Settings* are virtually abstract and unlocalized, and the scene frequently appears angular and distorted, suggesting a bad dream. The properties are few and symbolic.

2. *The action* of the play is still broken into episodes, and these may represent stages in the hero's life or a sequence of visions as seen through his subconscious mind, as in a dream play.

3. *The characters* for the most part remain nameless and impersonal, often moving grotesquely: Kaiser always calls them *Figuren*, 'figures'. They always represent some general class or attitude, their characteristics being emphasized by costume, mask or make-up, so that the conflict of forces seem to be bare manifestations of energy.

4. *Crowds* are also impersonalized, and move with mass rhythmic movements, often mechanically. In another essay of 1922, *'Formung von Drama'*, 'Shaping the Play', Kaiser states that the

stage is able to make concrete the forms of human energy.

5. *The dialogue* is increasingly clipped, fragmented and unreal. It became known as the *Telegramstil,* 'telegram style'. This would be suitable for logical disquisition, were the language not also so inflated and over-heated. A rain of punctuation marks is showered on the lines as words appear to be inadequate to cope with the experience.

6. *The style of acting* is hard to reconstruct from the text, but expressionist films have established its general characteristics. Known as the 'ecstatic' style, it was intense and violent, and expressed tormented emotions. Actors might erupt in sudden passion and attack each other physically. Speech was rapid, breathless and staccato, with gesture and movement urgent and energetic —eyes rolling, teeth bared, fingers and hands clutching like talons and claws.

Kaiser's plays have a machine-like precision, but his sense of the stage is always strong and he is always concerned to channel the excitement of expressionism into workable theatre. He is conscious of space and the opposition of forces upon it, and he makes good use of lighting and perspective effects and different levels. And for all the feverishness in performance, the devices of expressionism produced a cold, logical drama, and threw the weight on to the play's thesis. Kaiser's plays of ideas are therefore never 'discussion plays', and in dramatic method they stand diametrically opposed to the plays of Bernard Shaw and Bertolt Brecht.

The most important play of the Czech playwright Karel Čapek (1890–1938) was influenced by Kaiser's *Gas.* This was *R.U.R.: Rossum's Universal Robots* (1921), a piece of expressionistic science fiction which brought its author a world-wide reputation, and also coined the word 'robot' (from the Czech word for 'slavery'). R.U.R. is an international company which manufactures machines that almost behave like human beings. These robots rebel and conquer the human race, but they cannot reproduce themselves unless they acquire the qualities of human love — which, for the convenience of an optimistic curtain scene, two young robots manage to do. The robots are heavily symbolic of the technology which Čapek believed could overwhelm mankind, but the mode of the drama is one of tepid realism which fails to match the momentous theme.

In any case, robots are not the best material with which to create three-dimensional characters. Nevertheless, the mechanical gestures and movements of the actors playing the robots provided a norm of stylized performance which impressed audiences everywhere.

*R.U.R.* was soon followed by another allegorical morality play, which Čapek wrote with his brother Joseph (1887–1945), who died in a concentration camp. This was *From the Life of Insects* (1922), variously titled *The Insect Play* or *And So ad Infinitum*. Its simple symbolism, with butterflies used to satirize triviality, beetles selfishness and insularity, and ants the warlike possibilities of the totalitarian state, introduced a balletic element into the performance of the play, and it was very popular for a short time.

The politically-inspired plays of Ernst Toller (1893–1939) were as bleakly pessimistic as Kaiser's, although perhaps more acceptable because of their religious overtones. After seeing *Masses and Man*, James Agate decided that Toller was a poet and not a propagandist. Toller's plays began to appear soon after the First World War, and caught the disillusionment of the times, especially since many had been written in prison at Niederschoenenfeld, Munich, where he was serving a 20-year sentence for revolutionary pacifist and communist activities. Although Toller was of a radical

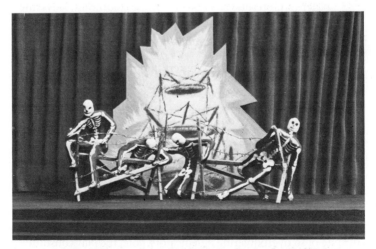

15. Toller, *The Transformation*, 1919. Production by Karl Heinz Martin and design by Robert Neppach. Model of stage set.

persuasion to the end of his life, his plays are not narrowly based, but speak to the whole condition of mankind and of general human suffering.

His first play, *Die Wandlung* (*The Tranformation*, 1919), was autobiographical. Its hero is Friedrich, who patriotically enlists in the army, but returns disillusioned from the war to renounce his former nationalism and espouse instead a belief in the international brotherhood of man. The play therefore traces the growth of a revolutionary in thirteen *Stationen*, and proceeds on two levels, realistic and expressionistic, mixing scenes from the war with those of Friedrich's subconscious imagination. The first scene opens gruesomely with the dead rising from their graves, and another depicts the skeletons of soldiers crawling through barbed-wire entanglements.

But the play that made Toller's name international was *Masse-Mensch* (*Masses and Man*, 1921). This, he explains in the preface to the printed play, he drafted in prison as if in a trance:

> It literally broke out of me and was put on paper in two days and a half. The two nights, which, owing to my imprisonment, I was forced to spend in 'bed' in a dark cell, were abysses of torment. My mind was tortured with visions of faces, daimonic faces, faces tumbling over each other in grotesque somersaults. In the mornings, shivering with fear, I sat down to write and did not stop until my fingers, clammy and trembling, refused to serve me.

The play is dedicated to the Workers and to

WORLD-REVOLUTION:

MOTHER OF NEW

POWER AND RHYTHM,

MOTHER OF NEW

PEOPLES AND PATTERNS.

RED FLAMES THE CENTURY IN BLOOD OF EXPIATION:

THE EARTH NAILS ITSELF

TO THE CROSS.

In spite of so overpowering a dedicatory note, the play constitutes a beguiling dramatic dialectic, based on the interaction of the individual and the mob, the intellect and mass emotion. The central character is 'The Woman', also named 'Sonia' after someone Toller knew. She is a pacifist and a humanitarian, and she urges the workers to strike. Instead, they call for war, and Sonia is unable to control them when they become violent. Indicted for starting a riot she had actually tried to check, she goes willingly to her execution.

In a comment on the play, Toller said that everyone shares Sonia's moral position, and yet at the same time everyone is one of the crowd, driven by the social situation and common impulse. In this, he thought, lay the tragic paradox of life. He was careful to indicate that Sonia is not to be regarded as an individual, but simply as representative of the humanitarian position. Her antagonist is 'The Nameless One', so-called because the masses have no name, and it is he who speaks for the materialistic mob. And as in Strindberg, characters appear in different roles: the Man of scene 1 is Sonia's husband, a government official who stands for conventional law and order, but in scene 2 he becomes the clerk who looks after bank business. In scene 4, a guard and a prisoner exchange masks, as if victor and victim were one. And even the Nameless One changes his role from that of a revolutionary to that of fate.

Again forms of realism and expressionism alternate. Four scenes are of stylized reality and three are 'dream pictures', although while the dreams are of more theatrical interest, in performance it is difficult to distinguish one from another. Scene 2, the first dream, is set in a stock exchange where bankers bid for government war contracts, and also establish an international corporation for soldiers' brothels. To conclude their negotiations, the bankers dance an unusual foxtrot:

> A VOICE. How about women?
> FOURTH BANKER. As many as you want.
>> Someone tell the doorman:
>> Five hundred
>> Gay
>> Young girls
>> Wanted here!
>> Meanwhile. . .
> THE BANKERS. We donate!
>> We dance!

Help
The unfortunates!
(*Music of clinking gold pieces. The Bankers in their high silk hats
dance a foxtrot around the exchange. The stage darkens.*) (translated
Louis Untermeyer)

Scene 4, the second dream, is of a prison yard in which the Condemned, with ropes round their necks, dance with their Guards
round the Nameless One as he plays a wild tune on a concertina
and coloured lights flash on and off. Scene 6 finds Sonia crouching
in a giant birdcage – a common expressionist image – and
caught in a shaft of light to suggest 'boundless space'. She is
accused of the death of the workers in the rebellion, and their ghosts
are suggested by giant shadows thrown up around her. Finally the
Prisoners appear, 'forms without faces'; they wear pointed caps from
which hang tattered rags that conceal everything except their eyes,
and they walk around Sonia's cage 'in a monotonous rhythm,
silently'.

*Masses and Man* was inventively staged by Jürgen Fehling and
designed by Hans Strohbach in the Berlin Volksbühne in 1921, and
we are lucky to have a sharp eyewitness report of the production
from Kenneth Macgowan and Robert Edmond Jones in their
*Continental Stagecraft* of 1922. Fehling had the barest of settings,
a 'deep box of black curtains', which had the effect of destroying
all realism and emphasizing the actor. In the centre was a low, broad
platform, upon which the action took place: 'It reduces setting to less
than symbol', was Macgowan and Jones's comment. When the curtains were parted, they revealed a great flight of steps, set against the
spatial lighting of the cyclorama. According to his note, Fehling
believed his staging reflected the spirit of the play:

In my production I attempted to suggest the twilight of the
soul by an elusive blending of the limelight rays... The
scenes were severely architechtonic, composed of light and
space. Platforms and flights of steps, draped uniformly in
black, served as a scaffolding for the actors, individually
disposed in geometric patterns, or massed in opposition to
the protagonists. . . . The stage, curtained and carpeted in
black, only occasionally opening on a domed horizon with

white or yellow lighting, and itself tinged with glowing light, gave the illusion of illimitable space and freedom for the imaginative visualization of scenes appropriate to the changing dramatic situation (translated Vera Mendel).

The acting style was one of intense energy. The first scene, which called for two men and a woman to sit at a table in the workers' meeting hall, was lit by three shafts of light, under which Fehling's actors crouched with clasped hands 'in the taut attitudes of wrestlers'. The dream scene of the stock exchange opened the curtains to disclose the clerk 'on an impossibly high stool, writing on an impossibly high desk, almost in silhouette against the yellow-lighted dome'. Mary Dietrich, playing Sonia, 'drives with such furious precision at the meaning of this woman that she stands out immediately as a sort of Christ-figure'.

Macgowan and Jones recognized Fehling's attempt to distinguish between scenes of reality and those of dream, the former being 'made of nothing but abstract plastic shapes, harsh, and harshly lit', and the latter 'sometimes painted and shaped in the slightly decorat-

16. Toller, *Masses and Man*, 1921. Production by Jürgen Fehling and design by Hans Strohbach at the Volksbühne, Berlin. Drawing by Robert Edmond Jones of the workers' rally.

ive spirit of expressionism' and 'lit with beauty and atmosphere'.
They found scene 5, the rally of the workers before their defeat, to
be the 'tremendous' scene of the play:

> The stage is again boxed in black. There are steps like the
> corner of a pyramid rising up to the right of the audience.
> Upon these steps gather the working people. You see a host,
> affrighted and cowering, in the twenty-four men and
> women who stagger upon the steps singing the *Marseillaise*.
> As they sway, locked together hand in hand, like men on a
> sinking ship, and the old song mounts up against the
> distant rattle of machine guns, the scene brings the cold
> sweat of desperate excitement to the audience that fills the
> Volksbühne... Suddenly there is a louder rattle of arms.
> The noise sweeps through the air. It drives into the souls of
> the huddling men and women. They collapse, go down,
> fall in a tangled heap. The curtains at the left loop up
> suddenly. There in the gap against the yellow sky stand the
> soldiers (p. 152).

17. Toller, *Masses and Man*, 1921. Production at the Stadt theater,
Nuremberg, 1921. Scene iii, the workers' rally. Margarete Hannen
as the Woman.

The authors were also impressed by the sixth scene, with Sonia in her cage, which was painted scarlet and placed in 'a misty, swimming emptiness'. There her accusers moved 'in a great circle of towering shadows that seem to hang in the emptiness of the sky', filling the air with recrimination. Eric Bentley may have been right to suggest that expressionist drama scarcely existed without its revolutionary staging.

The Berlin production of *Masses and Man* succeeded before a largely socialist audience. When it was produced in the Nuremberg Municipal Theatre soon after, it started riots which caused the play to be suspect and rarely played afterwards. In his autobiography *I Was a German*, Toller reported, 'Some people held that it was counter-Revolutionary in so far as it was an indictment of force; others insisted that it was pure Bolshevism because the apostles of non-resistance went under in the end' (translated Edward Crankshaw).

Toller's black pessimism did not abate. *Hinkemann* (1922) dramatizes the futility of warfare, and has its title character return from the trenches impotent and bitter. In addition he is humiliated when he sees his wife being unfaithful to him, and he is degraded by having to earn a living eating live mice for the entertainment of others. With its cynical title, *Hoppla, wir leben!* (*Hurrah, We Live!*, 1927) is the tragedy of a revolutionary, one Karl Thomas, who spends eight years in an asylum, only to return home to find that all his old comrades have become corrupt conformists. When he is falsely accused of the assassination of one of these former friends, now Minister of the Interior, Thomas, like Hinkemann, finally hangs himself. *Hoppla* is distinctive in displaying the influence of Erwin Piscator by projecting newsreel film along with the stage action — an early example of the 'mixed media' technique.

Both Kaiser and Toller believed in the necessity of an expressionist approach if the stage wanted to do 'more than take photographs', and it was their development of the genre that made German post-war drama internationally famous. They were indirectly responsible for experiments in Ireland by Sean O'Casey and Denis Johnston. In America, the Theatre Guild produced *R.U.R.*, *From Morn to Midnight* and *Masses and Man* (this last in a production by Lee Simonson which aimed at duplicating Fehling's work in

Berlin), and greatly influenced Eugene O'Neill and Elmer Rice. If the original German expressionism, limited from the beginning by its nihilism, is now as dead in Europe and America as it is in Germany itself, expressionist techniques are now part of the common pool from which many contemporary playwrights and directors draw.

# 7 New production styles in Germany: Reinhardt and others

*The Miracle* (1911)

Possibly the greatest director of modern times was the Austrian Max Reinhardt (1873–1943). He is chiefly known in Britain and America for the spectacular, the '*kolossal*', productions he sent to London and New York. On the evidence of such commercially successful productions as *The Miracle*, *Oedipus Rex* and *A Midsummer Night's Dream*, aimed particularly at a bourgeois audience, some critics considered him vulgar and romantic, his skill with visual stagecraft branding him as superficial. Yet Ernst Stern, his chief designer, could write of the décor for *The Miracle* as if it was expressionistic, its costumes 'as fantastic as the architecture, like something out of a feverish dream', while 'the scallops and hangings twisted and twirled in the dance of life like the flames of hell' (translated Edward Fitzgerald).

There never was a single Reinhardt style. Herbert Jhering said that he left behind no style, only productions. His touch could be as subtle and gentle as it could be powerful and overwhelming, and he could direct actors as readily in his little Kammerspiele as in his Grosses Schauspielhaus. Like Appia and Craig, he believed the theatre to be an all-embracing art, and accordingly drew upon any style or period to make his production work. Recalling his memories for the BBC in 1954, the English director W. Bridges-Adams considered that 'the distinguishing mark of a Reinhardt show was the unfailing rightness of his choice', and it has been said that if

Reinhardt did not actually found a movement, he started nearly every hare in the modern theatre.

Some of the misunderstanding about his work arose because of his impatience with the drab productions of the naturalists and his consequent assertion of visual theatre. But his versatility ensured that he was comfortable both with the realistic and the non-realistic play. He was well aware of contemporary developments in expressionism – as early as 1906 he had the Norwegian expressionist Edvard Munch design his production of *Ghosts* – and he was instrumental in bringing Swedish and German expressionism to the general public. He helped to initiate, and lent his reputation to, the Young Germany series in 1917, beginning with Sorge's *The Beggar*, and he followed this with, among many other new plays, Kaiser's *The Coral* and Hasenclever's *The Son* in 1918, and Kaiser's *From Morn to Midnight* in 1919. When he took Strindberg's *The Ghost Sonata*, with Paul Wegener as Hummel, to the Stockholm Dramatic Theatre in 1916 and 1917, and then *A Dream Play* in 1921, it was a revelation. Reinhardt also promoted the plays of Büchner (*Danton's Death* in 1916 and *Woyzeck* in 1921) and Wedekind (*Earth Spirit* in 1902, *Spring's Awakening* in 1906 and *Pandora's Box* in 1918), keeping them in repertory when *The Miracle* was taking Europe by storm. The truth is that, devoted as he was to Shakespeare, Molière, the Greeks and the German classics, all was grist to Reinhardt's mill. But he saw every play, new and old alike, with a new theatrical intelligence and insight, and it fell to him to try out the new material. He was astonishingly successful, a 'magician'.

Reinhardt entered the theatre in Salzburg as an actor, and soon joined Otto Brahm's company at the Deutsches Theater in Berlin in 1894, playing naturalistic Ibsen and Hauptmann. But Reinhardt was a restless creator. After 1902, he started an experimental cabaret, *Schall und Rauch* (*Sound and Smoke*), which he then transformed into his tiny Kleines Theater. By 1903 he was also directing at the Neues Theater in Berlin, and between 1902 and 1905 he was responsible for the production of some fifty plays. Finally, in 1905, he became Brahm's successor in the Deutsches Theater itself. Up to this time he attempted every kind of play, from Gorky's intensely realistic *The Lower Depths* at the Kleines Theater in 1903 to the expansive

*A Midsummer Night's Dream* at the Neues Theater in 1905. This was
the production that made him internationally famous. At the time,
he was aged thirty-one.

With its setting of great tree-trunks jutting from a rolling
grass-covered glade, the wood near Athens revolving for the
chase of the Athenian lovers, the fairies no longer the 'depressing
ballerinas' of so many Victorian productions, but, according to
Ernst Stern, 'slim and elegant girls in close-fitting green tights
and green wigs'; with its evocative adaptation of Mendelssohn's
music and its atmospheric use of light and colour seen through
spangled gauze; with such an effect as that of absorbing the
fairy train into Oberon's magic cloak to suggest the coming of
dawn, Reinhardt's production of *A Midsummer Night's Dream*
belonged to a kind of fantastic theatre that had never been seen or
equalled. The production was still valid when he took it to America
in 1927–8, and used it as the basis for the Warner Brothers' film,
directed with another emigré, William Dieterle, in 1934.

When Reinhardt first became a director, he recognized that
Brahm's naturalism was only one form of dramatic expression, and
that it could exhaust its creative freshness and even inhibit the poetic
powers of the theatre if applied pedantically to all plays alike. His
idea was to expand the art of the stage, and his change of heart
happily coincided with the explosion of symbolist and expressionist
playwriting. Faced also with the challenge of the classics, he turned
by inclination to the Austrian baroque of his birthright, and found a
solution in the Wagnerian concept of the *Gesamtkunstwerk*, the
total art work which would press all the arts into the service of
drama. It was Reinhardt's special talent to be able to translate the
words of a dramatic text into the movement, rhythm and mood of
dramatic music and dance. Inevitably he found support in the lighting and design ideas of Appia and Craig, then under fierce discussion, and was encouraged to reject the picture stage for a theatre
appealing directly to the senses.

He explored nearly every earlier period for its theatrical
characteristics, everything from the Greeks to the Japanese *Noh*
theatre. He created a huge *Oedipus Rex* in 1910, which he took to
London in 1912, and another giant production in the *Oresteia* in
1911. For both of these productions he chose the Zircus Schumann in

Berlin. Yet his *Oedipus* in Munich in 1909 had been played without the usual stage in a hall with an orchestral platform at one end and a semicircle of spectators sitting on tiers of seats; the palace was merely suggested by a tall screen against which spotlights picked out the action. On a slightly lesser scale, he turned to the drama of the Renaissance, particularly to Shakespeare, whom he admired above all. For an impressive *Merchant of Venice* in 1905, Reinhardt had Humperdinck write the music, and astonished audiences by such an effect as that of reproducing the noises of Venice to bring the city to life. A ritualistic *Winter's Tale* in 1906, a shockingly barbaric *Lear* in 1908, and a wittily balletic *Shrew* done in the manner of the *commedia dell'arte* in 1909 prepared the way for an outstanding Shakespeare cycle which he took to Budapest, Vienna and Munich in the 1909–10 season.

The French classical drama was a particular strength, with Reinhardt able to capture Molière's 'mood of minuet'. For *George Dandin* in 1912, he built a permanent setting within the Deutsches Theater, a formal garden pavilion against which the players moved like silhouettes. No one gave more attention to the German romantics, Goethe and Schiller, and Reinhardt mounted productions of the

18. Sophocles, *Oedipus Rex*. Production by Max Reinhardt at the Theatre Royal, Covent Garden, 1912. Oedipus and the suppliants.

intractable *Faust I* in 1909 and *Faust II* in 1911. Goethe's *Urfaust* was brilliantly presented in 1920 as a series of scenes created like tableaux of old Flemish pictures seen inside a single Gothic arch, designed by Stern so that its traceries could be adapted to any height. Reinhardt's invention was unbounded.

He gave equal weight to the modern classics, particularly to the recent symbolist plays of Ibsen, Maeterlinck and Hauptmann. The production of *Ghosts* in 1906 with Munch as designer turned his Kammerspiele into an oppressive prison shut in by expressionistic mountains, a trial run for the presentation of Strindberg's expressionism on the same stage. For a soulful and sensitive *Aglavaine and Sélysette* by Maeterlinck in 1907, Reinhardt used a simple setting of melancholy purple curtains. For Oliver M. Sayler's book about him, Reinhardt wrote of 'the eternal wonder of resurrection' whereby what is apparently dead can live again through the medium of the stage, and in drawing on the riches of the past, he explored in the most practical way the nature of theatrical convention, mixing one technique with another to meet each occasion. 'There is no one form of theatre which is the only true artistic form', he declared.

An essential characteristic of Reinhardt's work was his concern that the spatial relationship between actor and audience should meet the needs and style of each particular play. To this end he developed three major theatres in Berlin simultaneously, and in his career he worked in an astonishing number of different theatres and playing places, of which the following are the important ones.

1. *The Deutsches Theater* had been built in 1883 as a conventional proscenium-arch theatre with a comfortable capacity of 1,000. When Reinhardt took it over in 1905, he equipped it with the latest Fortuny indirect lighting system, in which the light was reflected from a cyclorama, and added a flexible proscenium opening and a revolving stage of the kind invented for Mozart at the Residenz Theater, Munich. Most of Reinhardt's productions took place at the Deutsches Theater, and it was this new equipment, together with the use of front and apron staging, that made the multiple scenes of Shakespeare's plays flow smoothly. For the *Urfaust* production mentioned above, the stage opening was reduced to about nine feet, framing the great Gothic arch in which the scenes of the play were presented. Faust was caught at his study table, his face lit by

light from his lamp. A cathedral scene was conveyed by a pillar against a black background, showing only the backs of women in prayer as they huddled together on steps. In the cellar scene, the arch was lowered almost to the heads of the four drunken men as they sang and quarrelled, so that, according to E. J. Dent, 'one imagined oneself as close to the actors as they were to each other'. Gretchen looked like a Madonna by Hans Memling, and stood habitually in a Memling attitude. With such exquisite tableaux, Dent could not help feeling that the play was performed as an excuse for the pictures, rather than the other way round.

2. *The Kammerspiele* (chamber theatre) was possibly Reinhardt's best invention. It was conceived in 1906, when he gave up the Kleines Theater he had found so very serviceable. It was built next to the Deutsches Theater, and it seated less than 300 people in leather armchairs. Its proscenium width was only 26 feet, and only three steps took the actor from the stage to the auditorium. It was ideal for plays produced on a smaller scale and played in a quieter way — chamber plays which called for close actor—audience rapport — and it was this Kammerspiele upon which Strindberg modelled his own Intima Teatern in 1907. On such a stage the setting could be spare, supplying merely a frame and a background, and leaning towards symbolism, while the acting could be relatively realistic. Acoustically sensitive, it was Reinhardt's favourite for plays of delicate feeling and wit, and he chose it for *Spring's Awakening*, *Ghosts* and *The Ghost Sonata*.

3. *The Grosses Schauspielhaus*. In 1919, after the war, Reinhardt built his 'Theatre of the Five Thousand' like a circus arena on the site of the Zircus Schumann. It was an uncomfortable monster seating 3,300. Nevertheless, it was remarkable for its ability to reproduce the idea of a Greek amphitheatre because of its 65-foot thrust stage and its suggestion of a Greek *orchestra*. Behind the open space, a proscenium arch, which could expand to 65 feet also, was merely a frame to house a huge plaster cyclorama suitable for vast lighting effects. Sections of the arena could be raised and lowered by hydraulic machinery, and the floor itself could be revolved. On occasion, Reinhardt would introduce into the auditorium platforms, steps, ramps or gangways, in an attempt to bring the action closer to

the spectator. The Grosses Schauspielhaus was conceived ideal-
istically as a theatre for the people, a place of entertainment for the
masses.

It was certainly suitable for the *Oresteia* of Aeschylus with
which it opened, but even then the great height of the theatre
dwarfed Stern's settings and made them difficult to light. Crowd
scenes were necessarily over-extended, while scenes of small detail
and close timing, like many in Shakespeare, were killed. Dent
reported that the resonance of the building's huge dome (playgoers
spoke of it as 'the cave') magnified every cough into a roar, and the
actors had to bawl to be heard at all. Heinz Herald, who had initiated
the Young Germany series of plays with Reinhardt in 1917, wrote,
'What at the Kammerspiele is a mere relaxation of the fingers, must
become a motion of the hand at the Deutsches Theater and a lifting
of the arm in the Grosses Schauspielhaus.' At a time of runaway
inflation in Germany, this theatre was, except for its operettas, both
an artistic and a financial failure.

4. *The outdoor theatre.* The celebrated example is Reinhardt's
use of the cathedral square in Salzburg for his production of Hugo
von Hofmannsthal's adaptation of *Jedermann* (*Everyman*) from 1920

19. The Grosses Schauspielhaus, Berlin, in 1919.

onwards. The façade of the Cathedral was used as a backdrop, fanfares were played from the *portières*, and the voice of God came from within. Other voices calling Everyman to Death were orchestrated to be heard first from the Cathedral, then to echo mysteriously from church towers in the city, and finally even from the mountain towering above. The light changed naturally from daylight to dusk, and from twilight to torchlight. Reinhardt reported, 'Traffic is completely stopped, and the whole city listens and watches breathlessly.' The rather sentimental Hofmannsthal version lacked the austerity of the original, and consequently, Bridges-Adams reported, 'on a *Jedermann* afternoon you might meet hard-boiled men coming away from the square in a very reduced state indeed'.

5. *The church production*, notably of Calderón's *Das Grosse Welttheater* (*The Great World-Theatre*) in Hofmannsthal's version for the Salzburg festival of 1922, when the play was presented in the Kollegienkirche. For this production, a platform was set up in front of the altar across the width of the church, and draped in scarlet. The scene was universally acclaimed in which Death, at first invisible in scarlet against the scarlet background, suddenly revealed himself in black and descended from a high pedestal to the rhythm of an invisible drum. As he stepped, he mimed the drumbeats with bones for drumsticks, tapping on a little drum of his own tied to his waist. In this fashion he danced a chilling *danse macabre* with each of his victims, King and Beggar, Rich Man and Farmer, Beauty and Nun, compelling each to follow the drum like a puppet jerked back and forth on strings.

6. *The ballroom*. In 1922 Reinhardt adapted Maria Theresia's great baroque ballroom in the Imperial Palace in Vienna, creating the Theater in dem Redoutensaal. The arrangement was a little like Copeau's Vieux Colombier in Paris, but on a larger scale: the bare platform was backed by flights of graceful stairs with no proscenium arch. A set for this stage was at most a modest decoration of formal screens, so that the actors played essentially without scenic suggestion, and thus without attempting realistic illusion. The Redoutensaal encouraged basic experiments in the art of acting, and was particularly suitable for neo-classical drama and after – Calderón, Molière, Goethe.

7. *The exhibition hall*. In 1911, at the prompting of Charles Cochran, Reinhardt hired Olympia, London's huge exhibition hall, since used to hold motor shows and athletic competitions. With a few suggestions of stained glass windows and nave doors, he and his designer Ernst Stern disguised Olympia to resemble the inside of a vast cathedral for the production of Karl Vollmoeller's scenario for the Gothic mystery play *Das Mirakel* (*The Miracle*). The production subsequently toured Europe, playing in Berlin's Zircus Schumann, and after the war it was revived at the Century Theatre in New York, newly designed by Norman-Bel Geddes. With music by Humperdinck, the play was otherwise a great spectacle, a pageant without words, and the production was an extraordinary exercise in sheer scale. Reinhardt chose Olympia because it had the largest covered floor space he could find, and into it he introduced thousands of lights, ten miles of cable, an orchestra of 200, a choir of 500 and a cast of 2,000. It was a theatrical wonder that has never been equalled.

Unfortunately, the simple, sentimental story of the play could not match the grandeur of its setting. Based in part on Maeterlinck's *Soeur Béatrice* (*Sister Beatrice*, 1902), *The Miracle* tells of a nun who is tempted to leave her convent for worldly pleasures. After a series of seducers and lovers, she is charged with witchcraft by the Inquisition, and reduced to being a miserable camp-follower, baby in arms. Meanwhile, the Virgin Mary has miraculously taken the nun's place in the convent, and maintains the deception until the nun returns, deserted and sick, degraded and disillusioned, ready to confess her sins and atone.

For this, Olympia became the nave of a vast cathedral, complete with Gothic columns and arches, and a stained glass window three times the diameter of the rose window in Notre Dame. Stern explained that the Gothic style permitted 'improbable and fantastically involved arabesques curled with flowers, leaves and fruit which, on closer examination, proved to be grotesquely distorted masks'. In the centre a large platform rose and fell, each time with a different interior set, a banquet hall, an inquisition chamber, and so on. Huge scarlet doors at the end of the nave opened to reveal an exterior scene of a single tree on a bare hillside. Needless to say, the giant stage dwarfed the actors, and much of the detail of performance was lost, but as an experiment in combining music, dance and drama on a vast scale the production was justified.

The costumes, as was said, were dreamlike and fantastic, and they answered the demands in the text for 'bosom, belly, leg and thigh'. According to Stern, 'The fashion was devilish, grotesque and mocking, recklessly extravagant and exaggerated. It grinned, so to speak; it mocked; it stuck out its tongue at the prudish.' And he believed the method of costuming the play helped the actors to appear larger than life.

Reinhardt managed his huge medieval crowd to capture every mood from sorrow to revelry. To strike the right initial key for the performance, he began with a miracle: before all the peasants and pilgrims, the sick and the lame, a cripple is healed, and the murmurs of the people became a long, slow, growing cry of adoration, capped by the choir's singing a crashing *Gloria*. One witness, Bridges-Adams, commented, 'Those who remember it will remember to the end of our days how it feels to behold a miracle.' Each episode was treated as one of symbolic action: the healing of the sick, the dance to the Devil, the burning of the royal palace, and finally the rising of the sun. Of the scene of banqueting and festivity, another witness, Huntly Carter, reported what he saw:

> Streams of coloured light, yellow, blue, and white, flaming through the latticed surface of square black boxes or prisms posed on storklike legs. Forty-seven electric fans drove up the yellow silken ribbons upon which the light from the forty arc lamps beat. The shrieks of the revellers filled up the intervals of the fiery effects as they made themselves felt in the conflagration overhead. For some moments we stood in the midst of blinding lights, flashing flames, and crashing winds. Then the bell rang and there was the silence and darkness of death (*The Theatre of Max Reinhardt*, pp. 232–3).

*The Miracle* was Reinhardt's attempt at recreating a Greekish experience for a modern audience, and his sensuous treatment of a spiritual theme was breathtaking. There remains the aesthetic paradox: if a director turns a theatre into a cathedral, and there creates a holy occasion, can he be accused of realism?

At about this time the working director was learning to plan each scene in his studio for its line and colour in relation to the whole, like a painter composing his canvas. One can immediately see the difference between the promptbooks written before the First World War and those written before the Second World War. The new director began to make use of a model stage and test his lighting effects in miniature against scale figures of his actors; on his model he could try the effect of light on costume and setting, and of mixing one colour with another. Reinhardt set the standard by drawing up the first *Regiebuch,* the detailed and complete production record of a play, which describes moment by moment what was done with a text to bring it to life. Because the copyright was held by the American promoter Morris Gest, the book for the New York production of *The Miracle* was the first of its kind to be published, in 1924. Not until 1966 did Reinhardt's widow allow another of the *Regiebucher,* that for the *Macbeth* of 1916, to be published, and the *Faust I* of 1909 was published in 1971.

Arthur Kahane, Reinhardt's *Dramaturg,* or literary advisor, called the *Regiebuch* 'a complete, detailed paraphrase of a play in the stage manager's language', a glimpse into the director's workshop. Prior to a Brecht *Modellbuch,* or a film or videotape recording, there was no more complete a record of a theatre production. From such a master plan could be developed explicit directions for each contributor to the play, the designer or electrician, actor or musician, and the text itself became one of the ingredients in a total conception. This procedure appeared to make the director the final authority in the theatre, and to confirm his role as a creator in his own right. It could also relegate the actor to the role of a puppet whose every move had to conform to the master plan. But in this way, Kahane wrote, Reinhardt created a new world with each production, and did not allow the theatre to be the servant of literature, but 'a thing in itself, following its own laws, its own path, a *theatrum mundi'*.

Even though he was well able to direct an actor in a quick, sensitive, realistic style, Reinhardt's inevitable reputation grew upon his ability to create spectacular crowd scenes. But even here, he did more than paint the stage with people. When Shakespeare's Julius Caesar was killed in the Grosses Schauspielhaus, he staggered down the thirty or forty steps from his throne, stabbed again and again by the conspirators as he reeled from side to side. When Portia's speech in the trial scene of *The Merchant of Venice* unexpectedly traps Shylock, Reinhardt's crowd broke the tension with an ecstatic shriek. These devices, whether human or mechanical, were always functional and symbolic. Indeed, behind each grand effect in a Reinhardt production lay a drive towards simplicity, the intention of accentuating some effect appropriate to each scene. Hofmannsthal wrote warmly of Reinhardt's 'poetics' of rhythm, by which he also organized stage time to equal his manipulation of stage space. The Reinhardt stage seemed to be a new medium of expression, one having 'a mysterious affinity to the tendency of modern painters' — Hofmannsthal was thinking of the expressionists — in which 'the figures stand out in space . . . as if charged by electricity'. Like the expressionists, Reinhardt used the arts, not to reproduce reality, but to bring about a striking image of the energy, life and spirit of the play he was working on. Nevertheless, directors are nothing without plays to direct, and Reinhardt returned repeatedly to the classics. It is hard to escape the conclusion that he was bigger than the expressionist drama he found in vogue.

As a Jew, Reinhardt's Berlin theatres were taken from him by the Nazis in 1933, and by the end of 1934 he was in America, never to return to Europe. Other German directors also contributed to the greatness of their theatre before Hitler. Jürgen Fehling has been mentioned as the imaginative producer of *Masses and Man*. The anti-realist Georg Fuchs (1868–1949) was a theorist who echoed the ideas of Appia and Craig, and wrote about the theatre as a Wagnerian synthesis of the arts as early as 1905 in his book *Die Schaubühne der Zukunft (The Theatre of the Future)*. Fuchs advocated the rejection of 'monkey-like imitations of everyday life', and the return of 'theatricalism' and ritualistic experience to the theatre. With the designer Fritz Erler (1868–1940), he founded the Künstler Theater, the Art Theatre, in Munich in 1907, and it is of particular interest that even at this early date, these two extended the stage over the orchestra pit so that the actors could play forward into the house. Sections of their stage floor could be raised or lowered, so that a variety of acting levels, set against a cyclorama of changeable colours, could abstract and universalize the content of the drama.

Leopold Jessner (1878–1945), director of the Berlin Staatstheater, 1919–25, and strong advocate of expressionism, was
Reinhardt's immediate disciple. Jessner was more ardent as an
opponent of realism and less catholic in his tastes, and stole some
of the attention away from his master with several startling experiments in explicitly symbolic staging. His inclination was to compose
his stage in three dimensions, especially vertically, and for scenery
he substituted a platform and steps set against a cyclorama, mixing
Appia's ideas about light with Meyerhold's staging devices. The
extensive use of steps was associated with his name, and *Spieltreppe*
or *Jessnertreppe* became a mark of his productions.

In Jessner's production of Shakespeare's *Richard III*, a great
central stairway became the acting area itself for the main scenes.
In the scene of Richard's coronation, the steps were covered in a
blood-red cloth, and the King stood on the top step while his subjects
huddled below him, all dressed in red. In the scene of his death,
Richard literally toppled down the steps to die at the hands of
Richmond's men, all dressed in white. In Jessner's production
of *Othello*, steps lent a force to the action when in the scene of the
Moor's arrival in Cyprus, he appeared on the top step at the back of

20. Shakespeare, *Richard III*, Gloucester becomes king. Production
by Leopold Jessner, design by Emil Pirchan at the Schauspielhaus,
Berlin, 1922.

the stage, and towered over his men, who fell back as he descended. Reporting on Jessner in *Continental Stagecraft*, Kenneth Macgowan believed that the steps were the key to each of his productions: they shaped the play, established its formal quality, banished scenic realism, and gave Jessner good opportunities for arranging his actors. Under such men as Reinhardt and Jessner, the stage became an *expression* of the play.

# 8 *Expressionism in Soviet Russia: Meyerhold*

### The Inspector General (1926)

Along with their German contemporaries, the new directors who sprang from the Moscow Art Theatre all felt the limitations of stage realism. 'The stage is a world of marvels and enchantment, it is breathless joy and strange magic', said the greatest of Stanislavsky's progeny, Vsevolod Meyerhold (1874–1940), and it is significant that Stanislavsky himself, the greatest of the realists, should feel a stirring of dissatisfaction with the mode he had promoted so convincingly. But in his autobiography he admitted that 'between the dreams of the stage director and their realization there is a tremendous distance' (*My Life in Art*, p. 437).

Even in 1904, the year of *The Cherry Orchard*, Stanislavsky had been attracted to the symbolist meanderings of Maeterlinck, and as a result of a questionable production of *The Blind* and *The Intruder*, had in 1905 set up a Studio of the MAT in Povarskaya Street in order to experiment with symbolism and other abstract styles, which he called 'impressionism'. The Studio, he wrote, was 'able to introduce impressionism in the theatre and find a beautiful and conventionalized scenic form for its expression' (p. 434). It was this studio that Stanislavsky generously gave over to Meyerhold's care, since he had wanted to work in a more contemporary spirit. Nor should it be forgotten that Stanislavsky was also willing to put on Andreyev's symbolic drama, *The Life of Man*, the 'black velvet' production of 1907 designed to suit its author's gloomy mysticism (see vol. ii, ch. 6), and even to invite the leader of the opposite camp, Gordon Craig, to Moscow in 1908 in order to prepare a symbolist *Hamlet*. And although Stanislavsky never lost his love for realism, he was prepared to stretch its meaning to include a notion of 'inner realism'. Finally, in spite of a history of quarrels with Meyerhold on artistic grounds, just before his death in 1938 Stanislavsky surprised Moscow by inviting him to be his assistant and eventual successor at the Opera Studio.

Meyerhold had joined the MAT in 1898, playing Treplev in *The Seagull* that year, and working for four years as a realistic actor under Stanislavsky until he broke with him in 1902. Meyerhold was devoted to Wagner, and was at first excited by the symbolists, enthusiastically reading Appia, Craig and Fuchs. However, he had turned against realistic production on grounds all his own. He accused realism of using only the vocal and facial expression of the actor, rather than his whole body, with all its posture, gesture and movement. Nor, with his ideal of 'passive', psychological action, could the realistic director ever clarify the shape and internal rhythm of a play by stylization. Realistic production exhibited 'morbid human curiosity', and it was painfully analytical and fussy with business. It always ran the risk of never seeing the play whole. And Meyerhold pointed out that the true Chekhovian mood did not come from the sound of crickets, but from the rhythm and lyricism of Chekhov's words.

To his remarkable run of revolutionary productions, Meyerhold brought a new vision of theatre. He moved into expressionism by reasserting the audience's 'right to dream', and he emphasized the 'plasticity' (his favourite word) of *physical* acting, contrived to compel his audience to share in a performance. He achieved a more external, objective and ironic treatment of a play by applying many neglected and forgotten techniques of performance, and several others he invented himself. The term 'stylization' became associated with his manner of production, the outer form expressing the 'inner synthesis'. In his book on Max Reinhardt, Huntly Carter quoted Meyerhold for a contemporary definition of the term in 1914:

> I consider it is impossible to separate the ideas of 'styliza-
> tion' from the ideas of generalization, convention and
> symbolism. By the 'stylization' of a period or a pheno-
> menon, I mean the use of all means that bring out the
> inner synthesis of the period or phenomenon, and that
> enable the latent characteristics of artistic works to be
> clearly presented (p. 82).

In the event, Meyerhold chose not to go the way of Wagner's synthesis of the arts, since he believed that the art of painting was limited by the stage, and that music in the theatre had always to be subservient to the drama. But he insisted that in each production the director and his actors had to discover the appropriate style and tone for the play they were presenting. This was especially necessary in non-realistic drama, where the 'inner music', the hidden rhythm of language and movement, had to be determined. A play's form came before its content. Only then could the actor convey and illustrate the truth of a play's inner feeling.

One key to understanding a Meyerhold production lay in his attitude to his audience. Unlike Stanislavsky, Meyerhold did not wish the audience to forget it was in a theatre. Stanislavsky worked as if the audience did not exist; Meyerhold made it the centre of the theatre event. He quoted Andreyev approvingly: 'The spectator should not forget for a moment that an actor is *performing* for him, and the actor should never forget that he is performing before an audience, with a stage beneath his feet and a set around him' (translated Edward Braun, from whose book *Meyerhold on Theatre* this and other quotations in this chapter are taken). For Meyerhold, 'dynamic' theatricality meant that attention was to be on the audience, not the stage. He wrote in 1907,

> We intend the audience not merely to observe, but to
> participate in a *corporate* creative act; the actor is left *alone*,
> face to face with the spectator, and from the friction
> between these two unadulterated elements, the actor's
> creativity and the spectator's imagination, a clear flame is
> kindled (pp. 60 and 62).

The idea behind this derived from I. P. Pavlov's fashionable theory of conditioned reflexes and association: what was put together on the stage should 'condition' a reflex in the audience so that, however unreal the convention on the stage, the 'reality' would be perceived by the audience if the formula was correct. In his search for each formula, Meyerhold borrowed freely from every known source: the theatres of China and Japan, the *Kathakali* dance theatre of India, the acrobatics of the *commedia dell'arte*, the classical arenas and the travelling booths, the medieval and Renaissance theatres, the circus and the music hall. He was irrepressibly inventive, mobilizing all the resources of the stage, ransacking the past, not just for historical replicas, but for any lively device which would bring down the barriers between the stage and the spectator.

After its beginnings in realism, Meyerhold's career developed rapidly. For a short time in 1905 he returned to the MAT's first studio at Stanislavsky's invitation. At that time Meyerhold was still under the spell of the symbolists, attracted to the idea of revealing the 'inner dialogue' buried in Maeterlinck's static, stylized drama. In his production of *The Death of Tintagiles*, Meyerhold set his actors against a simple backcloth, where they struck poses in a statuesque, 'iconographic' manner, and spoke in clear, calm tones to rid the play of any tension or gloom, and convey instead a quality of restrained harmony or 'ecstasy'. But so inanimate a play went contrary to Meyerhold's nature, and while he clung to the idea of simplicity on the stage, the livelier spirit of ancient tradition was beginning to grip him.

In 1906 Meyerhold was invited by Vera Kommissarzhevskaya to work with her company in St Petersburg, but to her considerable alarm he began to show his inventiveness as a director. For Maeterlinck's *Sister Beatrice*, the set was brought so far downstage that the sisters appeared to act in bas-relief, the crowd of beggars and others moving together in slow motion like a medieval frieze. The highly stylized *Hedda Gabler* of 1906, mentioned in vol. 1, ch. 5, was also set upon a deliberately shallow stage, 33 feet wide and 12 feet deep. But Meyerhold also ignored Ibsen's finely detailed stage directions, each one loaded with multi-symbolic implications, and imposed a plan of his own.

Each character in *Hedda Gabler* was allotted his own symbolic colour to match his mood and inner nature, Tesman in dull grey, Hedda in green, and so on, and each had a characteristic pose to which he returned. As the central character, Hedda also had a huge white armchair like a throne to which she withdrew. Pavel Yartsev, literary manager to the theatre and assistant director for the production, gives some impression of the stylized performance from this description of the first scene between Lövborg and Hedda:

> Throughout the entire scene they sit side by side, tense and motionless, looking straight ahead. Their quiet, disquieting words fall rhythmically from lips which seem dry and cold... Not once throughout the entire long scene do they alter the direction of their gaze or their pose. Only on the line 'Then you too have a thirst for life!' does Lövborg make a violent motion towards Hedda, and at this point the scene comes to an abrupt conclusion.
>
> Realistically speaking, it is inconceivable that Hedda and Lövborg should play the scene in this manner, that any two real, living people should ever converse like this. The spectator hears the lines as though they were addressed directly at him; before him the whole time he sees the faces of Hedda and Lövborg, observes the slightest change of expression; behind the monotonous dialogue he senses the concealed inner dialogue of presentiments and emotions which are incapable of expression in mere words (translated Edward Braun, p. 68).

But even this production was transitional. Once Meyerhold felt the restrictions of illusionistic theatre fall away, the possibilities for experiment were endless. His *Spring's Awakening* by Wedekind in 1907 was an adventure in multi-scenic staging, with all the sets of the play on the stage simultaneously, and a simple spotlight picking out the actors as required. In this way Meyerhold divided up the action while unifying the play.

Starting in 1908, he spent three years directing for the Imperial Theatres in St Petersburg, the Alexandrinsky and the Mariasky Opera, again making great inroads into what he called the bourgeois theatre of false realism. The outstanding production during this phase was of Molière's *Don Juan* at the Alexandrinsky in 1910. The production was glorified with the music of Lully and decorated magnificently by Alexander Golovin with the brilliant chandeliers and gilded costumes of a festive Versailles. But the real emphasis was on the acting, the true vehicle for the play. To ensure that every posture, gesture and expression should be seen, Meyerhold confined the action to the forestage he had built on a platform, the actors playing at the very edge – he was convinced it had been this way in the original production at the Palais-Royal. They played under bright lights, without curtains and with the house lights on, footmen-stagehands changing the props in full view. The actors worked essentially without the benefit of illusion. In this way Meyerhold appeared to open up the proscenium stage and move the play out into the auditorium, thus having the actor play to his audience and destroy the last vestige of realism's notorious 'fourth wall'. The theatre became a great ballroom and the spectators were able, it was reported, 'to inhale the air of an epoch'.

It was at this time that Meyerhold was studying the Elizabethan stage that Shakespeare had used, and the Molière production is a certain indication that Meyerhold was in the vanguard of those who rediscovered open staging in the twentieth century. Huntly Carter summarized as follows: 'Stanislavsky told the actor he must forget that he is on the stage. Taïrov told him he must remember nothing else. Meyerhold told him he must remember that he is one of the audience.'

Yet during this same period, Meyerhold was staging even more radical experiments in his 'Interlude House', the former Skazka Theatre in St Petersburg. Considering this activity to be a breach of contract, the Director of the Imperial Theatres asked him to use a pseudonym, so that in about 1910, Meyerhold also worked under the delicious name of 'Dr Dappertutto', after a character of E. T. A. Hoffmann. Dappertutto was a true *Doppelgänger*, a double who knew no limits in the eccentric use of the theatre.

The Russian Revolution of 1917 gave Meyerhold a unique chance to put more of his proliferating ideas into practice, since that event shattered the traditions of theatrical taste and convention like so many other Russian institutions. He was authorized to found a new theatre for a new society, and in 1920 he converted the Zon Operetta on Sadovaya-Triumfalnaya Street to his uses. Of the first production, Edward Braun comments, 'The derelict, unheated auditorium with its flaking plaster and broken seats was more like a meeting-hall; this was wholly appropriate, for it was in the spirit of a political meeting that Meyerhold conceived the production' (p. 163). Actors were planted in the audience to raise their voices as at a public meeting, and full audience participation was the aim. Meyerhold now threw himself into the work of uncovering the mysteries of new theatre techniques with the same enthusiasm that his pupil Sergei Eisenstein, the great film director, devoted to the art of film montage in the 1920s. It was this revolutionary theatre which, after many changes in its name, eventually became the Vsevolod Meyerhold State Theatre in 1926.

This was also the time when Meyerhold was able to work out in practice what he called 'biomechanics' in acting, and he enthusiastically geared his theory to Soviet-Marxist philosophy. In a lecture of 1922, he actually said,

> The work of the actor in an industrial society will be re-
> garded as a means of production vital to the proper organ-
> ization of the labour of every citizen of that society . . . It
> is equally essential to discover those movements in work
> which facilitate the maximum use of work time . . . In
> so far as the task of the actor is the realization of a specific
> objective, his means of expression must be economical in
> order to ensure that precision of movement which will
> facilitate the quickest possible realization of the objective
> (translated Edward Braun, pp. 197–8).

So it was that Meyerhold gave his actors daily exercises in 'dynamic' movement. The actor was to learn to exert maximum control over his body, which should be athletic and acrobatic, precise and quick. His physical control had also to extend to the space around him, to the props and the set, as well as to the other players.

Biomechanics involved work in three stages:
1. preparation for an action.
2. the state of mind and body at the moment of action, and
3. the reaction to what follows.

The actor must develop sharp reflexes and be totally coordinated. He must always have his thoughts under control, and be ready to jump into a scene without emotional preparation. Thus when Othello sets upon Desdemona in the apparent heat of anger, he must at the same time be able to control his actions perfectly. In direct opposition to Stanislavsky's theory, Meyerhold also argued that, in principle, an actor's posture determines his emotions and vocal expression, and not the other way round — when you are afraid, you run, and it is only after running that you express your fear by uttering sounds.

With this went Meyerhold's theory of 'pre-acting', which involved long pauses between an actor's lines. The pauses would be taken up with improvised mime designed to show his mind changing, and to prepare the spectator for what was to come. Pre-acting was not unlike life, as when one gesticulates before speaking, and Meyerhold cited the actor Lensky in the part of Benedick eavesdropping on his friends in Shakespeare's *Much Ado about Nothing*:

> For a long time he stands staring at the audience, his face frozen in amazement. Then suddenly his lips move very slightly ... from beneath the brows imperceptibly, gradually, there begins to creep a triumphant happy smile; the actor doesn't say a word, but you can see that a great irrepressible wave of joy is welling up inside Benedick...
> Now [his] whole body is one whole transport of wild rapture and the auditorium thunders with applause, although *the actor has yet to say a single word* (translated Edward Braun, pp. 205—6. Meyerhold's italics).

Along with this technique went another of 'sociomechanics', by which the actor revealed the social mask and psychological attitude of a character through the rhythm of his speech, movement and gesture.

Corresponding with this development in acting, Meyerhold created the 'constructivist' set. The term was taken from the new abstract sculpture of intersecting masses and planes, and the practice was to set the stage with an arrangement of platforms and ramps, ladders and catwalks, trapezes and wheels. These provided the acting areas of a play, and would be built as a permanent, but 'kinetic', set — essentially 'a machine for acting'. It was also a way of simplifying the needs of the actors, and making it suitable to the new acting style, whose acrobatics almost required machinery to attain maximum speed and effect. Like Brecht later, Meyerhold made sure that all stage equipment and lighting were fully visible to the audience, and even placed them in the house itself; they were never hidden illusionistically behind a proscenium arch. Nevertheless, it is hard to resist the suggestion behind the starkness of a constructivist set that the whole thing may have been simply a budgetary convenience – *The Magnanimous Cuckold* cost only 200 roubles to put on.

It was to be expected that the revolutionary Meyerhold would turn at this time to German expressionism, with its outright attack on industrial capitalism, as the best material for his constructivist experiments. He did indeed direct Toller's *The Machine Wreckers* in 1922 and *Masses and Man* in 1923. But the unrealistic idealism of German expressionism's 'new man' held little appeal for those who had undergone an actual, bloody revolution, and Meyerhold looked elsewhere. His first great experiment in constructivism was the 1922 production of a play by the Belgian expressionist and farceur Fernand Crommelynck, *Le Cocu magnifique* (*The Magnanimous Cuckold*, first produced in Paris by Lugné-Poe in 1920). Meyerhold directed it at the Actor's Theatre with students from his Theatre Workshop.

Recalling the French actor Mounet-Sully's axiom 'Chaque texte n'est qu'un prétexte' (Each text is only a pretext), Meyerhold was heretical when it came to butchering an author's work. So *The Magnanimous Cuckold* became the pretext for his treatment of Crommelynck's simple story of Bruno the miller, a man so jealous of his wife that he forces her to sleep with every man in the village in order to discover her lover.

To accommodate the set he designed with Lyubov Popova, Meyerhold stripped the stage of its curtains and borders, of every feature and decoration, right to the ugly bricks of the back wall. The actor was to be as if naked on the stage, 'starting all over again . . . like the first day of creation'. Then Meyerhold built on the stage floor an extraordinary construction of two tall skeleton frames, connected by a long board which ended in steps down to the stage floor. Behind this were arranged the vanes of a huge windmill and a great wheel in red and blue, with the letters CR-MM-L-NCK painted on it in white to make its spinning more noticeable. The wheel would revolve with a great clumping sound whenever Bruno was in a jealous rage. The acting space below the mill could be a courtyard or a dining-room or an office, as needed. Each character was dressed alike in blue overalls, and the emphasis was all on the acting and the actors, who performed in the manner of *commedia dell'arte* clowns and circus acrobats, full of dexterous tricks and grotesque poses and gestures. Braun quotes Boris Alpers's description of Bruno, played by Igor Ilinsky:

> Bruno . . . stood before the audience, his face pale and motionless, and with unvarying intonation, monotonous declamatory style and identical sweeping gestures he uttered his grandiloquent monologues. But at the same time this Bruno was being ridiculed by the actor performing acrobatic stunts at the most impassioned moments of his speeches, belching, and comically rolling his eyes whilst enduring the most dramatic anguish (p. 185).

Since the style revived that of the Italian comedians of the seven-

21. Crommelynck, *The Magnanimous Cuckold*, 1920. Production by Vsevolod Meyerhold and design by Lynbov Popova at the Actor's Theatre, Moscow, 1922.

teenth century, Meyerhold commemorated the tercentenary of Molière with this production. His directorial method was the very opposite of Reinhardt's: there was no lengthy period of gestation, no elaborate *Regiebuch*. Meyerhold was a director of inspired improvisations, and ready to change his mind at any moment.

By common consent, his greatest production was in 1926, that of Gogol's *Revizor* (*The Inspector General*, written in 1836). Meyerhold was anxious to find plays which suited the Soviet aesthetic, plays chosen to make their audience politically aware, and Gogol's little world of provincial officialdom looked not unlike that of St Petersburg. So he decided to upgrade the officials of the play and increase the number of civil servants. With the additional aid of techniques for audience participation, *The Inspector General* was to become a bold satire on the new bureaucracy, 'collecting everything bad in Russia into one heap'. The production has been called the finest in the history of Russian theatre, and is thought to have inspired a larger volume of commentary than any other in the history of the theatre itself.

In spite of its political overtones, Meyerhold in one sense turned Gogol's comic masterpiece about the petty clerk who is mistaken for a government official into something of a poetic play. Like Strindberg, Meyerhold thought in terms of musical form, and his production, done in fifteen scenes, followed the pattern of a sonata. He was concerned with tones and tempo, and all the words and movements were subject to a controlling rhythm. Some scenes were treated chorically, with one character intoning the lines to the accompaniment of repeated responses from the crowd. Emmanuil Kaplan has reported how well the word '*revizor*' (inspector) was used in the opening scene:

> Suddenly, as though on a word of command, at a stroke of the conductor's baton, everyone stirs in agitation, pipes jump from lips, fists clench, heads swivel. The last syllable of '*revizor*' seems to tweak everybody. Now the word is hissed in a whisper: the whole word by some, just the consonants by others, and somewhere even a softly rolled 'r'. The word '*revizor*' is divided musically into every conceivable intonation. The ensemble of suddenly startled officials blows up and dies away like a squall. Everyone

freezes and falls silent; the guilty conscience rises in alarm, then hides its poisonous head again, like a serpent lying motionless and saving its deadly venom (translated Edward Braun, p. 217).

When at the end of the play the letter is read which explains the ridiculous error that has been made, this chorus is heard again. In his book on Meyerhold, the critic Aleksei Aleksandrovich Gvozdev tells how the guests and petty functionaries grew nervous, made noises, laughed and gloated maliciously, and exulted and cackled. Then the crowd grew quiet for a time before the noise and the cries broke out again, stronger than before. Gvozdev compared this use of the chorus with the orchestration of the musical instruments in a large symphony orchestra.

The setting for the play was treated with comparable licence. The stage was enclosed in a half-circle of rich mahogany screens, polished until they shone. The screens contained thirteen double doors in a series, and from time to time the centre screens opened to enable a pre-set truck-stage to be rolled forward or pulled back. The set was hung with magnificent candelabra, and a note of luxury was struck in the design of all the props and costumes. But the furniture was subtly unnatural: a Récamier couch curved more voluptuously, a giant wardrobe bellied out more outrageously, than the real things, in order to match the grotesque postures of the characters. The whole stage was used – and more: in the inn scene, the enormity of Dobchinsky's news of the inspector's arrival was conveyed by having Dobchinsky tumble headlong downstairs and right out of sight into the orchestra pit. At the end of the play, the final dance overflowed into the auditorium.

The characters were splendidly dressed as for *opéra bouffe*. According to Mikhail Korenev, Meyerhold's assistant, the pompous Mayor 'was arrayed in an ornate shako and voluminous cloak, looking like some august field-marshal from the glorious campaign against Napoleon'. His feather-brained wife Anna Andreyevna was changed from the provincial coquette to 'a society beauty with a lustrous black chignon, and shoulders of gleaming alabaster rising from the rich silks which swathed her voluptuous figure'. These characters were presented essentially as they saw themselves. Khlestakov, the indigent clerk who was the cause of all the trouble, was given a double with a lugubrious look, an officer who helped the little clerk change into the imposing figure of the impostor. He also joined Khlestakov in dancing with Anna and her daughter Maria, the cynical presence of the double theatrically pointing whatever notion had entered Khlestakov's mind. And even for silent characters, Meyerhold invented business and mime, as an unusual transcript of some of the rehearsals indicates. Thus the Doctor in attendance on the Mayor was required to speak incessantly in German, and to keep on talking as he stirred a glass of medicine and from time to time passed the Mayor a spoonful, walked round the bed, knocked his chest, applied a mustard plaster to his feet and exhorted everyone to keep calm —all this without a word being understood, and without understanding a word spoken to him.

Each scene was brought to heights of stylization of a kind never attempted before. In the scene of the 'procession', 'a tipsy Khlestakov in voluminous cloak steered an erratic course the length of a balustrade with a sycophantic *corps de ballet* of town dignitaries matching his every stagger'. When Anna reminisced about her amorous cavalry captain, a succession of love-sick officers, each holding a bouquet, popped up from behind the furniture and histrionically committed suicide. For the 'bribery' scene, the drunken clerk dozed in an armchair centre-stage, while 'the rat-like faces of the officials' appeared in every doorway, each man tendering a roll of notes simultaneously. Khlestakov pocketed the money 'with the mechanical gestures of a clockwork doll', the whole episode seeming to have been his intoxicated dream. At the beginning of each scene the actors froze and then suddenly began to speak or move, as if they were puppets. At the end, after the wild dance through the house, there was a final tableau and a blackout for a few moments, and when the lights came on again, the live actors had been replaced by naked dummies, fixed in poses identical with those of the actors just seen, as if to suggest that such people would remain the victims of their silly fate for ever.

Such theatrical improvisations Meyerhold called his *jeux de théâtre*, his theatre games. They owed their origin to the business of the *commedia dell'arte* and to Molière, and they were characteristic of all of Meyerhold's last productions. As if to acknowledge their right to exist, he would list himself in the programme as 'the author of the presentation'. When in 1935 he produced an evening of one-act 'vaudevilles' by Chekhov, consisting of *The Jubilee, The Bear* and *The Proposal,* he found no less than thirty-three instances of a character's fainting, turning pale, clutching his heart or calling for water, all gestures belonging to Chekhov's most farcical style. So Meyerhold made the idea of fainting the leitmotif of his production, and called the show *33 Swoons.* He exaggerated each piece of business to the point of the ridiculous, and accompanied it with appropriate music, even if this was rather at the expense of the pace of the whole.

The socialist realist press was dismayed by Meyerhold's treatment of *The Inspector General.* From that time on, he was accused of being a reactionary and even an anti-social mystic. The word then used in criticism of those artists who did not conform to the aesthetic of socialist realism was 'formalist', and this was levelled at 'aesthetes' who had chosen 'to shun real life'. It was as a result of *Pravda's* attack on Mayakovsky's *The Bathhouse* in 1930 as a formalist work that the poet committed suicide. The official government position on formalism was stated in Zhdanov's speech of 1936. So Meyerhold found his work the object of scorn, and in 1938 his theatre was closed. In 1939 he publicly denounced socialist realism and was soon after arrested. His wife was murdered that same year, and Meyerhold himself is thought to have been shot in prison in 1940. Happily, in the cultural thaw after the death of Stalin in 1953, Meyerhold's reputation was rescued, and his writings were published in two volumes in 1968. They constitute some of the most important documents of twentieth-century theatre.

# 9 Expressionism in Soviet Russia: writers and directors

*The Life of Man* (1907), *Turandot* (1922)

Stanislavsky and Meyerhold did not stand alone in the years immediately before and after the Revolution in Russia. The first quarter of the twentieth century now appears to have been the richest period in the history of the Russian theatre.

Two Russian playwrights shared the leadership for the attack on realism, even if they somewhat uncertainly mixed both the symbolist and the expressionist modes they found in vogue in the west. Leonid Andreyev (1871–1919), who was also mentioned in volume 2, chose the way of Maeterlinck's soul-searching pessimism. He began writing plays in 1905 after he was successful as a story writer, and by 1916 he had written twenty full-length plays and eight one-acts. *The Life of Man* was written in twelve days in 1906, and although it was out of character for the MAT, Stanislavsky attempted to produce it expressionistically in 1907. It is a modern morality play in which Man is followed through five stages of his life from birth to death. Andreyev writes of these stages, not as 'acts', but as 'pictures' — in the manner of Dürer's woodcuts. As in its medieval prototype, the characters are not individualized, but bear the simple generic names of Old Woman, Young Man, and so forth. In the gruesome person of 'Someone in Grey', Man is at every step dogged by his fate, and at the last dies in darkness to the discordant and strident sounds of a modern orchestra.

It is interesting that Meyerhold should have staged this play in St Petersburg that same year. His approach was far more stark, using a bare stage and grotesquely exaggerated make-up for the characters. Meyerhold placed more emphasis on Someone in Grey, who stood with an expressionless face in a corner of the stage throughout the performance, holding a candle which ominously burned down a little more with each scene. Rather than represent the splendour and vanity of bourgeois life on earth, the dancers at the ball in the third scene, a chorus of Friends and Enemies, were made to move like regimented automata with lugubrious expressions on their faces as they danced to the discordant music of three exhausted musicians. Altogether a more pessimistic, and apparently more expressionistic, treatment. When in 1908 Andreyev rewrote the last scene, that of Man's drunken death in a tavern, he changed the chorus of Drunkards to one of grasping Heirs in order to echo the first scene's chorus of Relatives who were present at the birth. In many ways a seminal play, *The Life of Man* was heckled by members of the anti-Semite Black Hundreds who had been responsible for the massacre of the Jews on Easter Day, 1903, and it was subsequently banned in Odessa and other places where the authorities feared a civil disturbance.

A notable theorist of the new movement, Nikolai Evreinov (1879–1955) was a 'prolific writer and jack-of-all-trades, actor and director, playwright and musician. He succeeded Meyerhold at the Kommissarzhevskaya Theatre in 1908, and so he was able to exert a greater influence on theatre practice than Andreyev. He was one of the few who were ready to attack Chekhovian realism directly, and in his book *The Theatre in Life* (taken from the three volumes of essays, *The Theatre for Oneself*, which he had published between 1915 and 1917) he offered a sarcastic criticism of the MAT's work. If Stanislavsky had been logical about copying life in his production of Chekhov's *Three Sisters*, he said, he would have rented a small house in the suburbs of Moscow, the audience would have come under the pretext of looking for apartments, and then looked through a key-hole or a half-opened door, visiting the house in the morning, the afternoon, the evening, 'and even in the night, when you would behold it in flames'.

The theory behind Evreinov's notion of theatre was straightforward, and in some ways anticipated the theory of expressionism. Since in life we constantly 'role-play' as children or adults — in the clothes we wear and in the little rituals we practise — life in the theatre should be strongly 'theatricalized', and audiences should never be allowed to forget where they are. Evreinov's monodrama *The Theatre of the Soul* (1912) partly dramatized his theory. In this play the same character, Man, appears in three different roles, each an aspect of his total personality: the rational, the emotional and the spiritual. Accordingly, when Woman comes on the scene, she too appears differently to each of the sub-characters. Ever up-to-date, Evreinov also pursued the theory that a play should present its author's 'inner self' in such a way that the character would seem to be his *ego* to the spectator's *alter ego*. This Pirandellian approach to playwriting was taken up in Evreinov's play *The Chief Thing* (1919), which argues that a human being needs the illusion of happiness, and shows how the need may actually be supplied by theatrical illusion.

Evreinov was a writer clearly unsuited to proceed far into the age of Soviet socialist realism, and he emigrated in 1925. His introspective pessimism was as acute as Andreyev's, but the highly satirical and theatrical note he struck bore more obviously on expressionistic developments. Both of these dramatists caused a furore in their time, but both now rest among the forgotten.

Immediately influenced by Meyerhold was the director Alexander Taïrov (1885–1950), who broke away from the MAT in 1914 to found the Kamerny Theatre (chamber theatre) with his wife Alice Koonen. 'Little by little the theatre has turned into an experimental laboratory for psychopathological research', he argued, and set about bringing into existence a 'theatre unbound' in which all the arts would be synthesized. His vision included a stage populated with ballet dancers, mimes, music-hall comics, circus performers and opera singers. His productions were formally patterned with stylized movement and intoned speech — he even spoke of his actors as 'musical instruments'. He believed that actors, like dancers, should begin their training at the age of seven, and that their exercises should include acrobatics, fencing and eurhythmics. For his sets he drew upon Appia's ideas about light and space, as well as upon Meyerhold's constructivist levels, ramps and steps. Unlike Meyerhold, however, Taïrov believed that the actor should be given more freedom to improvise his own performance, and he tried to retain the kind of emotional intensity associated with a production by Stanislavsky. His most notable productions included Racine's *Phèdre*, Wilde's *Salomé* as an opera, and a *Seagull* played by actors dressed entirely in black against totally black curtains. This was hardly a theatre for the people, and Taïrov soon ran into trouble with the Party.

Stanislavsky's most dedicated and gifted student was the actor Yevgeny (Eugene) Vakhtangov (1883–1922). Vakhtangov was also caught up in the post-revolutionary reaction against realism, but less radically. He felt that Meyerhold's extreme techniques tended to suppress true feeling, and so he sought a way to temper theatricality with realism. Vakhtangov had joined the MAT in 1911, and was at first more realistic as an actor than Stanislavsky himself. When Vakhtangov founded the MAT's Third Studio in 1914, he put his theories into practice with great success. This theatre later took his name, and on his death its direction passed to Michael Chekhov, nephew of the playwright.

Vakhtangov called his approach one of 'fantastic realism', the 'fantasy' referring to the form and structure of the production, and the 'realism' to the treatment of a scene within the whole. It was a fusion of Meyerhold's theatrical inventiveness with Stanislavsky's search for psychological truth, and the double approach offered a creative treatment of actuality in the belief, as Vakhtangov said, that 'rightly found theatrical methods impart genuine life to the play upon the stage'. In this conception he followed the poet Mayakovksy's definition of art when he said that it was 'not a copy of nature but the determination to distort nature in accordance with its reflections in the individual consciousness' (quoted in E. T. Kirby's *Total Theatre*, p. 151). We might recognize this as another facet of expressionism. Vakhtangov's actor was able to recreate a realistic emotion, and at the same time be consciously aware of what he was doing. His audience saw *what* he was doing, and *how* he was doing it. Stage speech was not spoken to harangue the spectator, but to convince him without the use of stylization. Vakhtangov's convenient synthesis of styles has, in fact, pointed the way for much of modern production everywhere.

Before his early death, four major productions marked Vakhtangov's progress towards fantastic realism. He opened the new theatre of the Third Studio in 1921 with Maeterlinck's *The Miracle of St Antony*. Into scenes of intense 'inner realism' developed in the Stanislavsky way, Vakhtangov introduced exaggerated expressionistic devices in order to underline a point unambiguously. Grotesque make-up and gesture were used to satirize the French bourgeoisie — a miser, for example, would hold his hands palms up and with grasping fingers. The automatic movements of the figures turned the play into a grim farce. In the same year, Vakhtangov produced Strindberg's *Erik IV* at the First Studio, with Michael Chekhov in the title part. The stage was set with a labyrinth of passageways and stairs that suggested the twisted mind of the mad king, and much of the action was interpreted through his eyes. The courtiers were played like puppets, but, to make a powerful contrast, the common people were presented realistically.

While he was dying of cancer in 1922, Vakhtangov created his finest productions. One was Shloyme Ansky's Yiddish play *The Dybbuk* (1918), originally written for the MAT in 1914, but suppressed. It was first presented in Warsaw in 1920, and when the Hebrew-speaking Habima Theatre was legalized after the Revolution, Vakhtangov directed them in the Habima Theatre Studio in Moscow. It was this production that went on tour in 1926 and 1948. It was one of extreme discipline and precision, and played in the generally grotesque style of the ghetto's inhabitants, a style to match the mystic content of the play and help each character achieve a quality of reality in the rhythm of his playing.

Vakhtangov's final production, performed in the Third Studio

22. Gozzi, *Turandot*, 1762. Production by Yevgeny Vakhtangov at the Third Studio of the Moscow Art Theatre, 1922.

in 1922, was of Carlo Gozzi's original version of *Turandot*, his 'tragi-
comical theatrical Chinese fairy tale' of 1762. The story is of the
Princess Turandot and the three riddles which her suitors must
answer if they are not to be beheaded. As in any fairy tale, Prince
Calaf succeeds in winning her hand and saving his neck. The production was designed by a Cubist painter, I. Nivinsky, as a
Meyerhold-like composition of platforms, gangways and galleries,
and the action was made 'contemporary' by such devices as that
of having the King carry a tennis racquet in lieu of a sceptre. Characters from the world of the *commedia dell'arte* like Pantalone and
Truffaldino and Tartaglia were woven into the performance, and the
actors appeared to improvise their costumes and props — one
wrapped a towel about his head for a turban, another tied a scarf
round his chin for a beard.

In spite of these tricks, the presentation carried with it a
challenging ambiguity. On the one hand, the Calaf and the Princess
conveyed their suffering sincerely, so that the audience could
sympathize with them, but, on the other hand, each emotional effect
was ironically undercut for laughter. For example, William Kuhlke
described this piece of business:

23. Gozzi, *Turandot*, 1762. Design by I. Nivinsky, 1922.

When the actor playing Barach accomplished a small coup of inner realism by weeping real tears as he told Calaf of his mother's death, Tartaglia rushed from the wings with a shaving bowl, collected Barach's tears, and then displayed them to the audience as ironic 'proof' of the deep sincerity of Barach's portrayal *(Educational Theatre Journal,* May 1967).

The actors for this production had been able to don and doff the realistic mask at will, playing a role and commenting on it at the same time in a manner that Brecht was later to institutionalize. However, Vakhtangov's effect was not yet Brecht's *V-effekt (Verfremdungseffekt,* or alienation effect), since the Russian expected his audience to feel emotion in the regular way.

The total quality of this production of *Turandot* was gay and light-hearted. The actors put on their costumes, and the stagehands set the scene, in full view of the audience. The music was played on combs and tissue paper. Although the production had been worked out in fine detail, it had the joyful effect of spontaneity, as if it was an experience in dramatic creation happily shared by actors and spectators. The play ran for more than 1,000 performances.

In the spirit of the times, Vakhtangov conceived his theatre company as a 'collective', with the company itself choosing the play to be produced, and assigning a director from its own ranks. The director was not to be a despot like Meyerhold, but an equal contributor. He would merely submit his ideas for discussion and approval before rehearsals began, and in this way all members of the company would be partners in a creative enterprise. As it happened, it was only after Vakhtangov's death that the Vakhtangov Theatre tried to put these somewhat questionable ideals into practice.

Nikolai Pavlovich Okhlopkov (1900–66) studied under Meyerhold and modified his master's expressionistic style, but he was as much a showman and a dictator. Okhlopkov's important work began at the Realistic Theatre in Moscow, a very small building with a capacity of only 325. It had begun life as the Fourth Studio of the MAT, and Okhlopkov became its director in 1932. The story goes that he had been present at a lecture given by Maxim Gorky in which the audience had been forced by the shortage of space to sit all round the speaker on the platform, and as a consequence had been magnetized by him. Okhlopkov henceforth decided to produce in-the-round. He banished the formality of the proscenium arch by putting seats on the stage and arranging platforms for his actors all among and around the audience. He had actors performing in the aisles, and even on an overhead bridge. His series of what he called 'directorial sketches' at the Realistic Theatre were conceived as preparation for bigger productions to come — he nursed a hope for a popular theatre designed to hold 3,000.

One of the best western observers of modern Russian theatre, Norris Houghton, writes in *Return Engagement* that Stanislavsky had tried to banish the theatre from the theatre. In opposition to this,

> Okhlopkov says, in effect, 'We do not go to a theatre to forget we are in a theatre. We go to it because it takes us away from life. It is like going to the circus. There we accept the convention of the clown's white cheeks, his huge red mouth, and his enormous flapping shoes. We are not fooled into thinking this "real". He is a clown and that is enough for us.

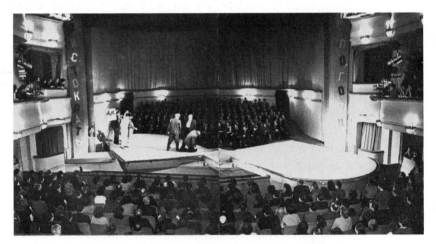

24. The Mayakovsky Theatre, Moscow, as adapted by Nikolai Okhlopkov for a production of Pogodin's *Aristocrats* in 1935.

Okhlopkov's intention was to bring the action to the audience, make the stage vividly three-dimensional, and in performance achieve an ideal of 'creative interplay' between actor and spectator.

His experiments with theatrical space brought down charges of formalism on his head, as other experiments had upon Meyerhold, but Okhlopkov was fortunate to be able to re-emerge after the death of Stalin. At that time it was he who introduced Brecht to Russia with a production of *Mother Courage*, and in 1962 he presented Euripides's *Medea* as a spectacle in the Reinhardt tradition in the vast Tchaikovsky Hall that had been originally designed by Meyerhold. For this production the centre of the auditorium was occupied, not only by Euripides's tragic chorus, but also by a complete symphony orchestra and a choir of a hundred voices.

Georg Tovstanogov spoke for the Russian theatre as a whole when he said, 'Meyerhold was form, Stanislavsky content. We believe it is a very good combination.' And it is true that these two great theatrical influences of modern times, although diametrically opposed, have in the tension set up between them produced a line of outstanding Russian directors and productions. Yet for all the experimenting with new techniques, it can hardly be claimed that the new Soviet theatre has resulted in many new playwrights or many good plays. Gorky wrote only two more plays after the Revolution, and Vladimir Mayakovksy's highly original satires *The Bedbug* (1929) and *The Bathhouse* (1930) received a very mixed reception.

# 10 *Expressionism in America: O'Neill*

*The Emperor Jones* (1920), *The Hairy Ape* (1922)

The attack on Gordon Craig as a designer by his American contemporary Lee Simonson (1888–1967) in his book *The Stage Is Set* in 1932 was an attack on a romantic by a practical man of the theatre. Simonson was caustic on the subject of Craig's ignorance of technical problems. Craig would design 'a towering cliff and set a cloud at its summit' in the expectation that 'matter would ultimately obey the spirit somehow, somewhere, sometime'. But Simonson's sarcasm did not mean that the American theatre was pleased to ignore everything that was not realistic. Simonson admired Appia to the extent of translating his works into English, and he and his fellow designer and director Robert Edmond Jones (1887–1954) not only assimilated the new theories of space and light, but successfully put them into practice.

Simonson joined Lawrence Langner to form the Washington Square Players in Greenwich Village in 1915 with the express intention of introducing New Yorkers to the new European drama, but in our story it is Jones who assumes a greater importance. It was Robert Edmond Jones who helped to start Eugene O'Neill (1888–1953) on his path as an experimental playwright. Jones had worked with Reinhardt in Berlin, and in 1915 he, George Cram ('Jig') Cook, Susan Glaspell and others formed the amateur group calling themselves the Provincetown Players, putting on summer productions in Provincetown at the tip of Cape Cod. When they moved soon after to New York, they kept their name, and it was this group that proved to be the seed-bed for non-commercial, avant-garde, home-

25. The Wharf Theatre, Provincetown, Massachusetts, in 1915.

grown playwriting and production. O'Neill joined the Provincetown Players in 1916.

Jones believed that, in common with other arts at that time, the theatre should articulate the sub-conscious mind. A director and his designer should soak themselves in the atmosphere of a play to discover its essential nature, and then try to create the physical dimension which would suggest 'the immanence of a visionary world'. Since the cinema could outdo the stage in pictorial realism ('Nothing can be so photographic as a photograph'), the coming of films should have liberated the stage from literal verisimilitude and given it back to the imagination. 'Think of it!', Jones wrote in his statement of belief *The Dramatic Imagination,* 'No more tasteful, well-furnished rooms with one wall missing'. At one time he wondered whether screen images could not be combined with those of the stage, thus simultaneously revealing the unconscious and the conscious mind, but he returned constantly to the argument that the theatre needed, not illusion, but allusion. His characteristic pronouncement was,

> Actually the best thing that could happen to our theatre at
> this moment would be for playwrights and actors and
> directors to be handed a bare stage on which no scenery
> could be placed, and then told that they must write
> and act and direct for this stage. In no time we should have
> the most exciting theatre in the world (p. 135).

His particular plea was for a simple platform, 'sparing in detail, rich in suggestion', one, like Shakespeare's stage, that would be capable of carrying a continuous flow of changing action. He wanted a stage animated by actors, not by its setting.

As a designer, Jones believed in using any simple, evocative device that would capture a play's atmosphere, and he drew freely upon symbolist and expressionist styles and ideas. In 1921 he designed for Lionel Barrymore's *Macbeth,* directed by Arthur Hopkins, and made this rather slow production a landmark. Kenneth Macgowan reported in *Theatre Arts Magazine* for April 1921 that throughout the presentation Jones 'attempted through significant form to create an abstract background expressing the spiritual relationships of the play'. The main scenes were surrounded by black curtains, with three giant silver masks suspended high above the set to suggest the mystic forces at work upon the characters. Asymmetrical Gothic arches seemed either to aspire to heaven, or, as the action demanded, to topple over. As a result, Jones's design encouraged 'a sensation of terrible, overpowering obsession', the scenery suggest- ing 'an emotional idea, instead of a physical reality'. In every case, Jones's designs for O'Neill's experimental plays, *The Emperor Jones* (1920), *Desire under the Elms* (1924), *The Great God Brown* (which Jones also directed, 1926) and *Mourning Becomes Electra* (1931), created a picture which went well beyond realism.

It was suggested in volume I that the basic impulse of the new American drama was towards Ibsen's, and then Chekhov's, realism, and certainly O'Neill continued to write realistic plays intermittently. However, for nearly ten years the Provincetown Players provided a stage for his anti-realistic experiments. Further, when the Washington Square Players became the Theatre Guild in 1918, European expressionism found a home in New York. So it was that through the 1920s and 1930s the Guild presented, not only the local product, but such plays as Kaiser's *From Morn to Midnight*, Strindberg's *Dance of Death* and Toller's *Masses and Man*. In a letter to the Provincetown Players in 1922, O'Neill said he wanted to produce Wedekind's *Earth Spirit*, Strindberg's *Ghost Sonata* and Andreyev's *The Black Maskers*.

All this is to suggest the extent of American interest in expressionism, and there was also a psychological reason to back this up. The conventional economic philosophy of laissez-faire in the United States, with its optimistic reliance on individualism, belonged to the period before the Armistice of 1918. The post-war years were troubled by an intellectual disillusion, and the disintegration of the so-called 'American dream'. The stage always catches the spirit of the times, and O'Neill turned to the new expressionism, and particularly to Strindberg, for a form which would better express his own disenchantment. He continued to draw closely-observed characters, and to write a new, distinctly American, dialogue in the realistic vein, but he recognized Strindberg as 'the precursor of all modernity' in the theatre, 'the greatest interpreter in the theatre of the characteristic spiritual conflicts which constitute the drama – the blood – of our lives today'.

The philosophy behind German expressionism as it was first conceived, with its intention of expressing the rebellious subconscious mind, scarcely travelled outside the country, but its techniques attracted O'Neill and a few other American playwrights. O'Neill's reading in Greek tragedy, Strindberg, Wedekind and Freud prompted him to turn to expressionism as a way of making a more personal statement. His association with Jones and the Provincetown Players ensured that he kept abreast of the latest developments, and could test the possibilities of such devices as those of interior monologue, symbolic characterization and masks. At the same time, O'Neill's urgent sense of tragic irony guaranteed that what he wrote was more than a superficial search for novelty, and his earnest example had much to do with the ability of the American theatre to break away at last from its European ties.

The evidence for O'Neill's interest in specifically German expressionism is a little contradictory. In his book on the playwright, Barrett Clark reports O'Neill as saying that he did not think much of Kaiser's plays, because they were 'too easy'. He also said that he had not seen an expressionistic play on the stage before he saw *From Morn to Midnight* in New York in 1922, that is, after he had written *The Emperor Jones* and *The Hairy Ape*. But George Pierce Baker's playwriting course at Harvard in 1914–15 had introduced him to German expressionism, and he had started to learn German. Certainly there are many likenesses between Kaiser's play and *The Emperor Jones* — its scene structure, the images seen through the eyes of the protagonist, and such expressionistic conceptions as the 'Little Formless Fears'. When Cook produced O'Neill's play for the Provincetown Players in 1920, European expressionism had been absorbed by a wholly American sensibility, and *The Emperor Jones* could even claim to be more satisfactory than its prototypes.

But the major expressionistic elements in *The Emperor Jones* belong to the patterning of the play's action. It is set out in eight scenes, which move in space from the palace at the edge of the forest through the forest and out again, and in time from dusk to dawn. Therefore, as Brutus Jones's role passes from that of emperor to that of slave, and as the play traces his change from egotism to self-knowledge, the forest and the night appear to embody the limitations of his mind. Yet the play begins and ends in a realistic manner, so that the six central scenes are a framed monologue serving to examine Brutus Jones's spirit. This arrangement demanded a good deal of the actor playing the title part, the black actors Charles Gilpin in New York and London in 1920, and Paul Robeson in London in 1924. The convention makes the play a study in the psychology of fear, intended to symbolize the conscience of mankind. O'Neill had taken to heart the Jungian concept of a 'collective unconscious'. The fact that Jones is a petty Caribbean dictator fleeing from those he has oppressed rather spoils the audience's chances of identifying itself with him in his agonies of mind, but the devices of expressionism are successful in making it possible to stage his superstitious fantasies as he hides in the jungle, especially the re-enactment of his immediate and his racial past.

Much of the power of the play is transmitted to the audience by the continuous beating of a tom-tom, which starts in scene one 'at a rate exactly corresponding to normal pulse beat — 72 to the minute — and continues at a gradually accelerating rate from this point uninterruptedly to the very end of the play'. This trick was used first in *The Drums of Oude* by Austin Strong, but various other sources for the play's special atmosphere have been proposed: Conrad's *Heart of Darkness*, the troll kingdom of Ibsen's *Peer Gynt*, O'Neill's reading of religious ceremonies in the Congo, and, when he visited Honduras, a bout of malaria which made the blood pulse in his ears. By a kind of hypnotism, therefore, the audience is intended to sense primitive fears and respond to voodoo magic. The paradox here is that these effects must be as real as possible if they are to work, an assumption which runs counter to the concept of expressionism. Such realism certainly contradicted the setting for the first production. With six required changes, the designer Cleon Throckmorton (1897–1965) was compelled to compromise with cut-out silhouettes set against a plaster cyclorama that had been erected on the tiny Provincetown Players' stage.

*The Emperor Jones* was received by the critics with guarded comments, but with enthusiasm by the public, who filled the small theatre for 204 performances. When the production was moved to Broadway, its success may also have killed the Provincetown Players, whose resources were divided and whose amateur freedom to experiment was dissipated. Jig Cook returned to the Cape in disgust. Today, the play is rarely played because its stereotype of the Negro is unacceptable. Yet, according to Travis Bogard in *Contour in Time*, the first production of *The Emperor Jones* took O'Neill and the Provincetown Players 'beyond any horizon they had envisioned', so that 'the American theatre came of age with this play' (p. 134). Bogard also believes that, because of its success, O'Neill felt obliged to give his whole effort to the art theatre movement in New York, and write only experimental plays. Any such decision was possibly strengthened by a fateful meeting in 1921 with Kenneth Macgowan (1888–1963), avant-garde critic and proponent of European expressionism. O'Neill, Macgowan and Jones together formed what the press called 'the triumvirate', and were a brilliant team who reorganized the company and called their theatre the Provincetown Playhouse.

The triumvirate had the common wish to assimilate new ideas from Europe. Between 1911 and 1917, visits to America by the Abbey Theatre, the Manchester Repertory, Max Reinhardt's company and the Ballets Russes were a revelation to theatre-hungry artists in New York. The publication in 1914 of Sheldon Cheney's *The New Movement in the Theatre* sounded a clarion call, and his *Theatre Arts Magazine*, which began publication in 1916, became the voice of the American avant-garde. The familiar demand was heard again: to return to an ideal of sincere and passionate theatre, one opposed to 'servile realism'. In 1919, Macgowan joined Cheney in editing *Theatre Arts*, and published another manifesto for the new American stage in *The Theatre of Tomorrow* (1921). With Jones, Macgowan toured Europe for ten weeks, and together in 1922 they published the enormously influential text, *Continental Stagecraft*. Macgowan was particularly enthusiastic about expressionism, and preached the new 'inner realism' of the unconscious mind, drawing upon the recently available studies of Freud and Jung to lend him support. With its advocacy of a new 'anti-realistic' and 'presentational' stagecraft, *Continental Stagecraft* was bravely dedicated to 'The Playwrights of America', and held up O'Neill's latest play, *The Hairy Ape*, as the example.

The Provincetown idea of expressionism at this time, as outlined by Macgowan in *The Theatre of Tomorrow*, was apparently simple. He considered that in *From Morn to Midnight* Kaiser had succeeded in 'getting past the surface of reality' and penetrating 'the basic stratum of man's psyche', and he added, 'To do this, I take it, is the purpose of expressionism' (p. 261). It might be thought that the character of Yank in *The Hairy Ape*, O'Neill's equivalent to Kaiser's Cashier, was already on too basic a level to penetrate far, or to be able to represent many of those in search of their identity. But this play aimed higher. In a letter of 10 June 1921, O'Neill records that he had seen the expressionist film *The Cabinet of Dr Caligari*, which opened his eyes to 'wonderful possibilities' he had 'never dreamed of before'. As a vehicle of social protest, and in its vivid effects of chiaroscuro, *The Hairy Ape* is closer to its German origins than *The Emperor Jones* ever was. It was written in less than three weeks, and directed by James Light and Arthur Hopkins at the Provincetown Playhouse in 1922.

Like the Cashier in *From Morn to Midnight*, Yank also seeks un-successfully to escape from the world he knows. He is the stereo-type of the New York waterfront tough, now king of the stokehold, where he is at home with his own kind. In the first production, Louis Wolheim was well cast in the part: he had taught mathe-matics at Cornell, and spoke French, German and Spanish fluently, but he also liked a fight, and his physical strength was enormous – it had taken four club-wielding policemen to subdue him when he got into a brawl outside the Astor Hotel. This Yank is set against Mildred Douglas, the genteel daughter of a millionaire, played by Mary Blair, and then on Broadway by Carlotta Monterey. Dressed from top to toe in white, with white crêpe de Chine dress, white cloak and white hat with flowing veil, she was altogether the anaemic 'white apparition' O'Neill had asked for. She shows the fashionable interest in the working conditions of the stokers, but when she actually sees the grime of the hold, the sooty skins of the men and the bestial looks of Yank, she is repelled. So the stoker deserts the ship to take his revenge, as well as to discover where he 'belongs' in human society. In New York city, he meets and attacks the elegant ladies and gentlemen walking on Fifth Avenue. Only in the gorilla he sees in the zoo in Central Park can he recognize his kin, but the animal crushes him to death in his cage. Ironically, the cage is reminiscent of the stokehold seen in the first scene of the play.

The costumes were by Blanche Hays. She managed to make a

gorilla suit from dyed goatskins, although these after a while
became 'overwhelmingly odiferous'. And it was she who suggested
the use of masks in order to indicate that the people on Fifth Avenue
were on a different order, and to ensure that they all looked alike
in their vacant expressions, with furs for the women and Prince
Alberts for the men. O'Neill took up the idea of masked characters
with enthusiasm, and even suggested that when Yank begins to
'think' in the fourth scene, he should enter a masked world, with
everyone appearing strange and alien, even his mates in the forecastle. O'Neill was to explore the use of masks in several plays to
come.

The set designs by Cleon Throckmorton and Robert Edmond
Jones were intended to be fully expressionistic. O'Neill made this
clear in his stage directions for the first scene:

> The treatment of this scene, or of any other scene in the
> play, should by no means be naturalistic. The effect sought

26. O'Neill, *The Hairy Ape*, 1922. Production by James Light and
Arthur Hopkins, at the Provincetown Playhouse, New York.
Design by Cleon Throckmorton and Robert Edmond Jones,
costumes by Blanche Hays. Scene v, with Louis Wolheim and
Harold West.

after is a cramped space in the bowels of a ship, imprisoned by white steel. The lines of bunks, the uprights supporting them, cross each other like the steel framework of a cage. The ceiling crushes down upon the men's heads. They cannot stand upright. This accentuates the natural stooping posture which shovelling coal and the resultant over-development of back and shoulder muscles have given them.

Travis Bogard believes that this image is too like the popular conception of brutish stokers, and the cramped space in the forecastle

27. Ernst Ludwig Kirchner, *Street, Berlin*, 1913. (Oil on canvas, $47\frac{1}{2} \times 35\frac{7}{8}$ ins. Collection, The Museum of modern Art, New York.)

of an ocean liner already too like a cage, to allow the scene to appear anti-naturalistic. Nevertheless, in the theatre of 1922, it was sufficiently unusual and striking. In the first production, the coal-blackened stokers moved in deadly unison like slaves, and, to complete the expressionistic picture, they shovelled rhythmically. As the scenes passed in succession, the distorted sets, the atmospheric lighting, the grotesque movements all grew increasingly expressionistic. The staccato, choric speech of the dialogue was echoed by the rhythm of ugly sounds made by the furnace doors, the grinding of metal, the crunching of coal, the roar of the flames and the throbbing of the engines.

In yet another respect *The Hairy Ape* managed to lend an expressionistic perspective to its subject. In its sequence of scenes, it is evident that the images projected are those seen by contrasting characters. To the narrow imagination of Mildred, brought up in her protected social circle, the stokers do indeed resemble apes in a cage, and it is as if the audience is to see the early scenes through her eyes. But the 'procession of gaudy marionettes' of scene 5, with the women excessively made up and over-dressed and with the men in top hats and tails, all moving like jerking robots and 'talking in toneless, simpering voices', is to be seen as Yank sees it.

The first night audience at the Provincetown Playhouse sat on its hard wooden benches in full evening dress, the women with their jewelry and the men with their gold-headed canes, not a little like the objects of satire before them. The applause was enthusiastic, but it was very much in doubt whether the audience could sustain Yank's viewpoint, without reverting to Mildred's. O'Neill acknowledged that the audience had difficulty in perceiving the intended symbolism, fascinated as it was with the unfamiliar images of the stage — it saw the stoker and not the symbol. In the *New York Herald Tribune* for 16 November 1924, he explained,

> They don't understand that the whole play is expressionistic. Yank is really yourself, and myself. He is *every* human being. But, apparently, very few people seem to get this . . . no one has said, 'I am Yank! Yank is my own self!'

It is hard not to sympathize with the audience, rather than the playwright.

Nevertheless, O'Neill's conception profoundly anticipates the thinking of the generation to come. Like Yank, man would struggle with his own fate and his divorce from an alien world. Unlike the animals, he no longer enjoyed his 'old harmony' with nature, nor had he yet acquired a spiritual harmony. Man's struggle, said O'Neill, 'used to be with the gods, but is now with himself, his own past, his attempt "to belong"'. On another occasion O'Neill explained that 'to belong' implied the understanding of one another. In spite of this, the play itself paints only a cloudy picture of the human spirit as a victim of materialism, and it raises questions about man's role in society without offering any answer. Some critics, like Patterson James of *Billboard*, could hear only vile language and see only a revolting subject.

In his *Herald Tribune* article, O'Neill said that a further intention behind expressionism was that 'it strives to get the author talking directly to the audience'. He indicated that he did not approve of the presentation of character as an abstraction, especially since no audience wished to lose 'the human contact by which it identifies itself with the protagonist of the play'. And it is true that the plays O'Neill wrote after *The Hairy Ape* move away from the extreme expressionist position: they are far more human. Increasingly, it was Strindberg's later style that became the model for O'Neill's studies in human suffering. When the renewed Provincetown Playhouse had a first season of 'Experimental Theatre' in 1924, it opened with *The Spook Sonata* (the title then current for *The Ghost Sonata*) and, significantly, O'Neill assisted in directing it and wrote its programme note. He described the achievement of *The Dance of Death* as one of 'super-naturalism', and considered *The Spook Sonata* to be what he called a 'behind-life' play. O'Neill's effort in his middle years was to write such super-naturalistic, behind-life plays himself. Emphasizing once again the need to reject 'the banality of surfaces', he believed that we should 'pass on to some as yet unrealized region where our souls, maddened by loneliness and the ignoble inarticulateness of flesh, are slowly evolving their new language of kinship'.

Between 1921 and 1926, O'Neill's experimental output was prolific, his plays being written faster than they could be produced. His pursuit of expressionistic forms continued at first less successfully with *All God's Chillun Got Wings*, directed by James Light with

Paul Robeson and Mary Blair at the Provincetown Playhouse in 1924. It was a psychological study of a mixed marriage, but the expected riots following upon a racial theme did not occur, and, perhaps for this perverse reason, the play was declared a disappointment. In the same year, *Desire under the Elms* cleverly integrated realistic and symbolic elements. The characters were authentic New England figures, while the frame setting of a house overshadowed by two oppressive elm trees permitted the audience to see the 'reality' of the characters inside the house, as distinct from the 'appearance' outside it. Thus in part II, scene 2, old Ephraim Cabot tells his adulterous wife Abbie his life story as she stares at the wall as if into his son Eben's room. Soon after, Abbie and Eben make love within the house, while Cabot, the embodiment of cold, unremitting Puritanism, goes off to the barn to sleep with his cows. With Walter Huston as Ephraim, Mary Morris as Abbie and Charles Ellis as Eben, this play ran for almost a year, encouraged along by attempts to have it banned from the New York stage. In London, there was no difficulty in having it banned.

*The Great God Brown* was O'Neill's most ambitious experiment to date. Directed and designed by Robert Edmond Jones at the Greenwich Village Theatre in 1926, the play dealt with the problem of being an artist in a materialistic society. The conflict in the soul was represented by two separate characters, the successful conformist William Brown (played by William Harrigan) and the artistic rebel Dion Anthony (played by Robert Keith). The name Dion Anthony deliberately evokes both the creative paganism of Dionysus and 'the life-denying spirit of Christianity' in St Anthony. The two protagonists compete first for the love of Margaret, the 'eternal girl-woman', an echo of Faust's Marguerite. Then they turn to the sensual Cybele, the Earth Mother. But this play is especially interesting for its extensive use of masks in a Pirandellian way: they both hide the truth of personality and show the changes made by the passage of time. Such an abstract treatment, however, worked against the realistic depiction of character and rendered the play somewhat bloodless. The audience was confused by the double personality of the mask, and what were intended as nuances of character came across as contradictions. For his part, O'Neill thought the problem was that the masks were too real and wanted them larger, but complained that the commercial theatre allowed neither time nor money for experiment.

*Lazarus Laughed* also experimented with the use of the mask. The play was revised many times, but its huge cast all but defied production. It was first performed, not in New York, but in the Pasadena Playhouse in California in 1928, and it has never had a production on Broadway. The play was a largely unsuccessful attempt to make a ritual act of Lazarus's return from the grave, able to exult at death and see true immortality. Lazarus remains unmasked, and his face grows younger, while the crowds who confront him in their hundreds wear masks like a chorus to convey the idea of their collective being. Also in 1928, Philip Moeller directed and Lee Simonson designed *Dynamo* for the Theatre Guild. This work attempted to represent the dynamo as the symbolic god of the machine age, and was intended to be the first part of a trilogy. Noël Coward dubbed it 'a womb with a view', and it was so much a failure that O'Neill abandoned the other two projected plays.

The trilogy *Mourning Becomes Electra* followed in 1931, directed by Moeller and designed by Jones for the Theatre Guild, with Alice Brady as Lavinia, Nazimova as Christine and Earle Larimore as Orin. The play was constructed like a Greek tragedy, but nevertheless relied upon modern Freudian notions of motivation, so that its essential core of psychological naturalism turned its intended tragic tone to bathos. O'Neill also intended the use of masks, but he saw that they would have called for a less realistic dialogue. He therefore attempted to retain a realistic picture of New England by settling for mask-like faces on his characters. The public was awed by the scale of this work, and only Robert Benchley in *The New Yorker* was unimpressed — it was not so much Greek tragedy, he wrote, as 'good, old-fashioned, spine-curling melodrama'.

O'Neill's use of masks for *The Hairy Ape*, *All God's Chillun*, *The Great God Brown* and *Lazarus Laughed* went well beyond expressionism. In articles written for *The American Spectator* in November and December 1932, he remarked that the eight-month run of *The Great God Brown* was extraordinary in view of its extensive use of so archaic a device, and argued that the time was evidently ripe for the reintroduction of such a 'necessary, dramatically revealing new convention'. The chief value of a masked drama was, he believed, 'psychological, mystical, and abstráct'. The mask also made the body of the actor as 'alive and expressive' as his face had been before, and intensified and emphasized the theme of his play. Finally, the success of the mask also pointed to the need for playwriting of greater depth: 'For what, at bottom', he asked, 'is the new psychological insight into human cause and effect but a study in masks, an exercise in unmasking?' This article, 'Memoranda on Masks', is a rare document for its time, but in the event, O'Neill's greatest plays of unmasking, those which best express the hidden conflicts of the mind, would be written only in the final, naturalistic phase of his playwriting career. *Long Day's Journey into Night* is his monument.

---

# 11 *Expressionism in America : after O'Neill*

---

*The Adding Machine* (1923), *Death of a Salesman* (1949), *Camino Real* (1953)

The influence of Eugene O'Neill on new American playwriting was immediate. In the Garrick Theatre in 1923, Philip Moeller of the Theatre Guild produced another American expressionistic play that was to gain international attention, *The Adding Machine* by Elmer Rice (1892–1967). His experiments with dramatic form and style in this play are extraordinarily radical and confident. In his first play, *On Trial* (1914), Rice had shown skill as a technical innovator, using a revolving stage in the manner of the 'flashback' in films, jumping back in time from a central courtroom scene to earlier scenes illustrating the lives of the characters. His ingenuity as a playwright and a director never deserted him, and he twice went to Soviet Russia to investigate the new stagecraft. In 1935 he became the state director of the Federal Theatre Project in New York, introducing the concept of the 'living newspaper', of which more later. In *The Adding Machine*, Rice's satirical theme was well suited to expressionist form, and the play remains as strong today as it was in 1923.

It was a play of general social protest, putting on the stage a vision of a dehumanized, mechanical society dominated by commerce. Like Kaiser's Cashier, the nameless Mr Zero, played first by Dudley Digges, is a book-keeper, a pawn whose life as a human adding machine is worthless, an assumption confirmed when after twenty-five years of service to his firm he is replaced by an actual machine. In a fit of anger, Zero kills his employer, but his execution as a murderer grants him only a short time in the Elysian Fields before he is ironically set to work on a heavenly adding machine; even then he is ejected from heaven as a failure.

The play's seven scenes make sharp symbolic statements to illuminate the tragedy of Zero in the expressionistic manner. However, in a letter to the *New York Times*, Rice discounted the possible influence of other expressionistic plays, saying that, in order to depict the 'inner significance' of events, he merely found it expedient 'to depart entirely from objective reality and to employ symbols, condensations, and a dozen devices which, to the conservative, must seem arbitrarily fantastic'. This, he supposed, was 'what is meant by expressionism'.

Design was by Lee Simonson. The bedroom of scene 1 had its walls papered with sheets of foolscap covered with columns of figures, and was lit by a single naked bulb. The scene consists of an endless monologue by Mrs Zero, played by Helen Westley, as she arranges her hair. Scene 2 has Zero seated on a high stool at a desk opposite a plain, middle-aged woman, one Daisy Diana Dorothea Devore, Zero's fellow book-keeper, played by Margaret Wycherly. When the Boss announces that Zero is fired, the sound of a distant merry-go-round is heard, and the floor begins to revolve. The music grows louder and the floor revolves faster until the words are inaudible and the Boss's jaws are seen only to open and close incessantly:

> The music swells and swells. To it is added every offstage effect of the theatre: the wind, the waves, the galloping horses, the locomotive whistle, the sleigh-bells, the automobile siren, the glass-crash, New Year's Eve, Election Night, Armistice Day, and the Mardi-Gras. The noise deafening, maddening, unendurable. Suddenly it culminates in a terrific peal of thunder. For an instant there is a flash of red and then everything is plunged into blackness.

Zero's neighbours are Mr and Mrs One, Mr and Mrs Two, and so on, representing the citizens of an automated society, and they file in and out in a double column, wearing identical hair and dress, although the colours of the wigs and clothes are different. They greet each other with a repeating formula, 'How de do, Mrs One' . . . 'How de do, Mrs Zero', and so on. In scene 4 these figures are also Zero's jurors, all sitting in a row with folded arms and staring stolidly before them. Finally they rise to their feet as one person and shout in unison, 'Guilty!'

Against the usual commercial fare on Broadway in 1923 — *Cyrano de Bergerac* at one end of the scale and *Ziegfeld Follies* at the other — the unrealistic devices of *The Adding Machine* fell upon the New York audience with force. In his foreword to the published text, Philip Moeller attempted a rationale for the play:

28. Rice, *The Adding Machine*, 1923. Production by Philip Moeller, design by Lee Simonson for the Theatre Guild at the Garrick Theatre, New York. Scene iv: Zero on trial, with Dudley Digges as Zero.

If 'expressionism' is objective seeing, as all observation must be, it is *subjective* projection; that is, all the half-understood 'hinterland' thoughts, all the yearnings and unknown suppressions of the mind, are exposed. . . Thus expressionistically Mr Rice has exposed the minds and souls of his people.

However, when the play was presented at the Court Theatre, London by the Stage Society, directed by W. G. Fay, in 1928, the critic James Agate was less impressed, and hunted about for reasons which probably expressed the feeling about expressionism in London, and fired them off in a memorable article entitled 'The Case against Expressionism'. It was simply untrue, wrote Agate, 'that clerks in a store are all exactly alike', and he went on to say that the myth about 'the down-trodden, soulless millions' was invented by 'somebody who had never met a mechanic outside an Institute'. So he came to his point and summarized the two objections to expressionism in the theatre as he saw it:

1. Its simplificatory method destroys the individuality in the dramatist, and
2. It annihilates imagination by being definitely more matter-of-fact than the representationalism which it would supersede.

Agate seemed to be pleading for a basic art of playwriting when he added wistfully, 'There was a time when a character had but to say, "And is old Double dead?" and mortality came over the stage like a cloud.'

In a lighter vein, expressionistic conventions were employed at about this time in a number of saccharine comedies on the New York stage. *Beggar on Horseback* (1924), an adaptation by George S. Kaufman (1889—1961) and Marc Connelly (1890— ) of Paul Apel's *Hans Sonnenstosser's Journey to Hell*, was an immediate financial success with its gentle satire on American philistinism. The play's central device was that of a dream in which one Neil McRae, a composer, finds himself married to Gladys Cady, the vulgar daughter of a wealthy businessman. The father is depicted in a golfing outfit with a telephone fastened to his chest, and the mother has a rocking chair attached to her back. In his dream, Neil is so miserable that he dispatches the whole family. The fantasy burgeons, and he is sentenced to produce cheap music in 'Cady's Consolidated Art Factory'. Happily, he wakes up and marries the girl next door — a comfortable ending. It is not difficult to imagine what the tempestuous young German expressionists of a decade before would have thought of this offshoot of their labours. However, as it turned out, Kaufman's practice of collaborating with many different co-authors prevented his developing a consistent style of wit for his comedies of American life.

Thornton Wilder (1897–1975) was another playwright of this period who embraced the opportunities granted by the expressionistic rebellion. His essay, 'Some Thoughts on Playwriting', advanced the theory that 'the theatre is a world of pretence', existing only by conventions. Because of this, 'it provokes the collaborative activity of the spectator's imagination' and encourages the audience to recreate the action of the play. The theatre also automatically 'raises the action from the specific to the general', so that, for example, Juliet becomes every girl in love, in every time, place and language. This idea may explain why Wilder continued to cling to the skirts of expressionism long after they had worn thin.

His clever one-act plays of 1931, *The Long Christmas Dinner*, *The Happy Journey to Trenton and Camden* and *Pullman Car Hiawatha*, all use simple stage devices to portray typical American families as seen caught in the dimension of time, and they prepare the way for his full-length plays to come. Thus in *The Long Christmas Dinner*, generation succeeds generation at the dining-table by the expedient of having actors enter through one portal trimmed with garlands of fruit and flowers to denote birth, and exit by another edged and hung with black velvet to denote death. These doors open and shut without visible agency. All the women are dressed alike in long gowns, and all the men in morning coats. As the women grow older, they draw shawls over their shoulders; the men indicate the passing years by adjusting white wigs on their heads. By these devices, it is readily suggested that ninety Christmas dinners have been eaten, all with imaginary food and imaginary knives and forks, and all in about thirty minutes' stage time. The other two plays also employ an impersonal Stage Manager as chorus to the joys and sorrows they introduce.

Wilder's first full-length play, *Our Town* (1938), directed by Jed Harris at Henry Miller's Theatre, New York, proved to be the most popular of all American expressionistic plays. It is a gently satirical saga of small-town community life in New Hampshire, a sentimental demonstration of the ordinary events of birth, marriage and death, and of the values we place on them. Wilder wrote a simple, colloquial idiom and created simple character types, but none of this would be remarkable were it not for the virtual absence of props and scenery on his stage. The bare stage not only sharpens the audience's perception of otherwise disregarded actions, the delivery of milk in the early morning, the feeding of chickens, and so on, because they are performed in mime, but also permits the play to deploy time freely, particularly to show the past at work in the present. A presentational device like the chorus figure of the Stage Manager (the prototype of Tom in Tennessee Williams's *The Glass Menagerie* and of Quentin in Arthur Miller's *After the Fall*) both generalizes the lightly sketched characters of George Gibbs and Emily Webb as symbolic of all young men and women who fall in love and get married, and also, with a touch of humour, manages to distance his audience from the sentiment and pathos of Emily's death in childbirth. The Stage Manager even succeeds in endowing

29. Wilder, *Our Town*, 1938. Production by Jed Harris at Henry Miller's Theatre, New York. The funeral scene.

these events with a little cosmic relevance – the *New York Times* found that the play gave life a 'strange, unworldly significance', and every reviewer used the word 'haunting' or one like it.

In the same vein, *The Skin of Our Teeth* (1942) was more challenging and less popular, for by a similar stagecraft this play tried to represent in the same characters the whole of creation and the history of mankind from the cave dwellers to modern New Jersey suburbanites as they survive every catastrophe from flood to world war. What might have been a profound and even moving experience in the theatre was more of an intellectual game in which the spectator spent his time trying to recall his knowledge of the past.

In the American theatre immediately after the Second World War, vestiges of expressionistic technique had not entirely disappeared. Both Arthur Miller (1915– ) and Tennessee Williams (1914– ) are essentially naturalistic in the way they see life, and their ear for dialogue is at bottom realistic – even if Miller is more like a prosaic Ibsen and Williams more like a poetic Chekhov. Nevertheless, both in the conception and the structure of their plays these two playwrights have strangely relied upon an element of expressionism.

In the 1958 introduction to his *Collected Plays*, Miller wrote an instructive note on the genesis of *Death of a Salesman* (1949):

> The first image that occurred to me which was to result
> in *Death of a Salesman* was of an enormous face the
> height of the proscenium arch which would appear and
> then open up, and we would see the inside of a man's head.
> In fact, *The Inside of His Head* was the first title.

The inside of the salesman's head was to reveal a mass of contradictions. When Miller declared, 'I wished to create a form which, in itself as a form, would literally be the process of Willy Loman's way of mind', his might have been the voice of an early expressionist: 'Any dramatic form is an artifice, a way of transforming a subjective feeling into something that can be comprehended through public symbols.' The form of *Death of a Salesman* emerged as that of the conventional two-act play, but so broken into episodic fragments by lighting and spatial changes that it conveyed the free association of the mind:

As I look at the play now its form seems the form of a confession, for that is how it is told, now speaking of what happened yesterday, then suddenly following some connection to a time twenty years ago, then leaping even further back and then returning to the present and even speculating about the future.

By such cinematic juxtapositons of time and place, the mood could be as its author wished it, satirical or lyrical.

Miller also pointed out that, although we can call *Death of a Salesman* cinematic in structure, 'it failed as motion picture' because, compared with the stage, 'the screen is time-bound and earth-bound'. In the theatre, the setting of the play remains unchanged — a skeleton of a small frame house with the front wall cut away. This setting distinguished the play's real from its imaginary events, and Miller explained how in act i the forestage between the house and the audience did double duty:

This forward area serves as the back yard as well as the locale of all Willy's imaginings and of his city scenes. Whenever the action is in the present the actors observe the imaginary wall-lines, entering the house only through its door at the left. But in the scenes of the past these boundaries are broken, and characters enter or leave a room by stepping 'through' a wall on to the forestage.

Miller preferred to change his scene verbally, keeping alive an image, as he said, through the image that follows it, whereas in the film each visual picture totally displaces the previous one. Thus it may be said that although the play's content was psychologically motivated and apparently naturalistic, the process of Willy's mind determined the pattern of the play. *Death of a Salesman* mixed the realistic and the expressionistic exquisitely.

Tennessee Williams has always written liberally of his artistic intentions, and provides a good case for testing them against achievement. In his 'Production Notes' to *The Glass Menagerie* (1944), he wrote of it as 'a Memory play', which could be presented with 'unusual freedom of convention'. From the German director Erwin Piscator he had borrowed the idea of scattering through the play titles and images projected on a screen, and Williams certainly thought of his episodic method as expressionistic. 'Expressionism and all other unconventional techniques in drama have only one valid aim, and that is a closer approach to the truth.' Such devices were not an attempt to escape from reality, but to find 'a more penetrating and vivid expression of things as they are'. He also believed that they were a step towards 'a new, plastic theatre', one replacing 'the exhausted theatre of realistic conventions'. This was the familiar tune, but in the event, the screen device got in the way of the direct impact of the play's action, and was wisely abandoned. Nevertheless, Williams continued to pursue the unorthodox, and in his preface to *The Rose Tattoo* (1951), he wrote of 'snatching the eternal out of the desperately fleeting', and considered this to be 'the great magic trick of human existence'. By whatever means, a play must be made to arrest time.

In 1953, Williams wrote his most expressionistic play, *Camino Real*. Writing in the *New York Times* of 15 March 1953, he suggested that this play was 'like the construction of another world'. It was,

30. Williams, *Camino Real*, 1953. Production by Elia Kazan, design by Lemuel Ayers at the Martin Beck Theatre, New York.

of course, the playwright's conception of the world he found himself in, and is especially expressionistic in conveying the viewpoint of its creator. *Camino Real* depicts a world largely evil, tyrannous and cruel. Written in free verse, the play is all fantasy, an allegory of life 'outside of time in a place of no specific locality'. Williams found that this mode gave him a special licence in the composition, 'the continually dissolving and transforming images of a dream', although this licence consequently demanded painstaking work on the form of the play. Both the author and its first director, Elia Kazan, worked to achieve a continuous flow in the episodic action, and Williams claimed that, of all the plays he had written, *Camino Real* was the one 'meant most for the vulgarity of performance'.

However, the play suffered from all the vices of avant-garde playwriting. It was short on characterization, thickly symbolist and consciously philosophical. Reception of the first production was predictably critical, although the revivals in New York in 1960 and 1970 were better appreciated. Some who found the play obscure were troubled by the loss of familiar conventions. Others shared with the author his sense of freedom. Williams claimed that 'a poem should not mean but be', and that 'symbols are nothing but the natural speech of drama'. He cited as an example of the play's symbolism Casanova's battered portmanteau, which is tossed out from the balcony of his hotel when he cannot pay the bill: 'While the portmanteau is still in the air, he shouts, "Careful, I have —" — and when it has crashed to the street he continues — "fragile — mementoes. . ."' But, paradoxically, when the spectator recognizes the symbolism in this incident, he finds it artless and obvious. Williams held that the terms 'dynamic' and 'organic', although fallen into disrepute in dramatic criticism by 1953, still defined the qualities he valued most in a play. Unfortunately, these are hardly the words that spring to mind in watching *Camino Real*, which lacks the touch of the poet felt in *The Glass Menagerie* and *A Streetcar Named Desire* (1947).

The period between the wars was one of great advances in American scene design and the domestication of expressionistic techniques. The artist whose versatile talents could most easily embrace the mixture of representational and presentational styles found in Miller and Williams in the 1940s was Jo Mielziner (1901—

76). Unlike Mordecai Gorelik (1899– ) with <del>r</del>
cerns, and Robert Edmond Jones with his mo<del>.</del>
approach to a play, Mielziner argued that the designer <del>s</del>
not to make a personal statement, but to share the director's inter
pretation of a play and the problems of staging it (*Designing for the
Stage*, 1965). In his own career, he moved from settings which were
'over-designed', and therefore more likely to be out of key with the
production, as well as lacking in practical applicability, towards
a greater simplification and flexibility. This concern for the
unity and integrity of the whole production was also evident in
the work of Lee Simonson (1888–1967), Norman-Bel Geddes (1893–
1958) and Donald Oenslager (1902–75). These designers made their
work express the play and not the artist, and they believed firmly
in collaborating imaginatively with the director. Designer and
director 'are, or should be', wrote Simonson, '*alter egos*'.

# 12 Expressionism in Ireland: the later O'Casey

### The Silver Tassie (1928)

We owe the first Irish expressionistic experiments to Ireland's
master of naturalism, Sean O'Casey (1880–1964). His avid reading
of Strindberg, Kaiser, Toller and O'Neill took him to the point of
defying Yeats's policy of a purely native drama at the Abbey Theatre,
Dublin.

Touches of expressionistic writing are to be felt even as early
as 1926 in O'Casey's *The Plough and the Stars*. In the brilliant act ii
of this play, the heated patriotic oratory of the shadowy figure outside the pub, heard in counterpoint with the increasingly noisy,
drunken voices inside, is halfway to creating a ritualistic effect of
the expressionistic kind. Act iv ends with an extraordinary amalgam
of symbolic effects: two British soldiers sit drinking tea beside the
body of Bessie Burgess, while offstage the sounds are heard of rifle
and machine-gun fire, cries of 'Ambulance!' and the ironic singing
of 'Keep the Home Fires Burning'.

Such mixtures and juxtapositions as these must be put down to O'Casey's desire to find an objective way of playwriting. He was a man deeply concerned for his country, but he refused himself a one-sided view, and his pacificist belief transcended the intense nationalism which obsessed his countrymen after the Easter Rebellion of 1916. In *The Plough and the Stars*, O'Casey's own political views are actually expressed by The Covey, an essentially comic Communist. To try to persuade a pretty girl to read Jenersky's *Thesis on the Origin, Development and Consolidation of the Evolutionary Idea of the Proletariat*, with so indigestible a title, when she is busy flirting, is hardly the way to encourage the audience to join the Party. Nevertheless, there is no denying that O'Casey enjoyed levelling barbs at hot-headed Irish nationalism and conventional Catholic morality. When heroic sentiment is heard in the early plays, he seems instinctively to distance his audience by introducing devices to undercut the clichés. And yet O'Casey's stage is never detached, but always remains solidly earthy and realistic.

O'Casey's interest in expressionistic techniques was the immediate cause of his break with Yeats and the Abbey Theatre, and the disastrous results of this quarrel can never be fully estimated. Act II of *The Silver Tassie* (1928) was a direct echo of German expres-

31. O'Casey, *The Silver Tassie*, 1928. Production by Raymond Massey, design by Augustus John at the Apollo Theatre, London, 1929. Act II: at the front.

sionism. 'Every feature of the scene seems a little distorted from its original appearance', reads the stage direction, and the set provocatively depicts the modern battlefield as some kind of hell. The scene is a ruined monastery, and it balances a broken crucifix which appears to point pathetically to the Virgin Mary, against a soldier spreadeagled on a gunwheel as field punishment like Christ on the Cross. The whole stage is overshadowed by a giant howitzer to make an overwhelming symbolic statement linking human suffering with Christian compassion. The Croucher is a character who symbolizes death, his face like a skull and his hands like the bones of a skeleton. He chants a grotesque version of Ezekiel like an auditory echo of the grisly set itself. Voices sing the Kyrie Eleison within the ruins, and these are picked up by the intoning of a bunch of wretched soldiers as they return from fatigue. Such effects, complex yet direct, constituted a powerful comment on the pallid products of the Abbey that followed the plays of Synge.

The choric repetitions and rhythms heard from the soldiers had actually surfaced at the end of act I, when the play's hero, Harry Heegan, thinks he may not return to the trenches:

> BARNEY.... No, no. We must go back!
> MRS HEEGAN. No, no, Harry. You must go back.
> SIMON, SYLVESTER and SUSIE (*together*). You must go back.
> VOICES OF CROWD OUTSIDE. They must go back!
> (*The ship's siren is heard blowing.*)

These auditory echoes seem to have been intended as a transition to the more startling effects of the second act, just as act III's cold, sanitary setting of a hospital ward, with impersonal jargon from the nurse, provide a parallel transition back to the realism of the play's end. Harry is the football player who is crippled in the war, his story conveying the simple theme of the youthful joy of life wantonly destroyed. Otherwise done in the realistic style, *The Silver Tassie's* aggressive mixture of the symbolic and the realistic makes the author's plea for peace both uncomfortably moralistic and warmly human. As an expressionistic experiment, it is more than interesting; as a work of dramatic art, it is a questionable success.

When he read the text of *The Silver Tassie*, Yeats was upset both by O'Casey's refusal to treat an Irish theme and by the non-realistic manner of the writing. At a time when Yeats's own plays were becoming more private in their symbolism, and increasingly formalized and idealized like the *Noh* drama of Japan, he chose to reject O'Casey's play on grounds of illegitimate content and form. Today we see the play as one of the important anti-war dramas of our time, but in 1928 Yeats considered that O'Casey wrote only out of his 'opinions', because he had never been in the trenches himself. In response to this, O'Casey asked, Had Shakespeare been at Actium, or Shaw at Orleans? The point was unanswerable.

Yeats was also perplexed by the expressionistic mixture of styles in the play, its truly experimental element. The other Abbey directors who read the manuscript, Lady Gregory and Lennox Robinson, had wanted the Abbey to produce the play, but they shared Yeats's doubts in the matter of its style. The success of R. C. Sherriff's sentimental realism in *Journey's End*, London's contribution to the anti-war genre that year, may have confirmed them in their opinion. In *The Silver Tassie*, O'Casey used realism only as a frame for the bigger allegory of war, almost like a trick to mislead the audience before he disclosed the ugly theme of the second act. That controversial scene was not without its faults, especially its loss of particularity in character and its awkward concoction of Cockney and rhetoric, but with no *Tassie*, the Irish National Theatre was left with only kitchen comedies.

*The Silver Tassie* eventually had its first production at the Apollo Theatre, London in 1929, when it was directed by Raymond Massey and designed by Augustus John. Charles Laughton as Harry Heegan and Barry Fitzgerald as the comic Irishman Sylvester guaranteed its success at the box office, but this was not the same thing as a trial by fire on Dublin's own stage. In 1934 Yeats made a gracious gesture of reconciliation with O'Casey, one which resulted in a first Abbey performance of the play in 1935. But not unexpectedly, it was immediately attacked by the Catholic press for its immorality, and by the President of the Gaelic League, who went so far as to urge that the Abbey itself should be abolished for undermining the national interest. In all this, Yeats took his share of the punishment, but it was too late. After his London experience, O'Casey recognized the narrow-mindedness of the Dublin audience, and he never returned to work there.

In 1929, the Abbey rejected another expressionistic play, written in 1926 by a new playwright, Denis Johnston (1901 – ). The play was about the Irish patriot Robert Emmet, and it was really a satirical treatment of Irish nationalism as a whole. In form it was a Strindbergian dream play modelled on Kaufman and Connelly's *Beggar on Horseback* of 1924. When it was sent back to him, Johnston ironically changed its title to *The Old Lady Says 'No!'*, and so it has remained ever since. He then offered it to the Abbey's new rival in Dublin, the Gate Theatre, which had opened in 1928 with the less parochial policy of presenting both Irish and continental experimental drama. The Gate immediately accepted Johnston's play (1929), but the Abbey's loss of *The Old Lady Says 'No!'* and *The Silver Tassie* within two years helped determine the decline of the Irish movement. The Abbey's acceptance of a government subsidy in 1925 not only provided it with a shield against financial competition, but also encouraged it to become a more bourgeois theatre.

In voluntary exile in England, O'Casey lost his connection with the Abbey company and its audience, and it became necessary for him to publish a play before producing it. He achieved the freedom to write in whatever way he chose, but at the same time he was denied the chance of working on his material in rehearsal. As a writer of somewhat undisciplined imagination, O'Casey could not afford to forego the requirement of being responsible to a stage he knew. For example, his first version of *Juno and the Paycock* had included the shooting of Johnny Boyle, with the death scene taking place on stage, but in the final copy this material was wisely cut in order to keep attention on Juno, the true centre of the play. After the unfortunate business of *The Silver Tassie*, O'Casey's plays suffered from a surfeit of untried, uncritical and often eccentric effects.

Thus his next work, *Within the Gates* (1933), was an attempt at a modern morality play which would satirize the years of the Depression. Formally, the play was a total immersion in the techniques of expressionism, complete with a setting which borrowed its idea for the lofty gates of a park painted on the front curtain from O'Neill's *Mourning Becomes Electra*. The action of the play centres on a Strindbergian dreamer, and the play is his vision. The setting is Hyde Park, and the pastoral image is extended by having a chorus of young boys and girls representing trees and flowers.

The play is made up of four scenes which pass from spring to winter and from morning to night — cycles of life. But these signs of the play's unity are illusory, for *Within the Gates* is otherwise a great rag-bag of dramatic scraps.

The action surrounds a Young Woman, the compassionate prostitute of melodrama, who is searching for her salvation. Her performance throughout stays largely on a single note of hysteria. The other characters are as unrealistic, and come in too great a number to be anything more than caricatures presented in a series of set-pieces, with lines that are over-blown and moralistic. They include a well-intentioned Bishop who nevertheless seduced the Young Woman's mother ('Life has passed him by', explained O'Casey), a Guardsman who is presently seducing a Nursemaid, two Evangelists who are also voyeurs, and a Salvation Army Officer who is attracted to the fallen woman he is supposed to save. The most that can be said for these characters is that for the most part they are not exactly stereotypes. Reviewing the London production of *Within the Gates* in 1934, the critic James Agate decided the whole thing was 'pretentious rubbish'.

Agate's judgment damaged the fortunes of the play, which needed informed advice rather than abuse. For in many ways *Within the Gates* was greatly daring. For example, it managed to create a symbolic moment of dancing on the stage of a kind which was to become almost the O'Casey signature. It had been part of Harry Heegan's image in *The Silver Tassie*, even in his wheelchair: an exultation over the miseries of life, a defiance of the oppressive elements in modern society, an assertion of the individual spirit against bigotry in all its shapes. To represent this spirit as movement and dance was just permissible in fantasy, but it was wholly out of keeping with realism. Just before her death, the young prostitute in *Within the Gates* moves unsteadily into a joyful dance with the Dreamer, who almost carries her in his arms before he lays her down. In *Red Roses for Me* (1942), the poor people of Dublin clap their hands and dance on the bridge over the Liffey. The open form of O'Casey's later plays permitted him to adopt such idiosyncratic moments of symbolism without strain.

The attack on O'Casey's style was an attack on anything which upset the laws of realistic illusion, and in his book of essays *The*

*Flying Wasp* of 1937, he returned to the fight with a direct attack on what he called 'the picture-frame age' of drama: 'The critics are still in the picture-frame age; they have lived all their lives there, and they want to die on the old doorstep.' He quoted Allardyce Nicoll with approval,

> We do not want merely an excerpt from reality; it is the imaginative transformation of reality, as it is seen through the eyes of the poet, that we desire. The great art of the theatre is to suggest, not to tell openly: to dilate the mind by symbols, not by actual things; to express in Lear a world's sorrow, and in Hamlet the grief of humanity.

And O'Casey adds,

> The rage for real, real life on the stage has taken all the life out of the drama. If everything on the stage is to be a fake imitation (for fake realism it can only be), where is the chance for the original and imaginative artist? (p. 123).

For the innocuous illusion of Noël Coward and Frederick Lonsdale, the current favourites in London in 1933, O'Casey put forward his Hyde Park of *Within the Gates* as a microcosmic image of the world, at once a criticism of the Church, represented by the Bishop and other do-gooders of the play, and a hope for mankind, seen in the generous spirit of his illegitimate daughter.

Despite the failure of *Within the Gates*, O'Casey continued to write plays coloured with variegated expressionist elements of his own. Subsequent plays of better quality and control, like *Purple Dust* (1940), *Red Roses for Me* (1942) and especially *Cock-a-Doodle Dandy* (1949), were all essentially expressionistic in treatment, but liberally mixed with the familiar O'Casey characterization of Dublin's low life. Each play was a new blast at realism: 'Take people off the street or carry them out of a drawing-room, plonk them on the stage and make them speak as they speak in real, real life, and you will have the dullest thing imaginable', he was still writing in *The Green Crow* in 1957. He considered *Cock-a-Doodle Dandy* to be his best play, symbolizing Ireland's fight for the 'joy of life' in the face of clerical, social and political repression. The play's incidents, O'Casey claimed, were based on fact. They included the ugly behaviour of a belligerent priest, the cruelty shown to a 'young, gay girl', the false piety of the elderly, 'the never-ending quest for money', and much more. Woven through all the scenes of the play was the central figure of the Cock, representing the joyful spirit of life.

Looking back over his career, O'Casey declared in the *New York Times* of 9 November 1958 that a play should be 'a part of life', and that it had to 'live in its own right'. Realism, however, tended to show life at 'its meanest and commonest'. So it appears that to the end of his life he was still justifying his decision to write *The Silver Tassie* as he did, and fighting the endless rear-guard action of the expressionist against the establishment.

# 13 'Epic theatre in Germany: Piscator and after

*The Good Soldier Schweik* (1928)

It is surprising that a disciple of Max Reinhardt, author of the 'magical' theatre, is to be credited with the invention of 'documentary', the factual theatre. He was the Marxist director Erwin Piscator (1893–1966), who developed expressionist theatre for left-wing 'agitprop' (the word a compound of 'agitation' and 'propaganda'). Working in the early years with Bertolt Brecht, Piscator formulated a plan for a drama which could be used for the public 'discussion' of political and social issues. They named their new dramatic form *'episches Theater'*, 'epic theatre'. Piscator's formative work was done in Berlin between 1919 and 1930, first with the nomadic Proletarisches Theater after 1920, then at the Volksbühne from 1924 to 1927, and subsequently at his own Theater am Nollendorfplatz (the 'Piscatorbühne'). When the Nazi Party gained strength, Piscator left Germany with so many others, in 1931 becoming for a time director of the International Theatre in Moscow, and then founding his own Studio Theatre of the Dramatic Workshop of the New School for Social Research in New York. Finally, after twenty years' exile, he returned to West Berlin in 1951, three years after Brecht's return to East Berlin, and opened the Freie Volksbühne in 1963.

Piscator's first production at the Volksbühne in 1924 was *Fahnen* (*Flags*) by Alfons Paquet, a production which embryonically contained all the chief elements of the Piscator method. The subject was the anarchist trials of 1886 in Chicago, and the treatment was one of frank propaganda presented as a sequence of narrative episodes, complete with a newsreader and musical pointing. The expressionist poet and dadaist Yvan Goll (1891–1950) had already tried out the use of photographs and film clips in *Die Unsterblichen* (*The Immortal Ones*, 1920) and in other plays, and Piscator's 'epic' characteristic in *Flags* was present in two screens, one on either side of the stage, upon which were projected photographs of the main characters, together with written summaries of the action in each scene. Piscator continued his long career by experimenting with every variation of this formula. In the same vein, he put together the *Revue Roter Rummel* (*The Rowdy Red Revue*, also 1924) with music by Edmund Meisel, and took it round the workers' meeting halls for the Communist Party. The revue presented a sympathetic picture of ex-soldiers as cripples and beggars, while caricaturing their wealthy masters in evening dress and top hats, and it was made up of fourteen episodes using song and dance material, films and slides. The audience that came to these shows was given a programme as fat as a pamphlet, crammed with commentary on the chosen topic.

Piscator's best-known production in these years was of *The Good Soldier Schweik*, which will be described in more detail below, but he applied his method to plays and novels as different as Schiller's *The Robbers*, treated as if it were the modern class struggle, and Tolstoy's massive *War and Peace*, which he dramatized with Alfred Neumann in 1936, tested at his Studio Theatre in New York in 1942, and finally produced at the Schiller Theater in West Berlin in 1955. In this unusual adaptation, the gentle Pierre assumed the role of narrator and lecturer, and moved large toy soldiers about the stage when he was not part of the action. In this double role, he could poise the stories of the families in the novel against the progress of the Napoleonic War.

Piscator's book, *Das politische Theater* (*The Political Theatre*, 1929, now translated into all the major languages) is an important autobiographical source which traces the beginnings of epic theatre. Piscator's intention was to imbue existing forms of drama, both naturalistic and expressionistic, with a new clarity, and so bring a pointedly social and moral purpose to the theatre. Above all, the stage was to be a political agency in the widest sense. It would be a scientific laboratory dealing in facts, which it would treat objectively. Brecht repeatedly acknowledged his debt to Piscator, who, he said, 'without doubt is one of the most important theatre men of all times', and in a lecture delivered in Stockholm in 1939, 'On Experimental Theatre', he argued that Piscator's method had transformed the work of the playwright, the actor and the designer by breaking 'nearly all the conventions' (translated John Willett).

Piscator believed that there could be no theatre without an audience, which should be the centre of the actor's attention. In spite of Stanislavsky, in spite of the development of realism and the creation of the 'fourth wall', the actor could never be truly natural on the stage — he must always speak more loudly than in life, try not to be masked by another actor, and so on. The actor should therefore accept the truth of this, and be 'natural' in a direct relationship with his audience. On an empty stage, shorn of the trappings of realism, the actor could rediscover his ancient mission, that of entertaining and teaching simultaneously. The theatre needed this new kind of actor, one neither of the declamatory nor the naturalistic school, one not improvising his emotions, but giving a commentary *on* his emotions. The new actor must play 'not only a result, but the thought which created the result . . . the roots and not the fruit alone, the seed and not the plant alone'. To achieve this, he needed a superior control and a new objectivity, so that he could discard the actor's usual egotism and become the mirror in which the audience saw itself.

'Epic theatre' is a term which has shifted its meaning according to the director who used it, but when Piscator chose it, he had in mind something of the Aristotelian conception of a tale told without having to observe the unities of time and place. Epic theatre therefore signified a performance free from the restrictions of realistic conventions, especially those of the tightly-knit well-made play. The epic play was to be a rational, rather than an empathetic, report on some social or political theme, and, free from realism, it would open out its content for inspection. It follows that Piscator was most comfortable adapting and dramatizing the novel.

Piscator became well-known for his advocacy and use of any mechanical device that might help him. Unlike Victorian stage machinery, Piscator's was used consciously to reflect a modern scientific society. From the beginning, it was the film used as an independent narrative device which enabled him to replace the lifeless scenery of the realistic stage, and he often projected more than one image simultaneously as a background to the acted play. In this way, newsreels and still photographs became a visual commentary upon, and an extension of, the drama, and assisted the actor in creating the desired objectivity. Lantern slides, placards and signboards, like the film, could contribute as atmosphere and background, and even provide a form of chorus by contrasting what was spoken with what was unspoken. A monologue could be illustrated, and a character's motives could be demonstrated.

Piscator's work also explored the uses of 'mixed media' in the theatre. Integrating film with live action is like mixing oil and water, however skilfully the director and the designer manipulate the images on screens and gauzes to match a two- with a three-dimensional medium. Yet the two can set each other off, film lending a modern, technological extension to the world depicted on the stage. Film clips can be timed to support, expand or comment on the stage action, the images on the stage and on the screens even suggesting cause and effect — the most commonplace arrangement was to have a political speech delivered on the stage, while behind the speaker the screen showed, say, the resulting horrors of the battlefield. In this way, the film could make a quick, generalized, usually emotive, statement at a moment's notice, and was particularly useful in illustrating the rambling historical narratives Piscator chose, where the general image was made to balance the particularity of the lines.

On a screen, an actor's image was of course usually giant-sized in comparison with what was seen on the stage, and so, against the reality of the life-sized actor, the screen image appeared to carry symbolic importance. Thus in a mixed-media play, the spectator is constantly teased by the conflict between the real and the illusory. For Friedrich Wolf's *Tai Yang erwacht* (*Tai Yang Awakes*, 1931) at the Wallner-Theater, with John Heartfield as designer, Piscator had a line of marching demonstrators carrying a series of empty banners upon which film images were projected as they crossed the stage, so seeming to bridge the gap between stage and screen. However, the effect was to make the audience too conscious of the artificiality of the trick — they laughed.

Piscator was keen to adapt for his purposes anything that modern science had invented. Like the actor of the Greek or the Elizabethan theatre, whose unlocalized stages could grant him freedom in time and space, the epic actor could find an equivalent freedom through the use of revolving platforms, conveyor belts and treadmills, escalators and elevators, motorized bridges, and rising and falling stage levels. By such devices the actor could become the narrator and the guide to the pictures shown. Not content with this, Piscator believed in using the colour organ and amplified sound and music, and he even turned his loud-speakers and searchlights on the

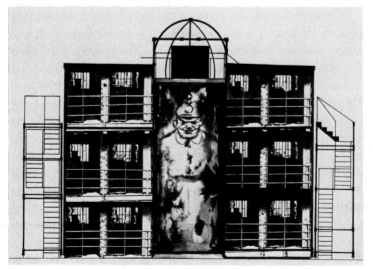

32. Toller, *Hurrah We Live*, 1927. Production by Erwin Piscator at the Theater am Nollendorfplatz, Berlin. Model of stage set.

audience. After 1953, he created a *Lichtbühne* or light stage by laying a stage floor of glass, in order to illuminate the setting from beneath as well as the top and sides. Piscator wanted his stage to be a 'play-machine', an 'arena for battling ideas'.

As a result of all this mechanization, Piscator's promptbook was like an engineer's manual. According to Brecht, the stage of the Nollendorftheater was so heavy that it had to be reinforced with steel and concrete supports. Moreover, each production required the assistance of several writers, as well as experts in history, economics and statistics, to back them up. As well as scenic construction and transparent settings, Toller's *Hoppla, wir leben!* (*Hurrah, We Live!*), which Piscator produced at the Theater am Nollendorfplatz in 1927, involved 10,000 feet of film projected by four projectors. His production of Alexei Tolstoy's *Rasputin* in the same year included the use of three screens set in a half-circle, with the actors playing in the middle on a circular stage.

His dramatization of Jaroslav Haček's comic novel about the First World War at the Theater am Nollendorfplatz in 1928 was one of the great events of the modern theatre. It had been previously

33. Max Brod and Hans Reimann, *The Good Soldier Schweik*, 1928. Production by Erwin Piscator. Drawing by George Grosz.

dramatized by Max Brod and Hans Reimann as *Abenteuer des braven Soldaten Schweiks* (*The Good Soldier Schweik*), and this rambling, picaresque subject seemed perfectly suited to receive the epic treatment. But before it could be presented, it had to undergo further rewriting by several hands, including Brecht and Piscator himself. In twenty-five scenes, the play tells the story of a simple Czech soldier conscripted into the Austrian army in 1914. Schweik is a genial little man who is so keen to obey orders that he unwittingly and repeatedly demonstrates the stupidity of the army authorities. Since much of the tale is an account of his journey from his house to the front line, rather than a picture of the fighting itself, the material lent itself to a free epic arrangement in which Schweik stood at the centre of events.

We are fortunate to have a lively account of the first production in Mordecai Gorelik's *New Theatres for Old*. The ingenious set consisted of three 'portals' one behind the other and taking up the depth of the stage. Between their supports two moving platforms ran from side to side like conveyor belts, with a translucent backcloth behind. This production marked the first appearance of Piscator's *'laufendes Band'* ('treadmill'), as such a conveyor belt was called. The backcloth became a screen against which satirical line-drawings by the cartoonist George Grosz could be cut out and mounted — the drawings for the play numbered about three hundred, and they have since been published by Malik Verlag in Berlin. The first projected drawing was of a pair of imposing Austrian generals, heavy with moustaches and medals, together with a judge with a face like a skull and a priest with a small crucifix balanced on the tip of his nose, and from time to time other drawings appeared. Piscator's first plan had been to have only one character, that of Schweik himself, played by a live actor, and all his tormentors represented as caricatures, but this proved to be too limiting.

To the accompaniment of a Czech folk-song played on a hurdy-gurdy, the conveyor belt first brought on to the stage the corner of a shabby room, where Schweik, played by the Austrian comedian Max Pallenberg, puffed contentedly on his pipe, while his landlady Frau Müller swept the floor. The location was Prague, where Schweik lived, a victim of rheumatism. Then the scene shifted to that of a beerhall, where the topic of conversation was the assassination of the Archduke Ferdinand. Back at his house, Schweik received his mobilization papers, while snatches of military propaganda were flashed on the screen. Frau Müller then pushed him in a wheel-chair to have his medical examination, as the streets of Prague passed by on the screen. Schweik waved his crutches enthusiastically and cried, 'On to Belgrade!' The examining doctor was another Grosz drawing, a huge face with a duelling scar and an enormous cigar, all projected on the screen, and he prescribed alternately, 'Physic and aspirin!' and 'Stomach pump and quinine!', excusing no one from duty.

Schweik was now in the army, and his travels began. Gorelik reported that the moving belt was very noisy and that the props placed on it tumbled about as it moved, but the total impression was fittingly comic and wonderfully well conveyed the idea of a crazily wandering soldier, the world changing around him as he went. The costumes of all the soldiers were grotesquely padded, making them seem like robots, and masks completed the wooden effect. Schweik at this point was made an orderly who was sent to Budweis on the Serbian front: a cut-out train was seen on the belt, while the land-scape rushed past on the screen. Unluckily, Schweik was arrested for pulling the communication cord, and was made to walk the rest of the way. It was a three-day march; paper snow fell profusely. On the screen a map of one of the towns on the route showed Schweik making a wide detour round the police. Then a caption read, 'Instead of going south to Budweis, Schweik marches in a straight line west' — in other words, he appeared to be lost. However, cap-tured with some other men as a deserter, he was bundled aboard another freight train, also a cut-out, and at last found himself on the battlefield. There Schweik was captured by his own side, only to be hit by shellfire for a final irony. As a last minute idea, literally half-an-hour before curtain time, Piscator had projected on the screen a procession of crosses moving towards the audience; the lights came up and the play was over. In another version, 'a legless beggar and half-a-dozen real cripples were engaged to parade across the stage, smeared with muck and blood and their missing limbs hanging out of their rucksacks' (C. D. Innes, *Erwin Piscator's Political Theatre*, p. 58). This jolly production was immensely success-ful with the general public.

The influence of Piscator's work has been strong in Germany, both before Hitler's accession to power in 1933, and with the popular revival of documentary drama since the Second World War. Brecht took part in many of Piscator's early experiments designed to 'increase the theatre's value as education'. As a poet, however, Brecht was less concerned with machinery and more with the uses of language, so that Brecht's epic theatre developed along different lines, as will appear. But western theatre generally found the Piscator approach rewarding, and cabaret-style political revue, mixing live actor, cartoon and film, is today almost a new dramatic genre in itself. It appeared in London, notably with Joan Littlewood's satirical picture of the First World War in *Oh, What a Lovely War!* (1963), and in Paris, notably in Roger Planchon's *Bleus, blancs, rouges ou les Libertins* (*Blue, White, Red or the Libertines*, 1967), with its subject the French Revolution. It was an essential ingredient in *Brassneck* (1973) by Howard Brenton and David Hare, where documentary sequences of historical events since 1945 introduced each scene. Mixed-media theatre may be Piscator's most important legacy.

The connection between Piscator and the architect Walter Gropius (1883–1969) lies in their common interest in developing a playhouse designed to serve any and every purpose in drama, while at the same time being capable of seating 2,000 people. In 1927 Gropius designed such a 'multiple' or 'flexible' theatre for Piscator, one which could accommodate arena, thrust or proscenium productions by means of a revolving acting-space and a block of seats which moved with it. Films or slides were to have been projected on a cyclorama at the rear, as well as on screens set all round and above the auditorium. The purpose was to have the audience in the middle of the action, thus furthering Piscator's idea of audience participation. The theatre was to be completely adaptable, and, Piscator wrote, 'as systematized as a typewriter'. Gropius called the concept '*Total Theater*'. 'The playhouse itself', he wrote, 'made to dissolve into the shifting, illusionary space of the imagination, would become the scene of action', all in the belief that 'while it is true that the mind can transform the body, it is equally true that structure can transform the mind' (translated Maria Ley-Piscator). This playhouse was never built.

The ideas behind the Piscator-Gropius concept of *Total*

*Theater* were most extensively tried out in the Bauhaus experiments. Gropius had founded a School of Fine Arts at the Staatliches Bauhaus in Weimar in 1919. It began as a school of design, but Gropius sought ways of bringing together the artist and the technician, and aimed for a common, functional style for the visual arts of painting and design, sculpture and architecture. His special interest in technology drew him to the examples of mechanized drama he found in Piscator's Studio, and he began to explore theatrical space and light at the Bauhaus itself.

34. *Study for the 'Triadic Ballet'*, 1922. Production by Oskar Schlemmer at the Staatliches Bauhaus, Weimar. Costume and stage design. (Gouache, ink and collage of photographs, 22⅝ × 14⅝ ins. (irreg.). Collection, The Museum of Modern Art, New York. Gift of Lily Auchincloss.)

Oskar Schlemmer (1888–1943) joined the Bauhaus in 1921, and took over its theatrical work from 1923 to 1929. Schlemmer conceived of the stage as a sculptor might, using actors as architectural and mechanical robots to 'transfigure the human form'. Costumes and masks were geometrical in appearance, and gestures and movements were angular and staccato, as if made by clockwork mechanism. Acting was seen as a spatial form, to be designed and lit like the dance, and the work of the Bauhaus has had considerable impact on modern ballet. Schlemmer's designer, László Moholy-Nagy (1895–1946), who also designed for Piscator, has been called 'the magician of stage vision' because of his ability to create effects on the stage of light and shadow in relation to space:

> Space is a reality. A reality, once it has been comprehended in its essence, can be grasped and arranged according to its own laws... These laws have to be studied so as to use them in the service of expression (translated Ley-Piscator).

This was heady stuff, and there was an intoxicating element in the mechanical ballets of the Bauhaus as it experimented with sound, light, space, form and motion.

The best achievement of the Bauhaus was *The Triadic Ballet*, directed by Schlemmer in 1923. It was so called because the performance consisted of three 'dances', each in a different mood marked by a different colour – 'gaiety' in yellow, 'solemnity' in red and 'mystery' in black. Significantly, the dances were designed for the costumes, and not vice versa, so that the actor's task was to bring out the character of the costume within the severe restrictions of its design. Thus, one costume was shaped like a rigid top, crowned by a wooden knob, so that every movement made by the actor inside the costume was accentuated, giving the spectator the impression that man was an automaton, a mere object in space and time.

The work of the Bauhaus also linked Piscator with the Futurist theatre of the Italians Marinetti and Prampolini. Both epic theatre and Futurist theatre saw the actor as a mechanized puppet, and drew upon various elements of vaudeville and the music hall, its noise and colour, its clowning and acrobatics. But the Futurist impulse, like that of the Bauhaus, was finally towards surrealism and an abstraction in drama which Piscator's primary interests could not accept. Piscator's concerns were first and last earthy, concrete, political. Where the Futurists tried to create violent stage images to stir the emotions, Piscator's ultimate wish was for the hard objectivity of a logical stage.

# 14 Epic theatre in Germany: early Brecht

*Baal* (1923), *A Man's a Man* (1926), *The Threepenny Opera* (1928)

Bertolt Brecht (1898—1956) entered the German theatre as one of a number of young playwrights at a time when stage production was in a whirl of experiment: realism was crumbling and new approaches were being put to the test. As we saw, Brecht acknowledged a special debt to Piscator and his idea of epic theatre; the two men worked together at the Volksbühne over the period 1919 to 1930, and Brecht had a hand in the famous production of *The Good Soldier Schweik*. Yet Brecht was also one of Reinhardt's assistants in his Deutsches Theater complex for a time, and was able to watch rehearsals for the great seasons of 1924—5 and 1925—6. In these years Reinhardt experimented with acting as role-playing, having the players mingle with the spectators as he had done for *Danton's Death* in 1916 and 1921. This was also the time when Reinhardt was trying out Pirandellian non-illusory devices, with actors stepping out of the play in *Six Characters in Search of an Author*, or improvising the action in Goldoni's *The Servant of Two Masters* as if they were a *commedia dell'arte* troupe. In addition to these great influences on Brecht's work, there were other powerful interests — in the energetic, scatalogical Wedekind, and in the recently rediscovered Büchner, a young revolutionary like Brecht himself, whose techniques in *Woyzeck* supplied exciting precedents for his early writing. And during this same period the young Brecht was avidly educating himself in every form of ritual playwriting he could find in Greek and Elizabethan drama.

Like others before him, Brecht would rebel not only against the ponderous style of German realism, but also against Reinhardt's baroque manner and the fever of the new expressionists. The expressionist hero had been messianic, a man of incredible vision, a poet — but at his worst a pompous ass. Brecht's disillusionment moved him to prick the expressionist idealism by substituting the *Gummimensch*, the 'rubber man', as an anti-hero. Such a one is a Kragler, the returning solder of *Trommeln in der Nacht* (*Drums in the Night*, 1922), who decides that the better part of valour is to make do with the pregnant girl who was unfaithful to him. As both a stage director and a playwright, Brecht was always watching his own and other experiments, borrowing and rejecting, modifying theory with practice, changing his ideas as each new production was conceived and tested. And during his career, Brecht never ceased to return to the past, particularly to the plays of Shakespeare and the eighteenth century, for material which seemed adaptable to his method and suitable for his themes. His many attempts to apply a didactic, and often political, ideology to the stage consequently resulted in a major new aesthetic for the theatre, one which has since proved eminently acceptable to the sceptical spirit of our time. What follows is a summary of Brecht's general approach to drama, although in fact he evolved it over many years.

Brecht's work embodied Piscator's way of epic theatre. Although Brecht inclined towards the more closed, 'parable' play which focused on a moral dilemma, his was still a narrative form, telling a story by the use of illustrative scenes, choruses and commentators, songs and dances, projected titles and summaries, and making use of much of the mechanical apparatus Piscator held dear. Brecht's special contribution was to envisage a particular role for the actor in all this, using him to help destroy conventional illusion. (It was the actor's task to put himself 'at a distance' from the character he was portraying and the situation he was involved with, in order to arouse a thinking, enquiring response in the spectator.)

Brecht's essay 'The Street Scene' provides the basic explanation of this approach. We are to imagine a traffic accident involving a driver and a pedestrian, together with a bystander on a street corner who witnessed what happened. When he tries to explain the accident to others afterwards, the bystander re-enacts what the

driver and the pedestrian did so that they can judge t
This kind of performance can be good theatre withou
the traditional artistic 'event'. The demonstrator is no ⸻ ⸻ ⸻ give
a perfect imitation of those who were involved in the accident, nor is
he required to cast a spell over his listeners. He is merely reporting
the incident, and no illusion of reality is necessary. Thus epic theatre
is at bottom non-illusory. It does not disguise the fact that it is only a
piece of theatre. Performance will make it clear that lines have been
learned, action rehearsed, stage equipment made ready.

Feelings and emotions may well be part of the experience for
the audience, but the actor is not asked to convey them himself.
Instead, just as in 'the street scene', the activity will have a social
purpose — perhaps to show who is guilty, or how to avoid such an
accident in the future. The purpose served must justify the effort
made. Brecht's epic theatre, like Piscator's, aimed therefore at a
political examination of society and its working elements, like the
class structure or the economic system. Brecht would produce
'*Lehrstücke*' or 'teaching plays', and 'insofar as they are good theatre,
they will amuse': he cited with approval Schiller's dictum that there
was no reason why a concern for morality should not be thoroughly
enjoyable. Brecht's was to be a didactic theatre for the scientific
age, and he saw drama as a critique of life, a critique which he
increasingly embodied in the structure of his plays.

The actor was to make clear to his audience his '*Gestus*' or,
demonstrable social attitude, his basic disposition. He would derive
his 'character' from the actions of the person he portrayed, not,
as is usual in drama, the actions from the character, which procedure
'shields actions from criticism'. And if the actor was to do his work
objectively, he would speak with a certain reserve or distance, or
repeat an action slowly, or stop to explain to the audience what he
was doing. By this behaviour the actor would create the desirable
'*Verfremdungseffekt*', the 'alienation effect' of epic theatre. In a play
which is distanced in this way, a transition in the action from
presentation to commentary, and vice versa, is characteristic and
constant.

So it was that acting as 'impersonation', even the purpose of
acting as 'imitation' in Aristotle's sense, was supplanted by
acting that was 'gestic' and 'epic'. Epic acting is acting that is

intended to be entirely natural, and Roland Barthes has pointed out
that 'the verisimilitude of [epic] acting has its meaning in the
objective meaning of the *play*, and not, as in "naturalist" dramaturgy,
in the truth inherent in the actor' (*Tulane Drama Review*, 37) — the
actor's reference point was always to be the meaning of the play.
Brecht's method was therefore diametrically opposed to that of
Stanislavsky and the drama of realistic illusion. Brecht's stage was
to be stripped of its theatrical magic, and the audience refused the
state of emotional, empathetic trance, a degrading condition he
associated with what he called the 'Aristotelian' theatre.

The idea of distancing lay at the very centre of Brecht's
theory, although it grew in importance only gradually, until it
was seen as essential for the inducement of a proper critical attitude in the spectator. As early as 1920, he wrote a note that
'humour is a sense of distance' (*Distanzgefühl*). He then made use
of the Marxist term '*Entfremdung*' or 'alienation', and sometimes
'*Fremdheit*' or 'strangeness', but after a visit to Moscow in 1935,
when he saw a performance of Mei Lan-fang's Chinese company, he
virtually coined the word '*Verfremdung*' to identify the quality he
recognized more clearly. Brecht saw that the symbolic Chinese
theatre never pretended there was no audience, and in his essay
'Alienation Effects in Chinese Acting' he compared this kind of
theatre with 'the acrobat who will glance at us for approval'. The
Chinese actor conveyed passion without having to be passionate
himself, and he was at all times in control, as in a ritualistic
performance.

As the theory developed, Brecht argued that all theatre
artists, from the writer to the lighting engineer, should work
together to induce the distancing effect and make the performance
truly objective. This idea, however, had nothing to do with the old
Wagnerian unity of the arts. In epic theatre each artist was to make a
*separate* contribution.

1. *The actor*, as we have seen, would 'show' rather than imit-
ate, and Brecht advocated a number of rehearsal devices to encourage this: the actor would speak in the third person, or in the past
tense, or even speak the stage directions (as in, 'He stood up and, since
he had nothing to eat, said angrily...') Gesture would consciously
indicate his inner feeling, as if the actor were visibly observing his

own movements. Direct address to the audience would be complete, unlike the traditionally hasty aside.

2. *The designer* of the set, following Piscator, would dispense with illusion and symbolism, and build according to the actor's needs. There would be no suggestion of a 'fourth wall', and, except for props, the stage would be bare, merely an open space on which to tell a story. Set changes would be made in full view of the audience, and if there had to be a curtain, it would simply be strung on a string across the stage. In this way stage and audience would be joined, not separated, and speaking directly to the house would be encouraged.

3. *The playwright* would structure his play episodically, preceding each scene with a written title, which would remain in position until replaced by another one, and offer an 'historical' account of the action of the scene. 'Historicization' was another of Brecht's concepts that was closely related to distancing — encouraging an awareness that an event had happened as if in the past, making the present look strange.

4. *The director* would arrange the blocking or grouping of the actors on the stage, not merely to achieve some formal beauty of good composition, but essentially to clarify the structure of human relationships in the play.

5. *The lighting designer* would abandon the idea of hiding the sources of light to achieve a mysterious effect that would draw the audience into the action. Instead, his apparatus would be perfectly visible, so that the spectator would be conscious he was in a theatre. The stage itself would be lit with a plain white light so that the actor would seem to be in the same world as the audience.

6. *The composer* of the music should express his idea of the play's theme independently, and so provide a separate comment on the action, which might often be in conflict with the activity of the characters. Unlike opera, in which aria and recitative are continuous, and music is used to reinforce the text, an epic production would have music and song which was in counterpoint with the action on the stage. At one time, Paul Dessau inserted

tacks into the hammers of his piano to make it sound like another speaking voice.

Certain of Brecht's earlier plays mark out his rapid development as an epic playwright. His first, *Baal* (1918), was a play of extraordinary maturity. It was written when Brecht was a medical student at Munich, and planned as a riposte to Hanns Johst's expressionistic idealism in *Der Einsame* (*The Lonely One*, 1917). Johst's play on the life of the playwright Christian Dietrich Grabbe had irritated Brecht with its exalted tone, its precious language and its cliché image of human suffering. *Baal* was also a play expressing moral indignation, but its central character, ironically named after the fertility god, was designed to be an obscenely anti-social and selfish hedonist, as a way of having him resist the demands of an anti-social world — an interesting forerunner of the characters Puntila and Azdak. The play was clearly conceived to shock and repel, yet it might be said to be lyrical in its arrangement of poetic interludes, and even in its callous, colloquial dialogue.

*Baal* opens with a mock expressionistic 'Chorale of the Great Baal', which is followed by twenty-two expressionistic scenes and ballads telling the hero's story. He is a ruthless cynic, drunken and sensual, and he spends much of his time in bar-rooms singing to a guitar. He seduces a series of women, one of whom, Johanna, becomes pregnant and kills herself when Baal turns her away. He also has a homosexual lover in his friend Ekart, whom he later murders in jealousy. Declaring the world to be 'the excrement of God', Baal finally dies in a filthy hovel in the Black Forest, ignored by the foresters who live there. Brecht loads his lines with the bestial imagery of feeding, sex and evacuating, and his poet without a conscience meets a fitting end in a dirty world.

*Baal* was first produced in Leipzig in 1923, and received a major production in Vienna in 1926 with Oscar Homolka in the title role. Needless to say, the play made no sense to its first audiences and was totally misunderstood. We can see now that Brecht was using his monstrous portrait of Baal to suggest ironically the larger one of modern man living a life of self-interest. Peter Ferran has suggested that in this treatment already lay the later Brechtian concept of a character's *Gestus*, and as a symbolic figure Brecht's Baal was as

romantic in his way as Johst's Grabbe. Five yea
*Threepenny Opera* would be equally misunderstood, b
profitable results for its author.

Brecht's gifts as a writer of dramatic verse and prose showed themselves strongly in *Baal*. The telegraphic style of expressionistic drama, made up of punctuated 'poetic' utterances, was radically changed. Brecht wrote in a realistic mixture of dialect and slang, with every line composed with its delivery in mind, capturing in tone and rhythm the exact quality of vitality intended in the speaker. Brecht's sense of the stage emerged particularly in his growing ability to write *gestische Sprache*, 'gestic language', which made the lines physically actable and conveyed the basic posture and attitude of the speaker as well.

In Brecht's second play, *Trommeln in der Nacht* (*Drums in the Night*, 1922), the epic theatre's use of placards and signs begins to appear; for the Munich production which won him the Kleist prize, slogans were posted in the auditorium. But the first play to embody epic characteristics with any rigour was *Mann ist Mann* (*A Man's a Man*), an anti-war comedy first produced in Darmstadt and Düsseldorf in 1926. It was revised for production at the Berlin Volksbühne in 1928 and at the Berlin Staatstheater in 1931, where it was directed by Brecht himself with Peter Lorre and Brecht's wife Helene Weigel in the chief parts.

*A Man's a Man* is a frankly didactic play full of the tricks of the circus, the cabaret and the music hall, devices which dispelled the last traces of expressionistic idealism and soul-suffering. Set in British imperial India, its ballads are cheeky parodies of Kipling, and its central character, the good-natured dock labourer Galy Gay is, in Eric Bentley's view, an elephantine mixture of Falstaff and Chaplin. It is Galy Gay who, by a series of misadventures, is persuaded to impersonate a missing machine-gunner at roll call, and who, in the course of the play's eleven scenes, is transformed into a 'human fighting machine'. With the new name of Jeriah Jip, he becomes the perfect soldier who single-handedly destroys a fortress in Tibet:

> A man's a man, says Mr Bertolt Brecht
> And that is hardly more than you'd expect.

romantic in his way as Johst's Grabbe. Five years' later, *The Threepenny Opera* would be equally misunderstood, but with more profitable results for its author.

Brecht's gifts as a writer of dramatic verse and prose showed themselves strongly in *Baal*. The telegraphic style of expressionistic drama, made up of punctuated 'poetic' utterances, was radically changed. Brecht wrote in a realistic mixture of dialect and slang, with every line composed with its delivery in mind, capturing in tone and rhythm the exact quality of vitality intended in the speaker. Brecht's sense of the stage emerged particularly in his growing ability to write *gestische Sprache*, 'gestic language', which made the lines physically actable and conveyed the basic posture and attitude of the speaker as well.

In Brecht's second play, *Trommeln in der Nacht* (*Drums in the Night*, 1922), the epic theatre's use of placards and signs begins to appear; for the Munich production which won him the Kleist prize, slogans were posted in the auditorium. But the first play to embody epic characteristics with any rigour was *Mann ist Mann* (*A Man's a Man*), an anti-war comedy first produced in Darmstadt and Düsseldorf in 1926. It was revised for production at the Berlin Volksbühne in 1928 and at the Berlin Staatstheater in 1931, where it was directed by Brecht himself with Peter Lorre and Brecht's wife Helene Weigel in the chief parts.

*A Man's a Man* is a frankly didactic play full of the tricks of the circus, the cabaret and the music hall, devices which dispelled the last traces of expressionistic idealism and soul-suffering. Set in British imperial India, its ballads are cheeky parodies of Kipling, and its central character, the good-natured dock labourer Galy Gay is, in Eric Bentley's view, an elephantine mixture of Falstaff and Chaplin. It is Galy Gay who, by a series of misadventures, is persuaded to impersonate a missing machine-gunner at roll call, and who, in the course of the play's eleven scenes, is transformed into a 'human fighting machine'. With the new name of Jeriah Jip, he becomes the perfect soldier who single-handedly destroys a fortress in Tibet:

A man's a man, says Mr Bertolt Brecht
And that is hardly more than you'd expect.

But Mr Bertolt Brecht goes on to show
That you can change a man from top to toe.
                                    (translated Gerhard Nellhaus)

Galy Gay's counterpart is Sergeant Bloody Five, a Kipling caricature,
the 'Tiger of Kilkoa', the 'Human Typhoon', who acquired his name
by shooting five Hindu prisoners without a qualm. A typical
sergeant when the sun shines, Bloody Five is consumed by lust when
it rains; furious at his own lack of self-control, he castrates himself
with a pistol. In these two characters we see Brecht's early propensity
to split his creations into two, as he does with Shen Te and Shui Ta in
*The Good Woman of Setzuan.*

A Man's a Man was received with mixed and uncertain re-
views, and was criticized for its lack of well-made suspense and
its failure to supply a character, even Galy Gay, with whom the
audience could sympathize. The play's vision of a man as a cipher,
both weak and cruel, and forced to conform to the requirements of
society, was obscured. The point was made in John Hancock's

35. Brecht, *A Man's a Man*, 1926. Production by Bertolt Brecht
at the Staatstheater, Berlin, 1931, with Peter Lorre as Galy Gay,
second from left.

production in New York in 1962, when everyone in the play wore a white mask except Galy Gay, who nevertheless little by little acquired one of his own before the last scene. *A Man's a Man* was Brecht's first play to extend the idea of a character by the use of a mask; others later were *Die Massnahme* (*The Measures Taken*), *Die Rondköpfe und die Spitzköpfe* (*Roundheads and Peakheads*), *The Good Woman of Setzuan* and *The Caucasian Chalk Circle* (see next chapter). The play which brought Brecht world-wide attention, and

36. Brecht, *The Threepenny Opera*, 1928. Production by Bertolt Brecht, design by Casper Neher at the Theater am Schiffbauerdamm, Berlin. Final scene, with Harald Paulsen as Macheath.

which possibly exemplifies his early epic manner best, was *Die Dreigroschenoper* (*The Threepenny Opera*, 1928). Inspired by Nigel Playfair's success with John Gay's *The Beggar's Opera* at the Lyric Theatre, Hammersmith, 1920–3, Brecht asked Elisabeth Hauptmann to translate the text into German, and he had found another English play for epic adaptation, having previously treated Marlowe's *Edward II* in 1924. He changed Gay's eighteenth-century scene to one of late nineteenth-century Soho in London, and with Caspar Neher as designer and Kurt Weill as composer, the new play ran for 400 performances at the Theater am Schiffbauerdamm in Berlin. It was subsequently made into a film in parallel German and French versions by G. W. Pabst in 1931, although Brecht fought a legal battle to have it suppressed because he considered the film too light weight. This film nevertheless remains our best film record of the early epic style. *The Threepenny Opera* was also produced at the Kamerny Theatre, Moscow in 1930, at the Théâtre Montparnasse, Paris in 1930 and at the Empire Theatre, New York in 1933, but London, the source of the play's original inspiration, did not see it until 1956, when it was produced at the Royal Court Theatre by Sam Wanamaker.

Where Gay had particular political targets for his delightful burlesque opera, Brecht attacked capitalism generally. There is war in the underworld of London when the thief Macheath and Peachum the receiver fall out. Peachum is 'The Beggar's Friend', supplying thieves with disguises as beggars — the Moscow production introduced the amusing idea of having normal men and women enter Peachum's shop on one side, only to emerge on the other as human derelicts. Macheath marries Peachum's daughter Polly, setting up the wedding in style with stolen furniture. But Peachum is angry, and betrays Macheath to the police. The law then appears in the person of Chief of Police 'Tiger' Brown (Gay's Lockit). Lucy, Brown's daughter, helps Macheath to escape, but he is again arrested when he is found frequenting his favourite brothel, and this time his neck is put in the noose. For a satirical conclusion, Macheath is given a pardon by the Queen, together with a handsome pension. In Pabst's film, he becomes a bank president.

The characters in Brecht's play are criminals as a kind of self-defence. Crime is seen to be a capitalistic enterprise, and

Peachum and Macheath have all the bourgeois virtues. Peachum sees poverty as a way of making money, and Macheath is a business-man who does not want his business disrupted, like Mother Courage in a later play. The satire lies in reproducing these attitudes in a criminal setting, and the image of corruption is complete when Macheath is given his royal pardon. However, audiences found it aesthetically satisfying to recognize an allegory which embraced both higher and lower classes, and merely to equate capitalists with gangsters did not have the caustic effect Brecht wanted. As a result, the play was popular with fashionable middle-class audiences everywhere.

In spite of this, there are many important technical advances in *The Threepenny Opera*. The curtain appeared to be nothing but a dirty sheet drawn on a string across the stage. A fair-ground organ stood at the back of the stage, with a jazz band on the steps in front of it. Coloured lights lit up when the music played. Free use was made of titles and drawings projected on screens in red satin frames on either side of the organ, and mock-religious signs were pinned on Peachum's walls, such as, 'It is more blessed to give than to receive' and 'Give and it shall be given unto you'. By these means, the audi-ence was persuaded to practise Brecht's notion of 'complex seeing'. And just as Gay made fun of the tradition of Italian opera, so the nineteen songs in *The Threepenny Opera*, based more on François Villon than on John Gay, were carefully planned to counter Wagnerian principles of music-drama: Brecht asked that setting, story and music should be 'mingled without mixing', each element making its own statement. In the production Brecht also developed the technique of having the actor speak against the music, and in his notes he insisted that the actor must not only sing, but 'show a man singing'. His experience in this play encouraged him in the composition of the operatic *Happy End* (the original title, 1929), which failed, and of *Aufstieg und Fall der Stadt Mahagonny* (*Rise and Fall of the City of Mahagonny*, 1930), which enjoyed a *succès de scandale*, with riots, whistling and applause descending on the performance in every German city where it was played. These plays also cemented the collaboration between Brecht and Kurt Weill, and prepared the way for the total integration of theatrical elements in the mature masterpieces which followed.

# 15  *Epic theatre in Germany: later Brecht*

*Galileo* (1943), *Mother Courage* (1941), *The Caucasian Chalk Circle* (1948)

From the time Brecht left Hitler's Germany in 1933 until his return to East Berlin in 1948 — fifteen years of exile which he spent in Switzerland, Denmark, Sweden, Finland, the United States, again Switzerland and finally Austria — this essentially pragmatic playwright was without a regular company to try out his plays. Yet these were the years of his masterpieces, *Leben des Galilei* (*Life of Galileo*, written 1938–9), *Mutter Courage und ihre Kinder* (*Mother Courage and Her Children*, written 1939), *Der gute Mensch von Sezuan* (*The Good Woman of Setzuan*, written 1938–40) and *Der Kaukasische Kreidekreis* (*The Caucasian Chalk Circle*, written 1943–5). The years 1941–7 in America, where 'The Method' was in the ascendancy and where epic theatre and its strange ways were meaningless, were largely lost to him. So he thought of his plays as '*Versuche*', 'attempts' or 'experiments', and restlessly he picked at his plays, wrote and rewrote them, knowing they were untried and hence unfinished. And he also resorted to the extensive writing of dramatic theory. No other playwright of this century has written so much about his work, and so his exile was not without a legacy. Never was there a better opportunity to raise the issue of judging intentions by results, although in the last twenty years of his life, his theories grew increasingly tentative and open-ended.

Brecht's most important statement of theory during these years was the 'Kleines Organon für das Theater' ('A Short Organum for the Theatre'), written near Zürich in Switzerland in 1948 and published in Potsdam in 1949. To this essay should be added a number of appendices which Brecht left after his death. Taken together, these statements may be taken as Brecht's mature aesthetic of the theatre. They constituted a final modification of the epic idea, and embraced the developing concept of what he called '*dialektisches Theater*', 'dialectical theatre'.

Brecht reaffirmed his earlier idea of social purpose, the commitment of a theatre 'fit for the scientific age'. The 'Kleines Organon' again attacked popular contemporary drama as 'a branch of the narcotics business', but the difference now was that the attack did not conflict with a revised notion of the theatre as entertainment. The 'critical attitude' and the 'solution of problems' were taken to be pleasurable. Otherwise the former complaint was heard again that current theatre induced a state of emotional trance, a form of sleep. What was needed was a theatre which would release impulses to transform 'the particular historical field of human relations' with which a play might be dealing.

To ensure that significant social impulses were visible in the characters and their actions, a special kind of acting was needed, one based on the alienation effect. Here Brecht returned comfortably to the acting and production technique he had spent his life focusing upon. His final definition was reduced to:

> A representation that alienates is one which allows us to recognize its subject, but at the same time makes it seem unfamiliar (translated John Willett).

The actor's movement, gesture and speech must be 'matter-of-fact', so that he would not wholly assume the character he was playing, and so that the audience would not easily empathize with him. The action would be performed as if it were an experiment, a demonstration, and on stage the difference between the actor and the character he was playing would be readily apparent. Today we should say that Brecht's actor was 'role-playing'.

Brecht's actor would have a viewpoint of his own, a social attitude, which would affect his posture, voice and facial expression. This was the former idea of '*Gestus*'. It was the 'story' of the play, what happened between people, that would provide the material for the audience to 'discuss, criticize, alter'. So, too, the structure of a play would be episodic, like a chronicle, to give the audience the chance to interpose its judgment. Indeed, all the theatre arts would work in their different ways to tell the story, but they would relate to one another in 'mutual alienation'.

37. The Theater am Schiffbauerdamm, East Berlin, in 1954.

⌈So Brecht felt less need to write didactic 'teaching plays'. At the same time he began to drop his use of the term 'epic', and at the end identified as 'dialectical' the kind of process by which he planned a scene to induce the critical attitude.⌉This development went along with his recognition of his own inability to bring about a completely distancing effect, and the discrepancy between theory and practice seems most glaring in the last plays.⌉ He riddled them with techniques of alienation, and yet in 1940 he admitted that German productions acted in the alienated manner had resulted in strong emotional responses. It seems that the spectator soon adjusts his perception to the new techniques, and is liable to find sympathy for a character even when it is not intended. Nevertheless, Brecht's great contribution to modern drama lay in his constant insight into the incongruities and contradictions of human motive, and his ironic approach to the material of his plays could produce an acute sense of ambivalence in his audience. Irony and ambivalence remained to the end the source of vitality in his drama.

When he returned to East Berlin, Brecht reunited many of the actors who had been dispersed by the war, and in 1949 he founded the Berliner Ensemble. This company, run by Helene Weigel (1900– 72), found a home in Brecht's pre-war Theater am Schiffbauerdamm, which became the company's own in 1954. According to an eyewitness, George Devine, it also found a dedicated audience, one which gave the productions 'an air of religious ritual'. It remains a question, however, whether Brecht ever found the audience of workers, either in Berlin or elsewhere, that he was working for, but at least the creation of the Berliner Ensemble finally gave him the chance to try out his theories using his own actors and his own stage and an audience he knew. It was the achievement of this company in the short time before Brecht's death in 1956 that has provided a unique example of epic theatre in performance.

In these excellent new circumstances, Brecht tested his scenes again and again in rehearsal, trying a variety of alternative ways, rewriting as the rehearsal progressed, arranging the actors so that the stage composition told the story, taking as many as nine months to put a play together. The disposition and movement of a scene's characters over the acting space generally provided the key to the point of the action, and at any significant moment would almost suggest a moral tableau in the manner of a Victorian domestic melodrama. It became important to find a way of keeping as careful a record of rehearsal decisions as possible.

The details of some of Brecht's productions have consequently been kept in what he called a '*Modellbuch*', a stage record that was far more than the usual promptbook or even a Reinhardt *Regiebuch*. It not only contained the patterns of movement and the positions of the actors as evolved by the director in rehearsal, but it also filed hundreds of photographs of each scene in performance, together with a detailed commentary explaining the principles behind the action. These *Modellbücher* reflected Brecht's scrupulous attention to detail and his concern for the exact word and gesture needed to achieve the effect he wanted. When challenged with the criticism that these records might limit the work of other directors who wished to produce the same plays, he retorted that any director would naturally wish to begin where his predecessor had left off. Brecht was here, of course, indicating his own way of working.

Unfortunately perhaps, Brecht set such a standard, and followed so idiosyncratic a path, that subsequent directors could not readily take his advice and begin where he left off. Yet their inability or unwillingness to carry out all that Brecht's idea of epic theatre demanded may have been fortunate in another way. Those directors all over the world who tried to follow him in the 1960s were compelled to accommodate the epic method to the demands of their separate audiences and their own native traditions, and this resulted in a rather more versatile treatment of Brecht's plays in the contemporary theatre than the existence of a *Modellbuch* would suggest. Purists in the Brechtian camp may groan, but the more various treatment of the masterpieces may have proved that they can survive all manner of handling as other great plays have before them.

*Galileo* was the most rewritten of Brecht's plays. With three versions completed over seventeen years, the revisions themselves tell the story of his development towards a dialectical drama. A first version was written in Denmark in 1938–9, and had a successful production by German refugee actors directed by Leonard Steckel in the Zürich Schauspielhaus in 1943, when the author was in America. A second version was written in English in an extra-ordinary collaboration with the actor Charles Laughton between 1944 and 1947. The only language the two men had in common was that of the stage itself, and a brilliantly stageworthy dialogue, as well as some radical changes in the scenes, emerged from their mutual attempt to communicate with each other by miming and demonstration. They did not hesitate to manipulate historical fact to emphasize Galileo's social betrayal, and made class differences between characters more pointed. In 1947 this version was given twelve performances in the Coronet Theatre, Beverly Hills, Los Angeles and twelve in the Maxine Elliott Theatre, New York, with Joseph Losey directing and Hanns Eisler composing the music. But the style was unfamiliar, and the notices were bad. The shape of the play was considered to be 'rambling and episodic', and lacking in any emotional peaks. Even Laughton's performance, popular as he was as a screen actor, was found to be baffling. The apparatus of alienation remained a mystery, and its challenges dismissed. A third version of *Galileo*, which drew upon both of the others for a final text, was begun in 1953, and had a production in Cologne in 1955 and in East Berlin in 1956.

The object of Brecht's dramaturgy in this play, and the source of the spectator's unease, is a duality in the central character. The play was written against the growing terror of atomic warfare, and Brecht was anxious that Galileo should not be the idealized scholar and scientist of history, the 'stargazer' remote from reality, but an ordinary man with earth-bound responsibilities. Indeed, Brecht chose this subject because in spite of Galileo's scientific discoveries it was hard to ignore the fact of his apparently shameful recantation when he was threatened with torture and death by the Inquisition. While it remains ambiguous whether this recantation was an act of cowardice or one of cunning, since Galileo's survival enabled him to carry on his work and smuggle a copy of the *Discorsi* out of the country, Brecht was at pains to stress that to recant was to rob science of its social importance, and permit the Church to reassert its primitive power over the people of that age. This he emphasized in revision: in the first version Galileo was shown to be carrying on his work in secret, but in the two later revisions he was represented as more and more unscrupulous, anti-social and even criminal.

The scenes in *Galileo* are therefore planned to secure ambivalent, dialectical, responses from the audience. Galileo is at once the great scientist, and the thief who steals the concept of the telescope from Holland. He goes to Florence to make some money 'to fill his belly', and yet while he is there he courageously defies the plague in order to continue his studies. More than this, every detail of characterization is introduced to fill out the character of Galileo as a complete human being. He is the sensualist whom we first see stripped to the waist as he enjoys his wash in cool water; it gives him pleasure to have his back rubbed. He enjoys drinking his milk, as well as his wine. As an old man he is still the glutton who greedily consumes a goose, that greasiest of birds. He shows up badly as a teacher, and when his work is interruped by a student, he betrays his irritation. As a father, be behaves unfeelingly towards his daughter Virginia and prevents her marrying, so that we see her later as a bitter old maid, happy to spy on her father for the Inquisition. When he recants in scene 13, as Galileo Laughton showed his degradation by assuming an infantile grin which indicated, in Brecht's description of the performance, 'a self-release of the lowest order'. Just as the recantation itself is not allowed to be a simple matter for praise or blame, so in such ways Galileo's contradictory personality is managed in every detail to inhibit the audience's facile reaction to him. Yet, for all the vivid realism of the action, Brecht required that the scenes should also appear like historical paintings, an effect assisted by the use of titles suspended behind the stage to lend the play the appearance of being a history lesson.

*Mother Courage* also had an early production by the German actors in exile in Zürich in 1941, when Brecht was in Finland. This play was to be his first production in Berlin after the war in 1949, with Erich Engel co-directing at the Deutsches Theater. The *Courage-Modell, 1949* was published in Dresden in 1952. Not only are the changes between the Zürich and Berlin productions illuminating, but the details of the final production are richly documented. This play, therefore, offers a special insight into the nature of mature epic theatre.

The settings for both productions were based on Teo Otto's Zürich design. This consisted of a permanent set of canvas screens lashed to wooden posts, with simple suggestions of location, like a farmhouse or the Commander's tent, introduced as necessary. Behind it all was a large white cloth, something less than a skycloth and certainly no cyclorama. The stage was virtually bare, and lit by a cold white light, with no modifications for night or day. Placards dropped from the flies, each indicating the change of scene from country to country, and captions were projected on to the screens. Four musicians sat in a box beside the stage, and in the Berlin production Paul Dessau's songs were introduced by a painted musical symbol like a drum or a trumpet lowered from the flies to indicate to the audience that the songs did not spring from the action. Orchestral music of a threatening character was used to accompany a quiet scene as an ironic commentary on the action.

The play was to represent war, said Brecht, as a 'business idyll'. War was a matter of business not only for the leaders, but also for Mother Courage herself. She needs the hostilities to continue for her own survival, while at the same time she fears what the soldiery can do to her family. Brecht wrote,

> With her eldest son she is afraid of his bravery, but counts on his cleverness. With the second she is afraid of his stupidity, but counts on his honesty. With her daughter she is afraid of her pity, but counts on her dumbness. Only her fears prove to be justified (translated John Willett and Ralph Manheim).

Eilif, the eldest, robs peasants and achieves a short-lived fame with his Commander, while Courage sells a capon in time of famine and makes money. When it is necessary to change sides from Lutheran to Catholic, the honesty of Swiss Cheese makes a prisoner of him, and Courage's bargaining over his ransom costs him his life. As for daughter Kattrin, she dies because she takes pity on other people's children. At the end of the play, the old woman is still following the army for a living. As Brecht said, she has learned nothing.

The Zürich production, directed by Leopold Lindtberg, presented the play as a lesson in pacifism, with war simply a natural catastrophe and Courage (played by Therese Giehse) its innocent victim. It was a success for the wrong reason. The critics found it a 'Niobe tragedy', with Courage a tragic figure of a woman who loses her children one by one, and they failed to see

the play as an epic conflict designed to show Courage as both victim
and villain. Brecht therefore inserted a number of new details
chosen to alienate the character more obviously. In the revised version, she is distracted by the sale of a belt buckle at the same time
as Eilif is being recruited into the army (scene 1). When the Chaplain
wants the shirts she has for sale in order to make bandages for the
wounded, she fights to keep them (scene 5). As the war proceeds, she
is shown to be doing well, with rings on her fingers and a chain of
silver talers round her neck (scene 7). Courage is both mother and
businesswoman, but in situation after situation, the two roles prove
to be incompatible and survival comes first. To make the scenes true
to his idea of reality, Brecht created a split character, an anti-heroine,
an inhuman woman who wants the war to go on, but at the same time
a natural mother who tries to protect her young. The wagon from
which she conducts business throughout the play becomes a symbol
of the dichotomy. It is essential for trade, and it is seen, like her life,
always rolling on. And yet, like one of Piscator's treadmills, it cannot

38. Brecht, *Mother Courage*, 1949. Production by Brecht for the
Berliner Ensemble at the Theater am Schiffbauerdamm, Berlin.
Scene xi, with Angelica Hurwicz as Kattrin on the roof of the
farmhouse.

go anywhere when placed on the revolve of th
just as Courage cannot change her nature. It is
motives in the play that makes it an excell
theatre. In *The Impossible Theater*, the Ameri
Blau found that the genius of the play was that Courage had been
corrupted by the same social forces that produced the war in the
first place; she has capitulated, and 'the capitulation is the chief
source of the drama's alienating effect'.

Nevertheless, even the more explicit treatment in Berlin did
not solve the problem of controlling the audience's response. The
Marxist critic Max Schroeder counted it a success for exactly the same
reason as before in Zürich, believing Courage to be 'a humanist saint
from the tribe of Niobe and the *mater dolorosa*'. An audience perceives
what it chooses to perceive, and certainly in a case of total ambiguity.
So the audience chose to see *Mother Courage* as a story about themselves, the common victims of war, doubtlessly recognizing in the
dilemmas of the play its own recent condition in war-torn Berlin. At
the end, when Courage is finally reduced to pulling the wagon alone,
her tenacity cannot be judged simply as an act of a predator and a
villain. Ernest Bornemann, writing in *Encore* in July 1958, summed
up the issue of Brecht's success or failure generally:

> Every play that was successful with his audience succeeded
> for the wrong reasons: only those passages that did not
> conform to his theories, that were unextruded remnants of
> conventional theatre, really moved his audience, while those
> passages on which he had worked hardest and which most
> lucidly demonstrated his theories of the epic stage pleased
> no one except his fellow-artists.

However, Bornemann was not dismissing Brecht's achievement:
when he also found that 'Every device which he had contrived to
destroy the "magic" of theatre became magic in his hands', he
pointed to the ultimate paradox.

In Berlin, Helene Weigel played the title part in a colder manner than Giehse had in Zürich. According to Eric Bentley in his
record of a visit to the Berliner Ensemble, in *In Search of Theater*,
Weigel was 'cool, relaxed and ironical', standing outside the role and
acting with 'great precision of movement and intonation'. But she

ᵣ introduced a great deal of realistic detail into her performance, lthough this realism in effect served only to make her more pathetic. In scene 9, where she is forced to beg in the Fichtelgebirge mountains in bitter weather, her tones grew dull and lifeless, like those of the poor whom Weigel had seen on the streets of Berlin. In scene 12, she hesitated as she was paying the peasants for Kattrin's funeral, and took back one of the coins she had given, accentuating the

39. Brecht, *Mother Courage*, 1949. Production by Brecht with Weigel as Mother Courage.

gesture by the click of her bag. As she harnessed herself to the wagon and began to drag it for the last time round the stage, the song from scene 1 was heard again, and no amount of military music could undercut the pathos of the moment. This production, although directed by Brecht himself, taught no lesson about war that was not already known; if anything, it demonstrated that at bottom human nature was frighteningly contradictory and unpredictable, an awesome mystery.

Brecht wrote most of *The Good Woman of Setzuan* in Finland, and in 1943 this 'parable play' also received a first production in Zürich, with Leonard Steckell directing. After the war it was perfromed in Frankfurt and Rostock, but it was not taken up by the Berliner Ensemble until after Brecht had died. In Britain it was produced at the Royal Court Theatre in 1956, with Peggy Ashcroft in the title part. The play is given a brief mention here because it takes to an extreme the dialectical device of the split character, as seen in Galileo and Courage. In 1933 Brecht and Kurt Weill had written a ballet for Weill's wife Lotte Lenya, *Die Sieben Todsünden der Kleinburger (Anna Anna)*, known in English as both *The Seven Deadly Sins* and *Anna—Anna*. In this, two sisters are both named Anna, the emotional Anna expressing herself by dancing, and the rational Anna by singing. Reason and instinct are here two aspects of the same personality, but represented on the stage simultaneously. A related idea is present in *Herr Puntila und sein Knecht Matti* (Mr *Puntila and His Man Matti*), written in Finland at about the same time as *The Good Woman of Setzuan*: Puntila is generous when he is drunk, but mean when he is sober. These plays all extend the ambiguity of character by representing it visibly on the stage.

In *The Good Woman of Setzuan*, three gods descend from above looking for signs of goodness in human beings. They find them in a prostitute, Shen Te, when she shelters them, and they reward her with money to open a tobacco shop. With her new-found prosperity, she is immediately besieged by poor relations and every other beggar, so that in self-defence she has to assume the person of her ruthless male cousin Shui Ta, in order to drive the parasites away. That is the beginning of a series of *Doppelgänger*, 'doubles', situations. The message here is that it is impossible for a good person to survive in the world without being corrupted. Hence, the world should be changed. Conflicts in the human personality have been transformed into moral dilemmas in the last plays, and in *The Good Woman of Setzuan*, the representation of two contrasting attitudes to life in what appear to be two different persons when in fact they are one, made the dilemma transparent to audiences. At the same time, this device was adopted at the cost of a certain simplification of character, and only Azdak in *The Caucasian Chalk Circle* could match Galileo and Courage in depth and complexity.

*The Caucasian Chalk Circle* was written in America, the last play Brecht wrote in exile. It was given its first production in English at Carleton College, Minnesota in 1948, and had its first Berlin production in 1954. This play has proved to be Brecht's most popular since *The Threepenny Opera*, and it is easy to see why this is so. The play was another parable, and Brecht gave it a semi-political frame, in which two collectives in Soviet Georgia dispute the ownership of a piece of land. The purpose of this frame was to historicize the core of the tale and make it a play-within-a-play; it also provided a reason for retelling the ancient Chinese legend of the chalk circle. However, it is possible to ignore or forget this prologue entirely, so that the inner play seems to be presented as a romantic folk-story, complete with story-teller. Its subject, the contest between the common people and their rulers, is told in terms of the love shown towards a child, and it has exactly the attractions of a folk-tale or a simple melodrama. The central character, the peasant girl Grusha, has the immediate appeal of a pathetic victim of injustice, since her maternal instinct leads her into one difficulty after another. The more she does the right thing, the more she must make personal sacrifices — even to the point of taking a husband to give the child a father and losing her own fiancé in the process. Brecht could not have conceived a more moving story.

The Berlin production was loaded with all the epic elements. A ballad-singer, using Paul Dessau's simple score, not only provided the narrative link between the many scenes of the play, but also pleasantly distanced the action by singing of it in the past. Five musicians sat on the stage with the singer, but otherwise the stage was virtually bare in the usual way. The Governor, his Wife and the Prince, with the palace officials, wore grotesque masks, clearly isolating them as villains. Probably to reduce the pathos, Grusha was played by a plain actress with thick legs and seemed less glamorous. Azdak, the wise old rogue who becomes the judge after the revolution, was a Rabelaisian character who delighted the audience by choosing Grusha over the Governor's Wife as the one to keep the child. No one noticed that Brecht had ironically reversed the decision in the original, which was that the true mother should win. He made his point that ties of blood do not always count, and the audience had the total satisfaction of seeing poetic justice done. *The Caucasian Chalk Circle* is therefore hardly the best example of the effective workings of epic theatre practice, but it is a clear-cut comedy of ideas.

The production of Brecht's plays in Britain and America has been notably weak and insipid. The strong tradition of naturalistic playing doubtless contributed to the anaemic productions done in English since the war, since the acting, by epic standards, has generally lacked the sharp definition of continental performance. When Jerome Robbins chose to direct *Mother Courage* on Broadway in 1963, restraint characterized the production. He even dispensed with the obligatory revolve, so that Courage's endless and agonizing passage across the stage with her wagon was politely reduced by Anne Bancroft to an occasional push or pull that seemed of little account in her momentous journey across Europe. When the actor in a play by Brecht misses the point of his character, he falls back upon the sort of conventional type-playing that Brecht spent his life trying to eliminate. The result might be called 'debilitated epic'.

Is it yet possible to judge what Brecht's theatrical reforms may have achieved? Prolific and dedicated as a playwright, a director and a philosopher of theatre, he is the outstanding example in modern times of a theatre artist who believed it necessary for every area of stagecraft to undergo a regular radical rethinking. At all times restlessly creative himself, but often working under the most difficult circumstances, he insisted that the vitality of drama depended upon constant testing, discussion and revision, a never-ending process. He was the complete man of the theatre, and he has attracted by his vision every director who ever found the business of mounting a play a truly imaginative challenge in dramatic communication. His theories of a logical theatre, and his pursuit of multifarious devices for distancing the stage and manipulating his audience, have moved modern drama towards a new kind of comedy, dry and intelligent, but not necessarily without compassion, and often powerful as theatre. )

---

# 16 *Epic theatre in Germany after Brecht*

---

*The Visit* (1956), *Kaspar* (1968)

In 1949, the theatre historian Allardyce Nicoll could write about Brecht in *World Drama* that it was 'doubtful whether either his works or the style he cultivates are likely to cause more than a ripple on the surface of the dramatic current'. Nicoll devoted only one paragraph to the playwright and director who had the single most profound impact on all branches of theatre since the Second World War. Following the establishment of the Berliner Ensemble, and its visits outside Berlin, Brecht's plays were revived everywhere in the rest of Europe, and, after a boycott following the erection of the Berlin Wall, also in West Germany. During the 1960s, even Russia overcame her mistrust of Brecht's 'formalism' and took him up. The publication of some forty volumes of his works in German began. Theatre artists responded to his new standards of dramatic economy, and started to rethink their purposes in stage design, in the structuring of a play, in its kind of language, and in the actor's relationship with his audience. Leading directors like Giorgio Strehler (1921–   ), founder of the Piccolo Teatro in Milan, Peter Brook (1925–   ), Britain's most visionary director, Jean Vilar (1912–71), director of the Théâtre National Populaire at Avignon and the Palais de Chaillot, and Roger Planchon (1931–   ), director of what is now the Théâtre National Populaire at Villeurbanne near Lyons could not resist exploring his new territory in their own ways. But nowhere has Brecht's influence been felt more strongly than in the German-speaking countries.

The rejuvenation of a writer's theatre in Germany after the hiatus of the Hitler years owes everything to Brecht. Dialectical drama in one form or another proved to be inherently theatrical, and Brecht taught the German playwright to turn the mirror away from his subjective self and transmute his expressionistic fervour to a calculated social criticism. He produced a generation of political playwrights. Theatre of the absurd was a French and not a German genre, and German writers turned to Brecht and not to Beckett and Ionesco for a lead. Zürich had been the centre of Brecht production during the war, and not unexpectedly Switzerland early found two major Brechtian enthusiasts in Frisch and Dürrenmatt, both German language dramatists working out of Zürich.

Max Frisch (1911– ) knew Brecht's work well, and had met him in 1948; he was also attracted to the expressionism of Thornton Wilder, and yoked Brecht's alienation effects with Wilder's imaginative leaps in time and place. In an epic twenty-four scenes, Frisch's *Die chinesische Mauer* (*The Chinese Wall*, 1946) represents on stage the building of the Great Wall of China, and simultaneously the atomic warfare of the twentieth century. The one makes the other seem silly. Masked figures from literature and history from Romeo and Juliet to Napoleon move through the play as in a cabaret, and lend yet another level of timelessness to the stage. Granted these vast perspectives, contemporary man is intended to learn his lesson.

The play which made Frisch's reputation, however, was the apparently absurdist *Biedermann und die Brandstifter*, produced in Zürich in 1958, and known in Britain as *The Fire Raisers* and in America as *The Firebugs*. It was a dramatic parable that was simpler and more forceful than anything in the absurdist theatre. In Brechtian fashion, the play is subtitled *'Ein Lehrstück ohne Lehre'* ('A morality without a moral'), and it offers a sinister little comedy which tells the improbable tale of Biedermann – a respectable 'Everyman' – who welcomes arsonists into his house in the vain belief that he can stop them setting it on fire. The play is distinguished by a chorus of comic firemen, a grotesque parody of the chorus in a Greek tragedy, which is there to undercut any moralistic pomposity. It also uses a clever simultaneous setting, so that we see on the stage at the same time both the living room where Biedermann is feasting his guests and the attic where, with outrageous irony, cans of petrol are being stored and the fire is being set. Frisch contrived to have his Biedermann actually give the intruders a box of matches with which to start the conflagration. The political allusion to the businessmen who gave their support to Nazi Germany did not lie too deep.

More frightening, however, was *Andorra* (1961). This play tells the story of Andri, who has been brought up to believe he is a Jew. When it is disclosed that he is not really Jewish after all, he nevertheless accepts the role that society has imposed upon him. He willingly accepts persecution, torture and execution when the country is overrun by the neighbouring anti-Semites from whom he came in the first place. Max Frisch had been explicitly interested in the political and moral role of Switzerland in the face of the Nazi aggression all around it, and *Andorra* makes a sly comment on the problems of neutrality.

Equally pessimistic, if more caustically comic, are the satirical plays of Friedrich Dürrenmatt (1921– ). Like Frisch, he was attracted both to Brecht and to Wilder as epic playwrights. In his Zürich lecture of 1954, *'Theaterprobleme'*, 'Problems of the Theatre', Dürrenmatt argued that tragedy was now impossible, since a tragic hero presupposes a quality of individual vision and a sense of personal responsibility, whereas today we are collectively guilty. Comedy, on the other hand, presupposes 'a world in the making, being turned upside down', and all we can hope to achieve is 'the tragic out of comedy', the 'abyss which opens suddenly' (translated Gerhard Nellhaus). Dürrenmatt's occasional papers give a good idea of his disposition of mind as a playwright: he admires Aristophanes for the surprises in his ideas, Christopher Fry of *A Phoenix Too Frequent* and *The Lady's Not for Burning* as 'a new Attic comedian' prepared to change the world into a comedy, and the caricaturist Ronald Searle whose schoolgirls display his grotesque wit. A genuine comedian, says Dürrenmatt, is never cosy – he bites, and in such comments Dürrenmatt is finally describing the characteristically bitter 'black comedy' of the post-war years.

Some years before Beckett and Ionesco had attracted attention, Dürrenmatt had chosen the word *'grotesk'*, 'grotesque', to explain his stylistic manner, one which deliberately set provocatively extreme images on the stage. He also chose not to change this word to 'absurd'. Absurdism implies an absence of purpose in life, where the grotesque, closer to expressionism, assumes a level of normal reality from which the writer has departed. Dürrenmatt's celebrated example is of Scott of the Antarctic: it would be absurd if he were a block of ice talking to other blocks of ice, but grotesque if he were trapped in a refrigerator near a busy street. His first play of importance, *Romulus der Grosse* (*Romulus the Great*, 1948), portrays the last Roman emperor as a total failure as a soldier and a ruler. In the face of the enemy, he devoted himself to raising chickens. But the play emphasizes Romulus's calm logic when all about him flee in panic, and his reasonableness and objectivity in an inchoate universe produce a special brand of exquisite tragi-comedy.

Dürrenmatt continued to explore the mixture of tragic and comic elements as a way of controlling stage and audience. He skirted surrealism in *Die Ehe des Herrn Mississippi* (*The Marriage of Mr Mississippi*), which was directed by Hans Schweikart at the

40. Dürrenmatt, *The Marriage of Mr Mississippi*, 1952. Production by Hans Schweikart at the Kammerspiel, Munich.

Munich Kammerspiele in 1952. The set was Ubuesque in its wild contradictions:

> A room whose late-bourgeois magnificence and splendour will not be altogether easy to describe. Yet since the action takes place in this room and in this room alone, since in fact we may say that the events which follow represent the story of this room, an attempt must be made to describe it. The room stinks to high heaven. In the background are two windows. The view from them is bewildering. To the right the branches of an apple tree, and behind it some northern city with a Gothic cathedral; to the left a cypress, the remains of a classical temple, a bay, a harbour. So much for what lies outside . . . (translated Michael Bullock).

For all this, the author asks that the setting be done realistically – 'Only so will it be able to disintegrate. The unreal and fantastic may safely be left to the text, to the author.' In *The Marriage of Mr Mississippi* we meet the fascinating Anastasia, who 'consumes an immoderate quantity of men'. One of them is Florestan Mississippi, the public prosecutor who has sent so many to their deaths, and at the end of the play these two poison each other. However, such a surrealistic presentation and so bizarre a plot hint at more a lack of authorial control than its presence, and the result is somewhat shrill.

Dürrenmatt wrote prolifically and had an international success with *Der Besuch der alten Dame* (*The Visit of the Old Lady*, 1956, known in English as *The Visit*). It was this play which was adopted to its author's great advantage by the Anglo-American team of Lynn Fontanne and Alfred Lunt, although with some damaging changes in the translation by Maurice Valency. It is the tragicomedy of Claire, a girl who was seduced and driven into prostitution, but who returns an elderly woman of immense wealth. With artificial limbs and a crowd of grotesque servants about her, she presents a truly nightmare figure. Determined to take a savage revenge on her seducer Alfred Ill, as well as on those who treated her badly when she was helpless, she coldly bribes the townspeople to have him killed and deliver his body to her. This they do. But it is still Claire's tragedy. When she promises Ill a mausoleum on Capri where he will enjoy 'a beautiful view', her love and her hate for him have become one. This was a probing and technically original masterpiece which has proved its imaginative quality by the variety of interpretations that have since been urged upon it, from the psychological and socio-economic to the Christian and metaphysical.

Dürrenmatt's experiments doubtless arise from the freedom he feels as a Swiss neutral in a world of polarized ideologies. He feels no obligation to pursue a particular theory or practice, but believes instead in the plurality of dramatic modes. His success has come from his unrestricted experiments with audience response, and, more recently, from testing theatre games after the manner of Wedekind, Pirandello and Wilder – he admires Wilder's 'dematerialization' of place in *Our Town* and *The Skin of Our Teeth*. Dürrenmatt was also attracted to the wit and social criticism of the nineteenth-century Austrian actor and playwright Johann Nestroy, whose *Einen Jux will er sich machen* (*He Wants to Have a Fling*, 1842) was the source play for Wilder's *The Matchmaker*. Dürrenmatt's more recent theoretical statements say frankly than he no longer considers drama to be a literary form, and in his introduction to *Porträt eines Planeten* (*Portrait of a Planet*, 1970) he wrote,

> For me, the stage has become a theatrical medium and not a literary platform. To put it more bluntly, I no longer write my plays for actors, I compose them with actors. I have abandoned literature for theatre.

The later plays increasingly suggest that this is so. The popular *Die Physiker* (*The Physicists*, 1962) teases its audience and dips into the absurd with its madhouse of scientists believing themselves, or pretending to be, Einstein, Newton and Möbius. The scurrilous *Der Meteor* (*The Meteor*, 1966), a light comedy of the macabre in which a Nobel Prizewinner is unable to die when all about him manage it so easily, was greeted in Zürich with a predictable mixture of cheers and boos. In *Die Wiedertäufer* (*The Anabaptist*, 1967), the evangelist is also an actor and director, so that the play is presented as an ironic play-within-the-play. *Play Strindberg* (1968) is a clever reworking of Strindberg's *The Dance of Death*, and Dürrenmatt explained, 'Out of a bourgeois marriage tragedy developed a comedy about bourgois marriage tragedies' (translated James Kirkup). He transformed Strindberg's lengthy and literary dialogue into a crisp series of ritualistic bouts as in a boxing match, and the married protagonists Alice and Edgar have delighted audiences by stinging each other with clipped verbal repetitions instead of consuming each other with Strindberg's slow mutual torture.

A little senior to Dürrenmatt is the Marxist playwright, living in Sweden since 1939 and now a Swedish citizen, Peter Weiss (1916–82). The play which brought him fame after its production at the Schiller Theater, Berlin in 1964, with requests for production from Brook, Planchon and Ingmar Bergman, was the *Marat/Sade*, and this was partly discussed in considering the impact of Artaud in the previous volume. Weiss had been a heavily Strindbergian symbolist before he discovered the clarity and force of Brecht, and the *Marat/Sade* showed the change by its use of a narrator, its songs, and its running debate between de Sade and Marat. Brook's production at the Aldwych in 1965 extended its possibilities as a stage vehicle, since the mixture of widely different idioms, those of epic theatre and theatre of cruelty, far from invalidated one another. Gertrude Mander believes that, instead of leading the theatre one more step from illusion, 'no amount of clever pastiche writing, or naturalistic or pantomimic shock effects' could disguise the fact that the Brook *Marat/Sade* was theatre 'at its most illusionist' (*Drama*, summer 1971). Michael Patterson thinks the play 'a juxtaposition rather than a synthesis of the two styles' of Brecht and Artaud (*German Theatre Today*, 1976), and argues that while Konrad Swinarski's Berlin production stylized the play and weakened the sense of a play-within-a-play for the sake of Brecht, Brook's realistic madmen were born of Artaudian emotion and obscured the central debate. The play has since proved to be even more malleable, for when it was played in East Germany, Marat, who speaks for society in the play, was presented as an orthodox Marxist, while de Sade the individualist came a bad second, leaving the debate no longer open-ended. What was remarkable about the Brook production was how far mind and senses were in fact reconciled, as only in the theatre they could be. The lunatic idiom can lend a special licence to a director, as it had to the author:

In such an environment you can say virtually anything. Amongst lunatics you've got complete freedom. You can say very dangerous and crazy things, anything at all, and at the same time introduce the political agitation for which you're trying to get a hearing (translated Michael Patterson).

Nevertheless, events have directed Weiss's talents elsewhere, as will be seen in the next chapter.

The East German Peter Hacks (1928– ) sought out and worked with Brecht in the Berliner Ensemble from 1955, and there he learned that the theatre could play a political role in society. Hacks's plays are like Brechtian parables with a stronger political message. His work was at first held as an example, and he was awarded the Lessing Prize in 1957. Then he made the mistake of writing a satirical play which hit a sensitive target. This was *Briketts* (*Briquettes*), finally produced in Berlin in 1961 as *Die Sorgen und die Macht* (*Problems and Power*). The play was based on an actual incident in which miners complained about the quality of the coal briquettes they were producing. Hacks considered it to be an outstanding historical event when workers no longer fought capital by producing shoddy goods, but demonstrated a new communal responsibility in wanting to produce the best goods possible. The authorities, however, did not read Hacks's paradoxes and antitheses as he intended them, and the play had to be rewritten. When Walter Langhoff finally put it on the stage, it was received with indignation as negative criticism of the régime, and it was withdrawn.

The need to fill a gap at the Deutsches Theater Festival of 1965 gave Hacks a second chance, and he seized it boldly with *Moritz Tassow* (1964). This was a clever political parable in verse, which managed to disguise its attack on the government rather better. The play was also set in the near past, in 1945, so that the action might be judged at a distance. Even then, the play was considered 'obscene', and Hacks's career in the east was again in jeopardy. The style of *Moritz Tassow* is that of a pastoral folk-tale, and the plot is simplicity itself. Moritz is a Marxist peasant who tends the pigs, and, to hide his hatred of the Nazis, pretends to be deaf and dumb. When he does speak, he attempts a single-handed revolution and calls for a communist collective which he describes as a possible paradise on earth. Unhappily, the other peasants of this paradise are greedy, and the Utopia collapses after a few months. Mattukat, a government official, thereupon divides up the land and settles the matter. Belatedly, Hacks claimed that Mattukat was the real hero of the play, with Moritz, like Mother Courage, an example of how not to be a Communist. Hacks has not regained esteem in the eyes of the authorities, but his parables, and his comic peasants, like Moritz and Ulrich Braeker, the conscripted Swiss soldier fighting the Seven Years' War in *Die Schlacht bei Lobositz* (*The Battle of Lobositz*, 1954), moulded in the tradition of Woyzeck and Schweik, will survive.

To name these few senior German playwrights cannot convey the unusual vitality of contemporary German theatre, even if the critical issue of what makes good politics and what makes good drama remains uncertain. The plays of Jochem Ziem (1932–   ) lean towards ironic documentary, as in *Nachrichten aus der Provinz* (*News from the Provinces*, 1967), which works from newspaper clippings. Wickedly anti-Stalinist satire and grotesque symbolism characterize the plays of Hartmut Lange (1937–   ), like the verse drama *Der Hundsprozess* (*The Dog's Trial*, 1968), in which in a religious ritual before 'St Stalin', an Inquisitor, has the people decapitated and their heads replaced with those of dogs. The Bavarian Martin Sperr (1944–   ) leans towards a disconcerting realism, with a minutely observed character and dialogue, and the political parable behind his first play, *Jagdszenen aus Niederbayern* (*Hunting Scenes from Lower Bavaria*, 1962, produced in Bremen in 1966), the story of a village fool who tries to show he is like other men by raping and murdering a local girl, reverberates frighteningly in the mind.

In the 1960s, another issue clouded the scene, especially in the east. If your work did not conform to the socialist–realist idea, you ran the risk of being accused of 'formalism', that is, more concerned with form than with content. Yet paradoxically, those German playwrights who came after Brecht but who had no wish to tread in his footsteps, needed to write a formalistic drama to avoid the other charge of being an old-fashioned naturalist and an effete romantic. If they were to write critically and satirically at all, they felt obliged to construct a drama of individualistic ambiguities and alienation devices. In the bleak view of a leading article in the

*Times Literary Supplement* for 3 April 1969, 'Anything that smacks of formal stability — of order, structural balance and tradition — is distrusted as a symbol of the establishment.' So the bright young writers of the new German theatre, treading the razor's edge between the traditional and the modern, resorted to older tricks of symbolism and surrealism. A playwright's playwright (a phrase which embodies yet another definition of formalism) like the Austrian Peter Handke (1942–   ) is more acceptable to the critics than to the audience.

Nevertheless, Handke has brought yet more new life to the German theatre. If he has borrowed something from Brecht and something from the absurdists, it has been said that in his plays the nature of theatre itself is put on trial. Like Ionesco, Handke is not interested in plot and character, the conventional elements of drama, but he makes good theatrical use of apparently random words to inhibit the rational thinking of the audience, and to show the ways by which language shapes our minds and determines our lives. And like Brecht, he tries to make the commonplace seem strange and the cliché outrageous, keeping his audience constantly aware of the theatricality of the proceedings.

Handke's renewed attack on the theatre of psychological realism began with *Die Publikumsbeschimpfung* (*Offending the Audience*), first produced in Frankfurt in 1966. The audience is at first made to regard the theatre as of great importance, ushered in solemnly turned back if improperly dressed. Four speakers then schematically address the house, and inform the audience that there is to be no play and no action on the stage. Instead, the audience is congratulated upon having performed so well as an audience, before it is increasingly subjected to a crescendo of insults and verbal abuse. Unfortunately, when the play was first played in London by the Almost Free Theatre in 1972, the British audience annoyingly refused to be offended, but took the insults in good part. The truth may be that since Pirandello the modern spectator is all too familiar with theatre games, and Brecht may have reminded us how artificial the theatre experience is once too often.

Handke named this kind of play a '*Sprechstück*', a 'play for speaking', that is, a play which offers no picture of the world other than that which lies in the words themselves, a stylized linguistic exercise. *Kaspar* was produced in 1968 simultaneously in the Theater am Turm, Frankfurt, with Claus Peymann directing and Wolf R. Redl as Kaspar, and in the Städtische Bühnen, Oberhausen, with Günther Büch directing and Ulrich Wildgruber as Kaspar. It depicts man as a product of language, as if Handke were dramatizing a theory of structural linguistics. Like the real Kaspar Hauser of Nuremberg who was kept prisoner in a chicken coop for sixteen years, emerging fully grown in 1828 as if he had never met another human being, the Kaspar of the play is an autistic boy who is taught to speak. In his introduction Handke wrote,

> The play *Kaspar* does not show how things REALLY ARE or REALLY WERE with Kaspar Hauser. It shows what is POSSIBLE with someone. It shows how someone can be brought to speech by speech. The play could also be called *Speech-Torture* (translated Nicholas Hern).

The interest in him is not historical or scientific, but lies in his almost Beckettian metaphysical implications.

Three impersonal voices-off, transmitted by loudspeaker, teach Kaspar to speak, and these voices embody another concept, that of *Einsager*, a word suggesting interior persuaders, 'in-sayers'. They first eliminate the one sentence Kaspar knows, 'Ich möcht ein solcher werden wie einmal ein andrer gewesen ist', 'I want to be a person like somebody else was once' (translated Michael Roloff), and then indoctrination may begin. As he learns to speak, so Kaspar begins to embody all the illogic and prejudice of the words themselves, but at one point reaching a climactic and triumphant 'I am who I am.' However, the words begin to lose their meaning in this process towards consciousness when four other Kaspars, like clones all wearing identical costumes and masks, ironically also exhibit the skills the original Kaspar has learned — their proliferation mocks the very individuality he seeks, as if he were one of the masses. They accompany his verbal efforts with a cacophonous speech, and when five identical Kaspars sink on the sofa, their original masks of astonishment have changed to ones of contentment. Finally Kaspar lapses into nonsense, and his last words are, 'I am I only by chance'. When the curtain closes, it knocks over all the Kaspars like wooden skittles.

The German word *Kasper* means 'clown', and Kaspar wears a white face and baggy trousers. But Nicholas Hern in his book on Handke has pointed out that Kaspar is not a clown, but an everyman. Instead of reducing all performances to duplicates of each other, the mask and the dialogue free every new actor to play the part differently. The Beckettian stage directions suggest that Kaspar

41. Handke, *Kaspar*, 1968. Production by Carl Weber at the Chelsea Theatre Centre, 1973.

is like a Beckettian puppet figure — he gropes his way through a gap in the curtain and bumps into the furniture like a comedian on the music-hall stage. Yet it is as if he is placed in the critical framework of a play by Brecht. Handke asks that the stage not represent a room, but only a stage, so that the audience is not to watch a story unfold, but experience a theatrical event. And, indeed, Handke has the gift of granting his audience insights into human behaviour that it can never have anticipated. It is hard not to be impressed by his technical resources of verbal and visual wit, and his power to call up the astonishing symbolic and parabolic forces of the stage.

42. Handke, *Kaspar*, 1968. Production at the Theater am Turm, Frankfurt-am-Main, with Wolf Red as Kaspar.

# 17 *Documentary theatre after Piscator*

*War and Peace* (1955), *The Representative* (1963)

Piscator's reputation was not widely known in Britain or America until his adaptation of Tolstoy's *War and Peace* was produced by the Bristol Old Vic in 1962 in Bristol and London, and by the Association of Producing Artists (the 'APA') off-Broadway in New York in 1965. By then the Berlin production was ten years old, the adaptation was almost thirty years old, and what was once conceived as a warning against the re-arming of Germany had broadened to become a generally anti-militarist document. Piscator's dramatic practice had largely been perfected in the adaptation of novels (*The Good Soldier Schweik, All the King's Men, Requiem for a Nun, An American Tragedy*), which he believed to be as natural a process as the dramatization of the classical epic poems by the Greeks, or of the Bible in the mystery plays through much of Europe in the middle ages. However, any criticism of the adaptation of the modern novel for the stage turned on the inevitable cutting down of its content and the exteriorization of its inner experience — in other words, of the expressionistic treatment needed to present it in the theatre. We may judge whether such criticism was not finally misplaced. Piscator himself dismissed it. He aimed at another ideal — a form of theatre narrative not unlike the Chinese 'spoken book'.

Piscator discovered that the kind of material suitable for his political theatre was not to be found in the usual plays written for the stage, either in their form or their content. Nor were a rigid proscenium staging and the typical box set sufficiently flexible to contain his broader content. He quoted Paul Klee: 'The purpose of art is not to portray the visible, but to make visible.' Commentary, placards, selective spot-lighting, film — any device should be at the disposal of the stage when it was to be used to exhibit a social document. *War and Peace* was a case in point. The novel was not to be reduced to the tragic but necessarily oversimplified love story of André and Natasha, nor to the humanitarianism and personal insights of Pierre. Instead, theatrical means had to be found to relate the great exterior subject of the war with Napoleon to the intimate human problems it created in its path. This objective was paramount, and was separate from the difficulties associated with the breadth and scope of the novel, the complexity of its plot and the abundance of its characters. All this provided an ideal preparation for the next step in the creation of documentary drama, the adaptation for the stage of broad themes from life itself, done without losing the warmth and intimacy of the human element and identifiable characters.

It was also clear that epic, documentary theatre (the so-called 'docudrama'), which at its best is factual and thought-provoking, must be at odds with the Wagnerian idea of a synaesthesia of the arts, intended to make a primary appeal to the emotions of the audience. For a play to be didactic, other sacrifices might also have to be made. Character might be impersonal, representative and even stereotyped at the expense of the individuality of realism. A more purposeful and directed dialogue might be simplified, less colloquial and more abstract. Humour, if any, was likely to be broad, and comic business could lean towards slapstick. Where agitprop was limited by the narrow purposes of its propaganda, documentary drama also inhibited the subtlety and imagination of the stage by its need to deal in facts. In particular, the vivid mechanical devices developed by Piscator over the years — newsreels, photographs, slogans, and so on — were essentially visual rather than verbal, and the drama could suffer from being less precise and fine. In any case, Piscator had little respect for the text of a play he directed, and was always ready to alter a script to accommodate his machinery.

Noise and movement were characteristic of Piscator's documentary stage, so that the actors had frequently to shout above the sound of the moving parts. He therefore developed a style of depersonalized performance, calling it 'objective' acting. It reflected his experience of seeing the Japanese *Kabuki* theatre in Berlin in 1930, and at bottom objective acting meant that the actors should address the audience rather than each other.

Piscator's years in America first touched the work of the Group

Theatre in New York. In 1936, Lee Strasberg produced as epic theatre Piscator's play *The Case of Clyde Griffiths*, the title given to his adaptation of Dreiser's *An American Tragedy*. The evidence advanced by the counsel for the defence was presented in flashback scenes on different stage levels, and the audience was addressed as if it was the jury. In *The Fervent Years*, however, Harold Clurman said he found this treatment too cold for American audiences. Paul Green's *Johnny Johnson*, also directed by Strasberg in 1936, was an anti-war satire which echoed *The Good Soldier Schweik*. The good soldier Johnny spreads laughing-gas everywhere in order to undermine the will to fight, and as a result he is examined by a psychiatrist who inevitably seems more insane than his patient.

Piscator's methods of epic theatre also effectively served the development of the 'Living Newspaper', which emerged in both Russia and America. The American Federal Theatre Project under Hallie Flanagan Davis (1890–1969) was established in 1935 to ease unemployment in the acting profession after the Depression, and the Living Newspaper was part of its work. The film director Joseph Losey thinks it to have been his own concept, with Arthur Arent as its chief writer and a newspaper man, Morris Watson, as its administrator. The object was to make drama out of journalism, and a living newspaper production was advertised as a 'publication' or an 'edition'. In *Theatre Survey* for 1962, John Gassner described the form as 'an amalgam of motion-picture, epic theatre, *commedia dell'arte* and American minstrel show techniques'. It also used elements of the circus, the music hall and the ballet. A character representing the man-in-the-street would ask a question, and 'a series of presentational devices consisting of scenes, demonstrations, slides, lectures and arguments' provided the answer. Thus, *Triple-A Plowed Under* (1936) exposed the problems of the farmers. *One-Third of a Nation* (1938) treated the issue of slum housing conditions, mixing facts with dramatized incidents against a tenement background designed by Howard Bay.

The Federal subsidy ended in 1939, when Congress felt uneasy about the radical emphasis in so many of the plays it had sponsored, so temporarily ending the rapid development of what many thought of as a new dramatic form. Nevertheless, documentary drama experienced an extraordinary revival in the 1960s. In England, it

sprang up again in Stratford, East London with the Brechtian Joan
Littlewood's *Oh, What a Lovely War!* (1963), in Stoke-on-Trent with
Peter Cheeseman's work at the Victoria Theatre, beginning with
*The Jolly Potters* in 1964, and at the Aldwych Theatre, London with
Peter Brook's production of *US* (1966). But the most vigorous de-
velopment has been in the German theatre.

When back in Germany, Piscator directed three documentaries
of importance for western theatre. *Der Stellvertreter* (in Britain *The
Representative*, in America *The Deputy*) by Rolf Hochhuth (1931– )
was first played in the Freie Volksbühne in West Berlin in 1963.
Its political subject made it natural that Hochhuth should ask
Piscator to stage it: it dealt with the failure of Pope Pius XII to inter-
cede for the Jews in Nazi Germany. It was a laboured piece, and the
addition of 25,000 words of the author's provoked an outcry against
untrustworthy documentaries. But it was effective and sensational,
and did much to stimulate the documentary revival.

*In der Sache J. Robert Oppenheimer (In the Matter of J. Robert*

43. The Living Newspaper, *One-Third of a Nation*, 1938, at the Federal
Theatre, New York. Stage set by Howard Bay.

*Oppenheimer)* by Heinar Kipphardt (1922– ) was directed by Piscator in 1964. This play was more soberly based on the hearings of a Personnel Security Board set up by the Atomic Energy Commission in America in 1954, and its text was sifted from 3,000 pages of typescript. Kipphardt confessed to being uneasy about using the stage in this way, even for a theme like that of the scientist's responsibility for the manufacture of weapons of destruction. He went so far as to add a postscript to the published work, saying that it was intended to be only a shortened version of the investigation, and that it would not damage the truth. Less sensational than *The Representative, Oppenheimer* nevertheless enjoyed a success because of its court-room form.

The third production was *Die Ermittlung (The Investigation)*, for which Peter Weiss drew on reports in the *Frankfurter Allgemeine Zeitung* of the 1962–4 War Crimes trial concerned with the atrocities at Auschwitz. The play was produced by Piscator in 1965 at the Freie Volksbühne, and simultaneously in seventeen other German theatres; it also received a reading in London, directed by Brook at the Aldwych. This play was criticized as merely exploiting the horror of the event, although Piscator defended it as a work of art on the grounds that the records had to be selected and arranged for effect. Written in a colourless free verse, it does not lend itself well to reading, but in the Berlin production the speakers were strikingly lit, and delivered their lines impressively in a ritualistic manner.

Following this broadside, documentary drama has been widely attempted in many countries by both professional and amateur companies. Not only current events local and national, but also people still living, have been depicted on the stage, and this unusual development may yet prove to be Piscator's greatest contribution to the modern theatre. Weiss has turned to the documentary form with enthusiasm, composing plays or political revues in quick succession on the Angolan rebellion of 1961 (1967), Vietnam (1968), the life of Trotsky *(Trotski im Exil,* 1970) and of the poet Hölderlin (1971). These last two plays were less documentary than historical collages and flashbacks, as if seen through the eyes of the principal figure. However, in stylizing his material, Weiss has tended to flatten his historical people to creatures of two dimensions.

In 'The Material and the Models: Notes towards a Definition

of Documentary Theatre', a lecture delivered in East Berlin in 1968 at a 'Brecht-Dialogue', Weiss made it clear that he had chosen his new path deliberately. The documentary play, he said, was first concerned with documenting an event from authentic, factual material — letters and statistics, speeches and news reports in print or on film. However, although facts were the proper basis of a documentary play, such a play was likely to be written as a form of protest, so that the imaginative contribution of the individual artist lay in the choice and arrangement of the play's ideas. The documentary writer retains the content, but reworks the form. He wants what is universally valid, yet not as if the play were a spontaneous event, but as an image of a piece of reality:

> It is far easier [for street theatre] to enact the birth in the stable at Bethlehem in the middle of Trafalgar Square than a demonstration that has passed across the Square an hour ago (translated A. V. Subiotto).

It was for this sort of reason that Brecht chose to present his political plays in locations like Chicago, eighteenth-century London and Kipling's India. Characters like de Sade and Marat can be used as the impersonal mouthpieces of history, and it would be for the actors playing such characters to contribute their appropriate attitudes. The play would take the form of enacted scenes, demonstrations and illustrative flashbacks. The audience might find itself in the role of the accused, the accuser, the judge or the jury.

Nevertheless, the selectivity involved in this version of agit-prop drama is far more likely to be subjective than objective, and with each new documentary Weiss has lost something of his former reputation. His most severe critics find his theatrical effects 'dead at the centre', lacking humour and humanity, and his polemics too much of the tub-thumping variety. Other writers continued the policy of choosing sensitive subjects. Kipphardt gloried in *Joel Brand, Die Geschichte eines Geschäfts* (*Joel Brand, the History of a Business Deal,* 1965), on the subject of the Eichmann proposal to exchange a million Jews for 10,000 vehicles. The novelist Günter Grass (1927–   ), who had previously attempted a German absurdist drama, made his own contribution to the new vogue with *Die Plebejer proben den Aufstand* (*The Plebeians Rehearse the Uprising,* 1965), on the subject of the 1953 rebellion in East Berlin, done as a clever parody of Brecht and his Ensemble as if they were rehearsing Brecht's own version of *Coriolanus* – a Pirandellian convolution that would have appealed to Brecht himself. Peter Hacks wrote on Columbus, Frederick the Great, the officers' revolt against Hitler, and the assassination of President Kennedy. Hochhuth continued to write lengthy documentaries in verse, or rather a rhythmic prose which tended to reduce documentary authenticity by its decorative, even expressionistic, style. *Soldaten: Nekrolog auf Genf* (*Soldiers: An Obituary for Geneva*, or simply *Soldiers*, 1967) was dedicated to Piscator, and had as its target Winston Churchill's involvement with the death of General Sikorski and the bombing of Dresden. *Guerillas* (1970) went so far as to invent the story of a United States senator killed by the CIA for his revolutionary ideals, and *Lysistrata and NATO* (1974) mixed Aristophanes with the military acquisition of a Greek island for strategic purposes. The length of these plays raises questions about their stageworthiness, but their flat dialogue also made their history seem more dead than alive.

To summarize. No one would claim that any of these plays was a great dramatic achievement, but they have raised the issues for the documentary genre, and solved some of its problems. The inherent contradiction is that, although the content of documentary may be real, it can never be presented realistically – Weiss's rule was to secure the substance but change the form. Yet documentary can never be fully authentic, since to meet the limits of the stage, the material must be pruned, an inevitably subjective process. The words of an official transcript rarely help the creation of individualized characters, yet these are necessary if an audience is to follow the play (although Weiss had sixty-two witnesses for his Trotsky). Sometimes it is essential to invent a representative or a spokesman for a group where history has not supplied one (in *The Representative*, Hochhuth found it necessary to invent Father Riccardo, a Jesuit priest, to speak for the Jews). Above all, 'Documentary theatre takes sides', Weiss concluded: the playwright chooses his subject for this kind of treatment because he wants to invite a partisan judgment. It is a matter of keeping an artistic balance between fact and fiction, truth and imagination, as Shakespeare discovered long ago in writing his chronicle plays.

# 18 *Epic theatre in Britain*

*Serjeant Musgrave's Dance* (1959), *The Woman* (1978)

In Britain, Brecht's influence has been more apparent on directors and designers than on playwrights. The Berliner Ensemble paid two outstanding visits to London in 1956 and 1965, and where an ignorance of the German language left audiences in some confusion about Brecht's intentions, what the eye could see was less mistakable. Therefore, although interest in Brecht coincided with the advent of John Osborne's *Look Back in Anger* in 1956, the new 'kitchen sink' drama was generally unaffected by epic theatre.

As we saw, the director Peter Brook was early attracted to Brecht's methods, and in his preface to the *Marat/Sade* text placed on record that he considered alienation to be an effect of 'quite incredible power'. He found an opportunity to test this judgment in his production of *King Lear* for the Royal Shakespeare Company in 1962. This so-called absurdist production in fact owed rather more to Brecht than to Beckett. Not only was the set stark and severe, with rusted metallic sheets flanking a bare stage, but it was uniformly lit with a harsh white light in the characteristic style. Costumes were of heavy, worn leather, in imitation of Brecht's production of *Coriolanus*, and the props were few and simple. One great stone throne for Lear supplied the opening scene, and Paul Scofield played the King with cold detachment, all colour drained from his lines.

Even when Brook was taken with Artaud and the theatre of cruelty, the *Marat/Sade* of 1965 owed some of its power to its hard dialectical core, and mixing the cerebral and the sensory had electrifying results. But by this time the direction taken by the Royal Shakespeare Company under Peter Hall (1930– ) was already Brecht's. Hall's designer John Bury had worked with Joan Littlewood from 1954 to 1963, and had devised stark and earthy single sets for multi-scenic drama. The set for *The Wars of the Roses* sequence of

Shakespeare's history plays in 1962 reflected Brecht's spaₗₑ ₋₋
as did Hall's use of 'unglamorous' actors like Ian Holm for Henry V
and David Warner for Hamlet. The RSC's policy of bringing
Shakespeare up-to-date has meant a reduction of illusion and a
conscious theatricality, together with much realism of detail —
a combination Shakespeare would have understood.

Other British directors, notably George Devine, John Dexter
and William Gaskill, were also attracted to Brecht, with Joan
Littlewood and her Theatre Workshop setting the pace. Littlewood
had played Mother Courage at Barnstaple in 1955, the first production of the play in Britain. Startling when they came to London's
West End, her productions were rough and passionate. Like Brecht,
she wanted to create a popular theatre for a working-class audience
in opposition to a middle-class theatre of false values, but, like
Brecht, she failed. Nevertheless, a characteristically Brechtian production style of energy and vulgarity was seen in everything the
Theatre Workshop touched. Brendan Behan's *The Hostage* (1958),
with its casual interlacing of Irish songs and banter, was dubbed
'Dublin's *Dreigroschenoper*' by Penelope Gilliatt. The company collab-
orated in the making of an epic musical depicting the period immediately prior to the First World War: *Oh, What a Lovely War!*
(1963) was a music-hall medley of songs and sketches not unlike a
Brechtian cabaret production. Nostalgic and comic at the same
time, the material of the play was made up of authentic speeches
and ballads of the time like a documentary, and the epic from permitted the constant juxtaposition of one tone with another. Like
Brecht, Joan Littlewood was never satisfied with a production, and
she continued rehearsing even during the run of the show, constantly
coming up with new ideas. Under her guidance, the stage was
uniquely alive and lusty, in an endless state of experiment.

In the 1960s, a few new plays flirted with fashion and adopted
a superficially epic form. *A Man for All Seasons* (1960) by Robert Bolt
(1924—  ) put forward Sir Thomas More as a man of individual
conscience prepared to risk everything against the despotism of his
king, but unlike Mother Courage or Galileo, he was too much master
of his fate to provide much of a comment on society, and episodic
scenes linked by the commentary of a Common Man were unin-
formed by Brecht's basic ambiguities. *Luther* (1961) by John Osborne

(1929—   ) echoed *Galileo* in style and intention, bringing to the central figure a certain complexity — simultaneously an Oedipus complex and a terrible problem of digestion — which unfortunately put the emphasis on the man and not on his historical context. *The Devils* (1961) by John Whiting (1917–63), based on Huxley's novel *The Devils of Loudon*, was realistically documented, but could not rise much above the sensationalism of its subject. *Chips with Everything* (1962) by Arnold Wesker (1932—   ) assumed an episodic structure which nicely concentrated the ironies of life in the Air Force, but Wesker was happier with his former style of realism. *The Royal Hunt of the Sun* (1964) by Peter Shaffer (1926—   ) dealt spectacularly with Pizarro's conquest of the Inca of Peru, but the Conquistadors stood little chance of an equal hearing on the issues of the play.

Only John Arden (1930—   ) has consistently demonstrated real understanding of Brecht's intentions and has persisted in testing epic techniques on the English stage. As a result of seeing *Mother Courage* in London in 1956, he discarded the realistic style he had used in *Live like Pigs* (1958) and wrote the bitterly ironic *Serjeant Musgrave's Dance*, produced at the Royal Court in 1959, and later in Paris by Brook in 1963. This play had no success on the professional stage, but everywhere outside, and it probably remains the best Brechtian play in English. It is an anti-war parable in which Arden repeatedly disconcerts his audience with unexpected and paradoxical developments. Yet the sergeant and three soldiers who come to a northern English town in mid-winter to show the civilians the horrible results of Victorian militarism turn out to be deserters. But can they also be pacifists if they kill one of their number when he tries to go off with a local girl? And Musgrave himself is so much a fanatic that he must preach his message at gunpoint and threaten the citizens with a Gatling gun. He is an exact anti-hero, since the audience that sympathizes with his ends must be repelled by his means.

Arden enthusiastically adopted Brechtian ways with ballad commentary, and in *Encore*, the avant-garde theatre periodical which flourished at the time, he stated, 'I can see prose as being a more useful vehicle for conveying plot and character relationships, and poetry as a sort of comment on them.' So in *Serjeant Musgrave's Dance* Arden makes full use of song and direct address, and other epic devices, but the play does not depend only on their use. A dialectical structure stands firmly at its back, and the play refuses to comfort the spectator or confirm him in his beliefs. Moreover, unlike Courage or Galileo, Musgrave is wholly without attractive qualities. All these reasons may be responsible for the uncertain fortunes of the play in the commercial theatre, and in his uncompromising desire for objectivity and ambivalence in a play, Arden, for all he is one of the most incisive minds in the modern British theatre, may be his own worst enemy.

44. Arden, *Serjeant Musgrave's Dance*, 1959. Revival at the Royal Court Theatre, London, 1965. Left Ronald Pickup, centre Sebastian Shaw.

In *The Times Literary Supplement* for 3 March 1978, the critic
J. W. Lambert attempted to identify the problem of Arden's indif-
ferent success. On the one hand, Arden has written few plays which
'get the tone right'. Nor is this easy to do when his mixture of 'prose
and verse, speech and song, naturalism and caricature, buffoonery
and bitterness' keeps his content elusive to the point of obscurity.
On the other, Lambert points to 'a near-fatal absence of creative
spontaneity'. Arden intellectualizes his writing process as his favourite playwright Ben Jonson did, with, one feels, not dissimilar results.
Arden has been intoxicated with ballads, which in 1960 he argued
were 'the bedrock of English poetry', and imagines that some mythi-
cal English folk-culture is waiting to be tapped. The spirit of Ben
Jonson is present again when Arden draws a character, which seems
coarsely cut like a Jonsonian 'humour', and staged in the manner of
a medieval fairground.

The biggest obstacle to a frank enjoyment of Arden's plays
has perhaps been his determination to write a committed drama,
while refusing to be committed himself. If this is not wholly true, he
has defended the idea of detachment both on and off the stage. His
object was not to give his audience a cause with which to sympathize, but to show them a conflict from both sides. He said in 1975,

> Plays written to a received doctrinal formula do not, in
> the long run, enhance the art of theatre. I believe that one
> of the main qualities of this art is its capacity for continual
> and fruitful criticism of received ideas, particularly those
> ideas which the playwright holds most dear.

This neutrality is helpful in eliminating the agitprop variety of
drama, but the constant use of contradiction, reversal and irony
needed for writing in a totally sceptical way leaves the average
audience either confused or hostile. Others of Arden's provocative
epic theatre experiments of the 1960s, *The Happy Haven* (1960),
*The Workhouse Donkey* (1963) and *Armstrong's Last Goodnight* (1964),
may yet find their special audience.

The most successful Brechtian playwright in English, after
naturalistic beginnings with *The Pope's Wedding* (1962) and *Saved*
(1965), has been Edward Bond (1935– ). Bond caught the fever from
his director at the Royal Court, William Gaskill (1930– ), who

claimed Brecht as 'the great formative influence' upon him and on most of those who worked with him:

> It's an approach to theatre which is hard to define: it's partly a question of economy, of reducing things to their simplest visual state, with the minimum of furniture, the minimum of scenery and props needed to make a theatrical impression (*Plays and Players*, May 1971).

45. Arden, *The Happy Haven*, 1960. Production by William Gaskill at the Royal Court Theatre, London, with Frank Finlay and Susan Engel.

Such freedom might be attributed as much to Beckett's influence, but Brecht's work also contained the discipline of 'a certain sense of moral and political direction'. So it is with Bond. The banned *Early Morning* (1968) rests upon the massive alienation-effect of a lesbian relationship between Queen Victoria and Florence Nightingale which accentuates their Victorian milieu. The censored *Narrow Road to the Deep North* (also 1968) focuses on violence and injustice by distancing the horror with oriental masks. In plays of ranging imagination — *Lear* (1971, and also directed by Bond himself in Vienna in 1973) and *Bingo* (1973), representing Shakespeare's declining years in Stratford — the emphasis is always on the social context, rather than on the individual situation. *The Woman: Scenes of War and Freedom*, directed by Bond on the open stage of the Olivier Theatre in 1978, is in this tradition, and is his most ambitious work to date.

Irving Wardle of *The Times* pronounced *The Woman* 'a classical demolition job'. Bond had re-read the Greek tragedies, and from half-a-dozen plays by Sophocles and Euripides constructed a new story of the Trojan War. Paris and Helen, Hector and Achilles, all romantic heroism, were eliminated, and the action focused on Hecuba (Yvonne Bryceland) and her relationship with a new Greek leader, Heros (Nicky Henson), and his princess Ismene (Susan Fleetwood). Bond has said that the play sums up all the themes from his earlier plays, and placing them in a classical framework is to lend them a degree of timelessness: the play, said Bond, is about the present. The viewpoint is dominantly that of the women; indeed, the men seem like beasts. Moreover, the cause of the Trojan War is no longer Helen, but the stone statue of a woman, a dehumanized idol — the Goddess of Good Fortune which had been stolen by Priam when he took a young wife. But to regain this statue could never be a matter of justice, since the Goddess 'brings good fortune to whoever is destined to own her', a bleakly deterministic notion.

In the first part of the play, atrocities are piled one on another. Disguised as Trojan ladies, plague victims set upon three Greek guards. For her pacificism, Ismene is immured alive like her sister Antigone by her own people. Rather than see her grandchild Astyanax be dragged off and tossed to his death, Hecuba chooses to blind herself — although she manages to lose only one eye. Robert

Cushman of *The Observer* considered *The Trojan Women* of Euripides more moving because it concentrated on only one murder, adding that the boy's death in Euripides had 'a gloss of *realpolitik* that actually made it more hideous'. Bond is relentless in accumulating powerful symbolic images — Ismene's cries drowned by the Greek drums, her judges laughing in their ritualistic white robes, the great metallic wall designed by Hayden Griffin rising to reveal the Trojan inferno — all making the first act one of 'staggering skill'.

Part II begins in a wholly different mood. We are at a folk festival for fishing on some remote Greek island, with songs scored for voices and clarinet by Hans Werner Henze; there Hecuba and Ismene have somehow come together like mother and daughter. The scene is set for the humanitarian development of the play: 'We mustn't write only problem plays', said Bond; 'we must write answer plays'. But Heros has pursued Hecuba and the statue, and she must devise a trick in self-defence. He is persuaded to run a race with a crippled slave, a refugee from the Athenian mines, and now the lover of Ismene. In this symbolic race, Heros loses and forfeits his life. Polemical speeches in this half of the play build up its anti-war

46. Bond, *The Woman*, 1978. Production by William Gaskill at the National Theatre, London, Yvonne Bryceland as Hecuba (left) and Dinah Stabb as Cassandra.

statement, and end the story with a greater affirmation of life than was usual in this author.

The play has nearly a hundred parts needing some forty actors, and its length and scale urge attention, but the production met with the customary attacks. Reviewers remain ill at ease with Bond's violence, and with the startling juxtaposition of his visual images — what Tony Coult in the first book on Bond calls his 'scenes of theatrical daring', like the soldier in *Lear* who counts the stars as he dies, or the old man in *Bingo* who throws snowballs at Shakespeare. In favour of the play, John Peter of *The Sunday Times* thought it 'a chastisement of the world', a three-hour play which 'speaks like the bad conscience of our time'. But in general it was found dry of emotion, perhaps also suffering from that dehydration of feeling from which epic theatre is never quite immune. In his notes on acting the play (1979), Bond makes the point that he does not want his scenes played 'with the emotional urgency we would use to tell someone their house was on fire'. In the Brechtian way, he wants his actors to become 'the illustrations of the story as well as the speakers of the text', and not be 'swept by emotion (as in ham acting) or glued to the emotional base (as in method acting)'.

There may be more to Bond's sang-froid. He is an atheist: in an interview he spoke of being a child in North London 'terrified to think how God was love, and he killed his son for us and hung him up and tortured him and washed us in his blood'. But his vision is more ironic than sentimental, and the vast size of the Olivier stage, together with the large cast, may have added to the facelessness of the lesson: 'You might weep for Hecuba, but', wondered John Peter, 'would you weep for an archetype?' Then again, to quote a line from one of Bond's own poems, 'The imagination is one of the exact sciences.'

# 19 *Expressionist theatre: retrospectively*

Like the other modes of drama, expressionist and epic theatre manipulated reality in order that an audience should perceive it afresh. However, unlike the other modes, one can admire it without necessarily enjoying it. Its built-in effects of self-conscious theatricality and its devices of ironic distancing put the audience in a strange and special position of authority. The drama's patrons, of course, are always right, and the expressionist and epic style can invite them to turn a cold shoulder. In his essay 'A Dramatic Theory about the Audience', Dürrenmatt told the story of a performance of *The Physicists* given before an audience made up exclusively of nurses, who burst into unwanted laughter because the actor playing Möbius resembled a psychiatrist they all knew. We may conclude that an audience that is in any way 'politicized' can react with a unity and defiance the play may not always have power to control.

The first expressionists were prone to be recklessly subjective, and their link with the reality of the audience soon snapped. Once the audience at a fantasy begins to ask the dreamer awkward questions about cause and effect, and the relationship between the individual motive and the demands of society, it can assert a critical independence which may be either a disaster or a boon to the dramatist and his company of actors. Epic theatre adopted the presentational and externalizing elements of expressionism, and at the same time stripped away its inherent sentimentality, taking advantage of any new ground gained for a more objective stage. As a result, the developing epic style most reflected its environment, and best responded to the sensibilities of its place and period. Epic theatre reminded us that the political side of the theatre as a public institution is often primary and always present. The word 'political' is used in its widest sense — not only to describe a vehicle for propaganda (although this too), but also to allow the stage a legitimate role in public affairs. The drama, like any art form, deals in truth and beauty, but it is unfair to expect both to come together every time.

No question but expressionism and epic theatre reduced the dependence of drama on plot and character in order to make its public statements, and some will count this a loss. They also encouraged the growth of a director's theatre: with a fragmentary form, one lacking in the structural bonds of the well-made play, it is often only the director who can find a unity in the action and sense the whole occasion. The reins tend to gather in one person's hands, and Brecht, the leading exponent of epic theatre, was lucky to direct some of his own plays. Lack of a usual structure made this form the most adaptable of the century, and for this reason alone its offshoots will doubtless dominate the stage of the next.

Finally, to return to the first point. Epic theatre most readily responds to the topicality of the stage. All drama is 'now or never', and Sophocles or Shakespeare are good on the stage today because they wrote for the audience they knew in the past. In some such belief as this, the present study has tried to make it clear that, since in the last analysis a play and its performance are indivisible, the occasion paramount, we must look into the complete context in order to find out where the audience placed most value at the time. Then issues of theory and practice, and the way they seem to modify one another endlessly, will emerge as very basic matters.

# Table of events in the theatre

1 Realism and naturalism
2 Symbolism, surrealism and the absurd
**3 Expressionism and epic theatre**
[The entries in **bold type** are the subject of this volume]
Legend: w = written, p = produced, f = formed, d = died

| World events | Writers, artists and events in the theatre | Plays and productions |
|---|---|---|
| *1851* | | |
| Louis Napoleon president of France | 'Opera and Drama' w Wagner | |
| Great Exhibition, London | Ibsen directing in Bergen and Christiana (to 1862) Limelight in use | |
| *1859* | | |
| 'Origin of Species' w Darwin | | |
| *1861* | | |
| Italy unified | | |
| American Civil War (to 1865) | | |
| *1865* | | |
| Lincoln assassinated | | 'Tristan and Isolde' w Wagner 'Society' w Robertson |
| *1866* | | |
| | Saxe-Meiningen company f Georg II | 'Brand' p Ibsen |
| *1867* | | |
| Dominion of Canada | | 'Peer Gynt' p Ibsen |
| 'Das Kapital' w Marx | | 'Caste' w Robertson |
| Baudelaire d | | |
| *1870* | | |
| Franco-Prussian War (to 1871) | Dumas père d | |

| World events | Writers, artists and events in the theatre | Plays and productions |
|---|---|---|
| Dickens d | | |
| *1871* | | |
| Germany unified | 'Purpose of the Opera' w Wagner | |
| *1872* | | |
| | 'The Birth of Tragedy' w Nietzsche | |
| *1873* | | |
| | | 'Thérèse Raquin' p Zola |
| *1874* | | |
| | Saxe-Meiningen company on tour | |
| *1876* | | |
| telephone invented | Bayreuth theatre built | 'The Ring cycle' p Wagner |
| *1877* | | |
| gramophone invented | | 'Pillars of Society' w Ibsen |
| *1879* | | |
| | | 'A Doll's House' w Ibsen **Büchner's 'Woyzeck' published** |
| *1880* | | |
| George Eliot, Flaubert d | 'Naturalism in the Theatre' w Zola electric light in the theatre | 'Pillars of Society' ['Quicksand' in London] |
| *1881* | | |
| Dostoevsky d | | 'Ghosts' w Ibsen |
| *1883* | | |
| | Deutsches Theater, Berlin f Wagner d | 'Ghosts' p Stockholm 'The Wild Duck' w Ibsen |
| *1887* | | |
| | Théâtre-Libre, Paris f Antoine | 'The Father' w Strindberg |
| *1888* | | |
| | Dagmar Theatre, Copenhagen f Strindberg | 'Power of Darkness' w Tolstoy 'Miss Julie' w Strindberg |

| World events | Writers, artists and events in the theatre | Plays and productions |
|---|---|---|
| *1889* | | |
| Browning d | Freie Bühne, Berlin f Brahm | 'A Doll's House' p London and New York |
| *1890* | | |
| Van Gogh d | Freie Volksbühne, Berlin f Wille Boucicault d | 'Ghosts' p Paris 'Hedda Gabler' w Ibsen 'The Intruder', 'The Blind' w Maeterlinck |
| *1891* | | |
| Melville, Rimbaud d | Independent Theatre Company, London f Grein 'Quintessence of Ibsenism' w Shaw | 'Ghosts' p London **'Spring's Awakening' w Wedekind** |
| *1892* | | |
| Tennyson d | | 'The Weavers' w Hauptmann 'Widowers' Houses' w Shaw 'Countess Cathleen' w Yeats |
| *1893* | | |
| Maupassant, Tchaikowsky d | Théâtre de l'Oeuvre f Lugné-Poe | 'Mrs Warren's Profession' w Shaw 'Pelléas and Mélisande' w Maeterlinck |
| *1894* | | |
| | Brahm at Deutsches Theater | 'Arms and the Man' w Shaw 'Land of Heart's Desire' w Yeats |
| *1895* | | |
| first films made | 'La Mise-en-scène du drame Wagnérian' w Appia | 'A Doll's House' in America **'Earth Spirit' w Wedekind** |
| *1896* | | |
| Verlaine d | 'The Treasure of the Humble' w Maeterlinck | 'Salomé' p Lugné-Poe 'Ubu roi' p Jarry 'The Seagull' in St Petersburg |

| World events | Writers, artists and events in the theatre | Plays and productions |
|---|---|---|
| *1897* | | |
| Brahms d | Moscow Art Theatre f | |
| | Stanislavsky and | |
| | Danchenko | |
| *1898* | | |
| Mallarmé d | | 'The Seagull' p MAT |
| | | **'To Damascus' w** |
| | | **Strindberg** |
| *1899* | | |
| Boer War (to 1902) | 'Die Musik und die | 'When We Dead |
| | Inszenierung' w Appia | Awaken' w Ibsen |
| | Irish Literary Theatre f | 'Uncle Vanya' w |
| | Yeats and Lady Gregory | Chekhov |
| *1900* | | |
| Nietzsche d | Wilde d | **'To Damascus' p** |
| | | **Stockholm** |
| *1901* | | |
| Commonwealth of | | 'Easter' w Strindberg |
| Australia | | 'Three Sisters' w |
| Queen Victoria d | | Chekhov |
| **Freud's 'Interpretation of** | | |
| **Dreams'** | | |
| *1902* | | |
| | **Kleines Theater,** | **'A Dream Play' w** |
| | **Berlin f Reinhardt** | **Strindberg** |
| | Zola d | 'The Lower Depths' w |
| | | Gorky |
| | | **'Danton's Death' p** |
| | | **Berlin** |
| *1903* | | |
| Wright brothers' flight | | 'Shadow of the Glen' |
| | | w Synge |
| *1904* | | |
| Entente Cordiale | Abbey Theatre, Dublin f | 'The Cherry Orchard' w |
| Russo-Japanese War (to | English Stage Society at | Chekhov |
| 1905) | Court Theatre (Vedrenne | 'Riders to the Sea' w |
| | and Barker) | Synge |
| | Chekhov d | 'On Baile's Strand' w |
| | | Yeats |
| *1905* | | |
| | 'The Art of the Theatre' w | 'Mrs Warren's Pro- |
| | Craig | fession' p New York |

| World events | Writers, artists and events in the theatre | Plays and productions |
| --- | --- | --- |
| | **Reinhardt at Deutsches Theater** **Meyerhold at MAT Studio** | 'Man and Superman' w Shaw **Reinhardt's 'Midsummer Night's Dream', Berlin** |
| *1906* Cézanne d | Appia meets Dalcroze **Meyerhold in St Petersburg** **Reinhardt f Kammerspielhaus** Ibsen d | 'Partage de midi' w Claudel **'Spring's Awakening' p Reinhardt** 'Hedda Gabler' p Meyerhold |
| *1907* Dominion of New Zealand | **Intima Teatern, Stockholm f Strindberg** Jarry d | **'Ghost Sonata' w Strindberg** 'Playboy of the Western World' w Synge **'The Life of Man' w Andreyev** **'Murderer, the Hope of Women' w Kokoschka** |
| *1908* | 'L'umorismo' w Pirandello | 'The Blue Bird' w Maeterlinck |
| *1909* Ballets Russes in Paris | 'The Mask' ed. Craig (to 1929) Synge d | |
| *1910* Union of South Africa King Edward VII d | 'The Tragic Theatre' w Yeats Tolstoy d | **'Oedipus Rex' p Reinhardt** **'Dom Juan' p Meyerhold** |
| *1911* first Post-Impressionist exhibition | | **'The Miracle' p Reinhardt** Synge's 'Playboy' p New York |
| *1912* second Post-Impressionist exhibition | Debussy's 'L'Après-midi d'un faune' p Nijinsky | 'Hamlet' p Craig in Moscow |

| World events | Writers, artists and events in the theatre | Plays and productions |
|---|---|---|
| Titanic disaster | Brahm d<br>**Strindberg d** | Shakespeare at the Savoy p<br>Barker<br>**'Theatre of the Soul'**<br>**w Evreinov**<br>**'The Beggar' w Sorge** |
| *1913*<br>Freud's 'Interpretation<br>of Dreams' trans. into<br>English<br>'Sons and Lovers' w<br>Lawrence | Vieux Colombier f<br>Copeau<br>Stravinsky's 'Le Sacré<br>du printemps' p<br>Nijinsky | 'The Mask and the<br>Face' w Chiarelli<br>**'Danton's Death' and**<br>**'Woyzeck' p**<br>**Munich**<br>**'Burgers of Calais' w**<br>**Kaiser** |
| *1914*<br>First World War (to 1918) | **Kamerny Theatre,**<br>**Moscow f Taïrov**<br>**MAT Third Studio f**<br>**Vakhtangov** | Barker's 'Midsummer<br>Night's Dream'<br>at the Savoy |
| *1915*<br>Lusitania torpedoed | **Provincetown Players,**<br>**Washington Square**<br>**Players f New York** | **'Patricide' w Bronnen** |
| *1916*<br>Easter Rebellion, Dublin<br>Henry James d | Dada exhibition, Zürich<br>**'Theatre Arts' pub-**<br>**lished New York** | 'Heartbreak House' w<br>Shaw<br>'At the Hawk's Well' w<br>Yeats<br>'Right You Are' w<br>Pirandello<br>**'From Morn to**<br>**Midnight' w Kaiser** |
| *1917*<br>America enters the War<br>Russian Revolution<br>Jung's 'Psychology of<br>the Unconscious' trans<br>into English<br>*1918*<br>Armistice signed<br>Debussy d | Copeau in New York<br>(to 1919)<br>**Reinhardt's 'Das junge**<br>**Deutschland'**<br><br><br><br>**Wedekind d** | 'The Breasts of Tiresias'<br>w Apollinaire<br>'Parade' w Cocteau<br>**Kaiser's 'Gas' trilogy**<br><br><br>O'Neill's one-act plays<br>of the sea<br>**'Baal' w Brecht** |

| World events | Writers, artists and events in the theatre | Plays and productions |
|---|---|---|
| *1919* | | |
| 'Cabinet of Dr. Caligari' (film) made | **Reinhardt f Grosses Schauspielhaus, Berlin** | **'The Transformation' w Toller** |
| Renoir d | **Theatre Guild, New York f** | |
| | **The Bauhaus, Weimar f Gropius** | |
| *1920* | | |
| League of Nations f | **State Theatre, Moscow f Meyerhold** | **'The Dybbuk' p Vakhtangov** |
| | **Salzburg Festival f Reinhardt and Hofmannsthal** | **'The Emperor Jones' w O'Neill** |
| | Théâtre National Populaire f | **'Beggar's Opera' at the Lyric, Hammersmith** |
| *1921* | | |
| Irish Free State f | Atelier f Dullin (to 1938) | 'The Wedding on the Eiffel Tower' w Cocteau |
| | **MacGowan's 'Theatre of Tomorrow'** | 'Six Characters in Search of an Author' w Pirandello |
| | | **'RUR' w Karel Čapek** |
| | | **'Masses and Man' w Toller** |
| *1922* | | |
| Mussolini in power in Italy | MAT visits Paris and Berlin | 'Henry IV' w Pirandello |
| Irish Civil War | American Laboratory Theatre f | **'The Hairy Ape' w O'Neill** |
| radio broadcasting begins | **'Continental Stagecraft' w Macgowan and Jones** | **'The Magnanimous Cuckold' p Meyerhold** |
| 'Ulysses' w Joyce | Vakhtangov d | 'Turandot' p Vakhtangov |
| 'The Waste Land' w Eliot | | |
| *1923* | | |
| | **Schlemmer's Bauhaus Theatre (to 1929)** | **'Triadic Ballet' p Schlemmer** |
| | MAT visits New York | **'The Adding Machine' w Rice** |
| | Bernhardt d | 'Knock' p Jouvet |

| World events | Writers, artists and events in the theatre | Plays and productions |
|---|---|---|
| *1924* | | |
| Stalin in power in Russia | 'My Life in Art' w | 'Juno and the Paycock' |
| 'The Magic Mountain' w | Stanislavsky | w O'Casey |
| Mann | Copeau's school in | 'The Infernal Machine' w |
| Puccini d | Burgundy | Cocteau |
| | first surrealist manifesto | 'Desire under the Elms' |
| | **Provincetown experi-** | w O'Neill |
| | **mental season, New** | **Piscator's 'Rowdy** |
| | **York** | **Red Revue'** |
| | **Piscator at the** | |
| | **Volksbühne** | |
| *1925* | | |
| | Pirandello f Teatro | **Berg's opera** |
| | d'Arte, Rome | **'Wozzeck'** |
| | | 'Hamlet' in modern |
| | | dress |
| *1926* | | |
| British General Strike | Théâtre Alfred Jarry f | 'Plough and the Stars' |
| 'Metropolis' (film) made | Artaud and Vitrac | w O'Casey |
| | | **'Great God Brown' w** |
| | | **O'Neill** |
| | | **'A Man's a Man' w** |
| | | **Brecht** |
| | | **'Inspector General'** |
| | | **p Meyerhold** |
| *1927* | | |
| Pavlov's 'Conditioned | **Gropius designed** | 'The Spurt of Blood' w |
| Reflexes' trans into | **Total-Theater** | Artaud |
| English | Isadora Duncan d | **'Hurrah, We Live!'** |
| | | **w Toller p** |
| | | **Piscator** |
| *1928* | | |
| Thomas Hardy d | **O'Casey leaves Ireland** | **'Threepenny Opera'** |
| | Appia d | **w Brecht** |
| | | **'The Silver Tassie' w** |
| | | **O'Casey** |
| | | **'The Good Soldier** |
| | | **Schweik' p Piscator** |
| *1929* | | |
| Wall street crash: world | **Group Theatre, New** | 'Street Scene' w Rice |
| economic depression | **York f** | 'Amphitryon 38' w |
| first 'talkie' | Religious Drama Society f | Giraudoux |

| World events | Writers, artists and events in the theatre | Plays and productions |
|---|---|---|
| | **The Political Theatre w Piscator** Diaghilev d | **'The Bedbug' w Mayakovsky** |
| *1930* | | |
| D. H. Lawrence d | Baty at Théâtre Montparnasse | **'Rise and Fall of the City of Mahagonny' w Brecht** **'The Bathhouse' w Mayakovksy** |
| *1931* | | |
| | Lorca's La Barraca f Madrid Saint-Denis f La Compagnie des Quinze (to 1935) **Piscator's Drama Workshop f New York** | 'Noah' w Obey 'Atlas-Hôtel' w Salacrou **'Mourning Becomes Electra' w O'Neill** |
| *1932* | | |
| | first manifesto of the Theatre of Cruelty **Okhlopkov at the Realistic Theatre** | |
| *1933* | | |
| Hitler in power in Germany Roosevelt president in America (to 1945) | second manifesto of the Theatre of Cruelty | 'Blood Wedding' w Lorca **'Within the Gates' w O'Casey** |
| *1934* | | |
| | Jouvet at Théâtre Athenée Pitoëff at the Théâtre aux Mathurins | 'The Children's Hour' w Hellman 'Yerma' w Lorca |
| *1935* | | |
| Federal Theatre Project in America (to 1939) | Theatre of Cruelty f Artaud | 'Waiting for Lefty' w Odets 'The Trojan War Will Not Take Place' w Giraudoux 'Murder in the Cathedral' w Eliot |

| World events | Writers, artists and events in the theatre | Plays and productions |
| --- | --- | --- |
| *1936* Spanish Civil War first public television | Stanislavsky's 'An Actor Prepares' trans into English Pirandello, Lorca d | 'The House of Bernarda Alba' w Lorca 'School for Wives' p Jouvet |
| *1937* | | 'Golden Boy' w Odets 'Electra' w Giraudoux |
| *1938* Germany annexes Austria Munich agreement | Artaud's 'Theatre and Its Double' **Brecht's 'Street Scene'** Stanislavsky d | 'Les Parents terribles' w Cocteau **'Our Town' w Wilder** |
| *1939* Second World War (to 1945) | Yeats, **Toller**, Pitoëff d | 'The Little Foxes' w Hellman **'Galileo', 'Mother Courage' w Brecht** |
| *1940* Paris occupied, Battle of Britain Churchill prime minister | Barrault at the Comédie-Française **Meyerhold**, Lugné-Poe d | **'Good Woman of Setzuan' w Brecht** **'Purple Dust' w O'Casey** |
| *1941* Germany and Russia at war Pearl Harbor: America enters the War Joyce d | **Brecht in America (to 1947)** | **'Mother Courage' p Zürich** |
| *1942* | 'The Myth of Sisyphus' w Camus | 'The Flies' w Sartre **'Skin of Our Teeth' w Wilder** **'Red Roses for Me' w O'Casey** |
| *1943* | Antoine, Danchenko, Reinhardt d | 'Antigone' w Anouilh |
| *1944* D-Day landing in Normandy | German and Austrian theatres closed | **'Glass Menagerie' w Williams** |

| World events | Writers, artists and events in the theatre | Plays and productions |
|---|---|---|
| | Giraudoux d | 'Caligula' w Camus<br>'Huis clos' w Sartre |
| *1945*<br>first atomic bomb<br>United Nations f<br>Labour in power in<br>Britain | **Littlewood's Theatre<br>Workshop**<br>**Kaiser, Jessner d** | Giraudoux's 'Mad-<br>woman of Chaillot' p<br>Jouvet<br>**'Caucasian Chalk<br>Circle' w Brecht** |
| *1946* | | |
| *1947* | Compaignie Renaud-<br>Barrault f (to 1956)<br>Hauptmann d | O'Neill's 'Iceman Cometh' p<br>'Men without Shadows'<br>w Sartre |
| | Actors' Studio f New York<br>The Living Theatre f Beck<br>and Malina | **'Streetcar Named<br>Desire' w Williams**<br>Barrault p Kafka's 'The<br>Trial'<br>'The Maids' w Genêt<br>p Jouvet<br>**'Galileo' p in America** |
| *1948*<br>Israel proclaimed<br>Czechoslovakia<br>communist | **Brecht's 'Little<br>Organon for the<br>Theatre'**<br>Artaud d | 'Les Mains sales' w<br>Sartre<br>Barrault p Claudel's<br>'Partage de midi' |
| *1949* | Ionesco f Collège de<br>'Pataphysique<br>**Brecht, Weigel f<br>Berliner Ensemble**<br>Maeterlinck, Copeau,<br>Dullin d | **'Death of a Salesman'<br>w Miller**<br>'The Cocktail Party' w<br>Eliot<br>**'Cock-a-Doodle<br>Dandy' w O'Casey** |
| *1950*<br>Korean War (to 1953)<br>McCarthy hearings in<br>America (to 1954) | **Piscator back in<br>Germany**<br>Shaw, **Taïrov** d | 'Come Back, Little<br>Sheba' w Inge<br>'The Bald Soprano' w<br>Ionesco |
| *1951*<br>Festival of Britain | Vilar at the Théâtre<br>National Populaire<br>(to 1963)<br>Jouvet d | **'The Rose Tattoo' w<br>Williams** |

| World events | Writers, artists and events in the theatre | Plays and productions |
|---|---|---|
| **1952** | | |
| H-bomb tested | 'Saint-Genêt' w Sartre<br>Cage at Black Mountain<br>College | 'Waiting for Godot' w<br>Beckett<br>'The Parody' w Adamov |
| **1953** | | |
| East German uprising<br>Stalin d | Shakespeare Festival of<br>Canada<br>**O'Neill d** | 'The Crucible' w Miller<br>'Professor Taranne' w<br>Adamov<br>**'Camino Real' w**<br>**Williams** |
| **1954** | | |
| Algerian Civil War<br>(to 1962)<br>Matisse d | **'Theatre Problems' w**<br>**Dürrenmatt**<br>**Berlin Ensemble at first**<br>**Paris festival** | 'Amédée' w Ionesco |
| **1955** | | |
| | **Littlewood at Strat-**<br>**ford, East London**<br>Claudel d | 'View from the Bridge'<br>w Miller<br>'Ping-pong' w Adamov<br>**'War and Peace' p**<br>**Piscator** |
| **1956** | | |
| Hungarian uprising<br>Suez Canal crisis | English Stage Company<br>at Royal Court Theatre<br>**f Devine**<br>**Berliner Ensemble in**<br>**London**<br>**Brecht d** | O'Neill's 'Long Day's<br>Journey' p<br>**'Look Back in Anger'**<br>w Osborne<br>**'The Visit' w**<br>**Dürrenmatt**<br>'The Balcony' w Genêt |
| **1957** | | |
| Treaty of Rome<br>establishes European<br>Economic Community<br>first Russian space flight<br>Sibelius d | | 'Endgame' w Beckett<br>'The Blacks' w<br>Genêt<br>**'The Entertainer' w**<br>**Osborne** |
| **1958** | | |
| De Gaulle president of<br>France (to 1969)<br>Berlin airlift | | 'Picnic on the Battle-<br>field' w Arrabal<br>'The Birthday Party'<br>w Pinter<br>**'The Fire Raisers' w**<br>**Frisch** |

| World events | Writers, artists and events in the theatre | Plays and productions |
|---|---|---|
| *1959* | | |
| | Polish Laboratory | 'Roots' w Wesker |
| | Theatre f Grotowski | 'The Zoo Story' w Albee |
| | San Francisco Mime Troupe | **'Serjeant Musgrave's** |
| | f Davis | **Dance' w Arden** |
| | '18 Happenings' p Kaprow | |
| *1960* | | |
| | Peter Hall p Royal | 'The American Dream' |
| | Shakespeare Company | w Albee |
| | (to 1968) | **'The Happy Haven'** |
| | Camus d | **w Arden** |
| *1961* | | |
| American forces in Vietnam | Bread & Puppet Theatre, | 'Happy Days' w Beckett |
| Berlin Wall erected | New York | **'Andorra' w Frisch** |
| | La Mama Experimental | |
| | Theatre Club, New York | |
| *1962* | | |
| Cuban missile crisis | Ionesco's 'Notes and | 'Exit the King' w |
| Lincoln Center for the | Counter Notes' | Ionesco |
| Performing Arts opened | Esslin's 'Theatre of the | 'Who's Afraid of |
| New York (completed | Absurd' | Virginia Woolf?' |
| 1969) | | w Albee |
| | | **'The Physicists' w** |
| | | **Dürrenmatt** |
| | | Brook's 'King Lear' |
| | | for RSC |
| *1963* | | |
| President Kennedy | National Theatre f London | 'The Brigg' p Malina |
| assassinated | Brook's Theatre of Cruelty | **'The Workhouse** |
| | season | **Donkey' w Arden** |
| | The Open Theatre f New | **Littlewood's 'Oh,** |
| | York | **What a Lovely** |
| | Tzara, Cocteau, Odets d | **War!'** |
| | | **Hochhuth's** |
| | | **'Representative'** |
| | | **p Piscator** |
| *1964* | | |
| | Living Theatre in Europe | **'Marat/Sade' w Weiss** |
| | **O'Casey d** | Grotowski's 'Akropolis' |
| *1965* | | |
| | **second Berlin** | **'Marat/Sade' p Brook** |
| | **Ensemble visit to** | 'Saved' w Bond |
| | **London** | 'Frankenstein' p Beck |
| | Eliot d | |

| World events | Writers, artists and events in the theatre | Plays and productions |
|---|---|---|
| *1966* | | |
| | Kirby's Happenings | 'A Delicate Balance' w |
| | Craig, Breton, **Piscator d** | Albee |
| | | 'America Hurrah' w van |
| | | Itallie p Chaikin |
| | | **'Insulting the** |
| | | **Audience' w** |
| | | **Handke** |
| *1967* | | |
| | The Performance Group | 'Rosencrantz and |
| | f New York | Guildenstern Are |
| | **Rice d** | Dead' w Stoppard |
| | | 'The Architect and the |
| | | Emperor of Assyria' |
| | | w Arrabal |
| *1968* | | |
| Paris riots | 'The Empty Space' w | 'Paradise Now' p Beck |
| Stage censorship lifted | Brook | 'Dionysus in 69' p |
| in Britain | 'Towards a Poor Theatre' | Schechner |
| | w Grotowski | **'Kaspar' w Handke** |
| | **'Notes towards a Defini-** | |
| | **tion of Documentary** | |
| | **Theatre' w Weiss** | |
| *1969* | | |
| American moon landing | | Grotowski's 'The |
| | | Constant Prince' |
| | | 'Christie in Love' w |
| | | Brenton |
| *1970* | | |
| | International Centre for | Brook's 'Midsummer |
| | Theatre Research in | Night's Dream' |
| | Paris | 'AC/ DC' w Heathcote |
| | | Williams |
| | | 'Home' w Storey |
| *1971* | | |
| | Brook's Festival at | 'Old Times' w Pinter |
| | Persepolis | **'Lear' w Bond** |
| | Vilar, Adamov d | |
| *1972* | | |
| | **Weigel d** | 'Jumpers' w Stoppard |
| *1973* | | |
| Britain joins the Common | Hall at National Theatre | 'Nightwalk' p Chaikin |
| Market | | **'Bingo' w Bond** |

| World events | Writers, artists and events in the theatre | Plays and productions |
|---|---|---|
| | | **'Brassneck' w Brenton and Hare** |
| *1974* | | |
| | | 'Travesties' w Stoppard |
| *1975* | | |
| Watergate scandal in Washington | **Wilder d** | 'Norman Conquests' w Ayckbourn |
| | | 'Comedians' w Griffiths |
| | | 'American Buffalo' w Mamet |
| *1976* | | |
| Vietnam War ends | National Theatre opens | 'The Ik' p Brook |
| American Bicentennial | on the South Bank | 'Weapons of Happiness' w Brenton |
| *1978* | | |
| | | **'The Woman' w Bond** |
| *1979* | | |
| | | 'Betrayal' w Pinter |

# Bibliography

This is a comprehensive list of works, chiefly in English, covering the subject of expressionism and epic theatre in modern drama.

## EXPRESSIONISM

*An Anthology of German Expressionist Drama*, ed. Walter H. Sokel, 1963
*Seven Expressionist Plays: Kokoschka to Barlach*, ed. James M. Ritchie and Hugh F. Garten, 1968
*Vision and Aftermath: Four Expressionist War Plays*, ed. James M. Ritchie, 1969

Agate, James, 'The Case against Expressionism' in *Their Hour upon the Stage*, 1930
— *Red Letter Nights*, 1944
Buchheim, Lothar Günther, *The Graphic Art of German Expressionism*, 1960
Carter, Huntly, *The New Spirit in the European Theatre, 1914–1924*, 1926
Eisner, Lotte, *The Haunted Screen: Expressionism in the German Cinema and the Influence of Max Reinhardt*, trans. Roger Greaves, 1969
Furness, R. S., *Expressionism*, 1973
Gorelik, Mordecai, *New Theatres for Old*, 1940
Hill, Claude and Ley, Ralph, *The Drama of German Expressionism: A German-English Bibliography*, 1960
Kayser, Wolfgang, *The Grotesque in Art and Literature*, trans. Ulrich Weisstein, 1963
Kracauer, S., *From Caligari to Hitler*, 1947
Krispyn, E., *Style and Society in German Literary Expressionism*, 1964
Macgowan, Kenneth and Jones, Robert Edmond, *Continental Stagecraft*, 1922
Matuška, Alexander, *Karel Čapek*, trans. Cathryn Alan, 1964
Pascal, Roy, *From Naturalism to Expressionism: German Literature and Society, 1880–1918*, 1973
Perkins, Geoffrey, *Contemporary Theory of Expressionism*, 1974
Raabe, Paul, ed., *The Era of German Expressionism*, trans. J. M. Ritchie, 1974
Ritchie, J. M., *German Expressionistic Drama*, 1976
Samuel, Richard and Thomas, R. Hinton, *Expressionism in German Life, Literature and the Theatre, 1910–1924*, 1939

Scheffauer, H. G., *The New Vision in German Arts*, 1924
Sokol, Walter H., *The Writer in Extremis: Expressionism in Twentieth-Century German Literature*, 1959
Whitford, Frank, *Expressionism*, 1970
Willett, John, *Expressionism*, 1970

### Georg Büchner
— *Complete Plays and Prose*, trans. Carl Richard Mueller, 1963
— *The Plays*, trans. Geoffrey Dunlop, 1927
— *The Plays*, trans. Victor Price, 1971
— *Danton's Death*, trans. Stephen Spender and Goronwy Rees, 1939
— *Danton's Death*, trans. James Maxwell, 1968
— *Lenz*, trans. Michael Hamburger, 1966
— *Leonce and Lena, Lenz, Woyzeck*, trans. Michael Hamburger, 1972
— *Leonce and Lena*, trans. Eric Bentley, 1956
— *Woyzeck, Danton's Death*, trans. Henry J. Schmidt, 1969
— *Woyzeck*, trans. John Holmstrom, 1963

Benn, Maurice B., *The Drama of Revolt: A Critical Study of Georg Büchner*, 1976
Hamburger, Michael, *Contraries*, 1970
— *Reason and Energy: Studies in German Literature*, 1957
Hauser, Ronald, *Georg Büchner*, 1974
Jacobs, Margaret, *Introduction to Dantons Tod and Woyzeck*, 1954
Knight, Arthur H. J., *Georg Büchner*, 1951
Lindenberger, Herbert Samuel, *Georg Büchner*, 1964
MacEwen, Leslie, *The Narren-motifs in the Works of Georg Büchner*, 1968
Richards, David G., *Georg Büchner and the Birth of Modern Drama*, 1977
Schmidt, Henry J., *Satire, Caricature and Perspectivism in the Works of Georg Büchner*, 1970
Stern, J. P., *Re-Interpretations*, 1964
Strudthoff, Ingeborg, *Die Rezeption Georg Büchners durch das deutsche Theater*, 1957

### Frank Wedekind
— *Tragedies of Sex*, trans. Samuel A. Eliot, Jr, 1923
— *Five Tragedies of Sex*, trans. F. Fawcett and Stephen Spender, 1952
— *The Lulu Plays*, trans. Carl Richard Mueller, 1967
— *The Awakening of Spring*, trans. Francis J. Ziegler, 1909
— *Spring's Awakening*, trans. Tom Osborn, 1969
— *Earth Spirit*, trans. Samuel A. Eliot, Jr, 1914
— *Lulu, a Sex Tragedy*, trans. Peter Barnes, 1971
— *Pandora's Box*, trans. Samuel A. Eliot, Jr, 1923
— *Schauspielkunst: Ein Glossarium*, 1910

Best, Alan, *Frank Wedekind*, 1975
Elsom, J., *Erotic Theatre*, 1973
Gittleman, Sol, *Frank Wedekind*, 1969
Wedekind, Tilly, *Lulu: Die Rolle meines Lebens*, 1969

**Carl Sternheim**
    — *Scenes from the Heroic Life of the Middle Classes: Five Plays*, trans.
      M. A. L. Brown *et al.*, 1970
    — *The Mask of Virtue*, trans. Ashley Dukes, 1935
    — *The Snob*, trans. Eric Bentley, 1958

**August Strindberg**
*See* volume 1

**MODERN GERMAN DRAMA** *(see also* 'Post-war German Drama')
Bauland, Peter, *The Hooded Eagle: Modern German Drama on the New York
    Stage*, 1968
Bithell, Jethro, *Modern German Literature, 1880–1950*, 1959
Bruford, W. H., *Theatre, Drama and Audience in Goethe's Germany*, 1950
Closs, A., ed., *Twentieth Century German Literature*, 1969
Davies, Cecil William, *Theatre for the People: The Story of the Volksbühne*,
    1977
Dukes, Ashley, *The Scene Is Changed*, 1942
Eloesser, Arthur, *Modern German Literature*, 1933
Feise, E., *Fifty Years of German Drama, 1880–1930: A Bibliography*, 1941
Fuchs, Georg, *Revolution in the Theatre*, ed. Constance Connor Kuhn, 1959
Garten, Hugh F., *Modern German Drama*, 1959
*Goethe on the Theatre*, ed. John Oxenford, 1919
Hamburger, Michael, *Reason and Energy: Studies in German Literature*,
    1957
Hayman, Ronald, ed., *The German Theatre: A Symposium*, 1975
Heller, Erich, *The Disinherited Mind*, 1952
Lange, Victor, *Modern German Literature, 1870–1940*, 1945
Last, Rex William, ed., *Affinities: Essays in German and English Literature,
    Dedicated to the Memory of Oswald Wolff (1897–1968)*, 1971
Mason, G. R., *From Gottsched to Hebbel*, 1961
Reiss, Hans, *The Writer's Task from Nietzsche to Brecht*, 1978
Ritchie, J. M., ed., *Periods in German Literature*, 1966
Rose, William, *Men, Myths and Movements in German Literature*, 1931
Shaw, Leroy R., *The Playwright and Historical Change: Dramatic Strategies
    in Brecht, Hauptmann, Kaiser and Wedekind*, 1970
Sokel, Walter H., *Twentieth-Century German Literature*, 1959

**Oskar Kokoschka**
    — *My Life*, trans. David Britt, 1974

— *A Sea Ringed with Visions*, trans. Eithne Wilkins and Ernst Kaiser, 1962

Arts Council of Great Britain, *A Retrospective Exhibition*, 1962
Hodin, Joseph P., *Oskar Kokoschka: The Artist and His Time. A Biographical Study*, 1966
Hoffmann, Edith, *Kokoschka: Life and Work*, 1947
Plaut, James S., ed., *Oskar Kokoschka*, 1948
Schmalenbach, Fritz, *Oskar Kokoschka*, trans. Violet M. Macdonald, 1968
Wingler, Hans Maria, *Introduction to Kokoschka*, trans. Peter George, 1958

**Georg Kaiser**
— *Five Plays*, trans. B. J. Kenworthy *et al.*, 1971
— *From Morn to Midnight*, trans. Ashley Dukes, 1920
— *From Morn to Midnight*, trans. Ulrich Weisstein, 1967
— *Gas*, trans. Hermann Scheffauer, 1924
— *Gas II*, trans. Winifred Katzin, 1963

Kenworthy, Brian J., *Georg Kaiser*, 1957
Schürer, Ernst, *Georg Kaiser*, 1971

**Ernst Toller**
— *Seven Plays*, trans. Edward Crankshaw *et al.*, 1935
— *Brokenbrow* [*Hinkemann*], trans. Vera Mendel, 1926
— *Draw the Fires!*, trans Edward Crankshaw, 1935
— *Hinkemann*, trans. J. M. Ritchie, 1969
— *Hoppla!*, trans. Hermon Ould, 1928
— *The Machine Wreckers*, trans. Ashley Dukes, 1923
— *Man and the Masses*, trans. L. Untermeyer, 1924
— *Masses and Man*, trans. Vera Mendel, 1923

— *I Was a German: An Autobiography*, trans. Edward Crankshaw, 1934
— *Letters from Prison*, trans. R. Ellis Roberts, 1936
— *Which World — Which Way?*, trans. Hermon Ould, 1931

Spalek, John M., *Ernst Toller and His Critics: A Bibliography*, 1968
Willibrand, William A., *Ernst Toller and His Ideology*, 1945

**Max Reinhardt**
Carter, Huntly, *The New Spirit in the European Theatre, 1914–1924*, 1925
— *The Theatre of Max Reinhardt*, 1914
Coghlan, Brian, *Hofmannsthal's Festival Dramas*, 1964
Fiedler, Leonhard M., *Max Reinhardt in Selbstzeugnissen und Bilddokumenten*, 1975
Gorelik, Mordecai, *New Theatres for Old*, 1940
Reinhardt, Gottfried, *The Genius: A Memoir of Max Reinhardt by His Son*, 1979

Rothe, Hans, *Max Reinhardt: 25 Jahre Deutsches Theater*, 1969
Max-Reinhardt-Forschungsstätte, Salzburg, *Sein Theater in Bildern*, 1968
Sayler, Oliver M., ed., *Max Reinhardt and His Theatre*, 1924
Stern, Ernst, *My Life, My Stage*, trans. Edward Fitzgerald, 1951
*Theatre Research*, vol. v, no. 3, 1963
Volbach, Walther R., 'Memoirs of Max Reinhardt's Theatres, 1920–1922', *Theatre Survey*, fall 1972
Wellwarth, George E. and Brooks, Alfred G., eds., *Max Reinhardt, 1873– 1973: A Centennial Festschrift*, 1973

### RUSSIAN DRAMA AFTER STANISLAVSKY
Bakshy, Alexander, *The Path of the Modern Russian Stage*, 1918
Billington, James H., *The Icon and the Axe: An Interpretative History of Russian Culture*, 1966
Boleslavsky, Richard, *Acting: the First Six Lessons*, 1949
Bowers, Faubion, *Broadway, U.S.S.R.* [*Entertainment in Russia*], 1959
Bradshaw, Martha, ed., *Soviet Theatres, 1917–1941*, 1954
Brown, Ben W., *Theatre at the Left*, 1938
Carter, Huntly, *The New Spirit in the Russian Theatre, 1917–1928*, 1929
— *The New Theatre and Cinema of Soviet Russia*, 1924
Chekhov, Michael, *The Problem of the Actor: Memoirs*, n.d.
— *To the Actor: On the Technique of Acting*, 1953
Dana, H. W. L., *Drama in Wartime Russia*, 1943
— *A Handbook on Soviet Drama*, 1938
Gorchakov, Nikolai A., *The Theatre in Soviet Russia*, trans. Edgar Lehram, 1957
Gray, Camilla, *The Great Experiment in Russian Art, 1863–1922*, 1962
Gregor, Joseph, and Fülöp-Miller, René, *The Russian Theatre: Its Character and History, with Special Reference to the Revolutionary Period*, trans. Paul England, 1930
Gyseghem, André Van, *Theatre in Soviet Russia*, 1943
Houghton, Norris, *Moscow Rehearsals: An Account of Methods of Production in a Soviet Theatre*, 1936
— *Return Engagement: A Postscript to 'Moscow Rehearsals'*, 1962
Kochno, Boris, *Diaghilev and the Ballets Russes*, 1970
Komissarzhevsky, Feodor, *Myself and the Theatre*, 1930
Komissarzhevsky, Viktor, *Moscow Theatres*, trans. Vic Schneierson and W. Perelman, 1959
Kott, Jan, *Theatre Notebook, 1947–1967*, trans. Boris Taborski, 1968
MacAndrew, Andrew R., *20th Century Russian Drama*, 1963
Macleod, Joseph, *Actors Cross the Volga: A Study of the 19th Century Russian Theatre and of Soviet Theatres in War*, 1946
— *The New Soviet Theatre*, 1943
— *A Soviet Theatre Sketch Book*, 1951

Markov, Pavel A., *The Soviet Theatre*, 1934
Mayakovsky, Vladimir, *The Complete Plays*, trans. Guy Daniels, 1968
Reeve, F. D., ed., *An Anthology of Russian Plays*, 2 vols., 1963
Sayler, Oliver M., *The Russian Theatre*, 1922
Slonim, Marc, *Modern Russian Literature: From Chekhov to the Present*,
    1953
    — *Russian Theatre from the Empire to the Soviets*, 1962
Taïrov, Alexander Y., *Notes of a Director*, trans. William Kuhlke, 1969
Varneke, B. V., *History of the Russian Theatre*, 1951
Yershov, Peter, *Comedy in the Soviet Theater*, 1956

### Leonid Andreyev

— *Plays*, incl. *The Life of Man*, trans. Clarence L. Meader and Fred
    Newton Scott, 1915
— *Life as Theatre: Five Modern Plays*, trans. Christopher Collins, 1973
— *He Who Gets Slapped*, trans. Gregory Zilboorg, 1922
— *Judas Iscariot*, trans. W. H. Lowe, 1910, Walter Morison, 1947
— *The Life of Man*, trans. C. J. Hogarth, 1915
— *Savva* and *The Life of Man*, trans. Thomas Seltzer, 1920
— *Letters of Gorky and Andreev, 1899–1912*, trans. Lydia Weston, ed.
    Peter Yershov, 1958

Gorky, Maxim, *Reminiscences of Leonid Andreyev, etc.*, trans. Katherine
    Mansfield and S. S. Koteliansky, 1931
— *Reminiscences of Tolstoy, Chekhov and Andreev*, trans. Katherine
    Mansfield, S. S. Koteliansky and Leonard Wolff, 1934
Kaun, Alexander S., *Leonid Andreyev: A Critical Study*, 1924
King, Henry H., *Dostoevsky and Andreyev: Gazers upon the Abyss*, 1936
Newcombe, Josephine M., *Leonid Andreyev*, 1972
Woodward, James B., *Leonid Andreyev: A Study*, 1969

### Nikolai Evreinov

— *The Theatre of the Soul* (play), trans. Marie Patapenko and
    Christopher St John, 1915
— *The Theatre in Life* (essays), trans. Alexander I. Nazaroff, 1927

### Vsevolod Meyerhold

— *Meyerhold on Theatre*, trans. Edward Braun, 1969

Alpers, Boris, *The Theatre as a Social Mask*, trans. Mark Schmidt, 1934
Gourfinkel, N., *Vsevolod Meyerhold — Le Théâtre théâtral*, 1963
Hoover, Marjorie L., *Meyerhold: The Art of Conscious Theatre*, 1974
Symons, James, *Meyerhold's Theatre of the Grotesque: The Post-
    Revolutionary Productions, 1920–1932*, 1973

**Yevgeny Vakhtangov**
— *The Vakhtangov School of Stage Art*, ed. Nikolai Gorchakov, 1961

Markov, Pavel A., *The First Studio: Sulerzhitsky, Vakhtangov, Chekhov*, trans. Mark Schmidt, 1934

Simonov, Ruben, *Stanislavsky's Protégé: Eugene Vakhtangov*, trans. Miriam Goldina, 1969

**Eugene O'Neill**
Alexander, Doris, *The Tempering of Eugene O'Neill*, 1962

Bogard, Travis M., *Contour in Time: The Plays of Eugene O'Neill*, 1972

Boulton, Agnes, *Part of a Long Story: Eugene O'Neill as a Young Man in Love*, 1958

Bowen, Crosswell and O'Neill, Shane, *The Curse of the Misbegotten: a Tale of the House of O'Neill*, 1960

Cargill, Oscar, Fagin, N. Bryllion and Fisher, William J., eds., *Eugene O'Neill and His Plays: A Survey of His Life and Works*, 1961

Carpenter, Frederick I., *Eugene O'Neill*, 1964

Chabrowe, Leonard, *Ritual and Pathos — The Theater of O'Neill*, 1976

Chothia, Jean, *Forging a Language : A Study of the Plays of Eugene O'Neill*, 1979

Clark, Barrett H., *Eugene O'Neill: The Man and His Plays*, rev. 1957

Dahl, Liisa, *Linguistic Features of the Stream of Consciousness Technique of James Joyce, Eugene O'Neill and Virginia Woolf*, 1970

Deutsch, Helen, and Hanau, Stella, *The Provincetown : A Story of the Theater*, 1931

Engel, Edwin, *The Haunted Heroes of Eugene O'Neill*, 1953

Falk, Doris V., *Eugene O'Neill and the Tragic Tension: An Interpretative Study of the Plays*, 1958

Frenz, Horst, *Eugene O'Neill*, trans. Helen Sebba, 1971

Gassner, John, *Eugene O'Neill*, 1960

— ed., *O'Neill: A Collection of Critical Essays*, 1964

Geddes, Virgil, *The Melodramadness of Eugene O'Neill*, 1934

Gelb, Arthur and Barbara, *O'Neill*, 1962

Gupta, P. C., *The Plays of Eugene O'Neill*, 1944

Leech, Clifford, *Eugene O'Neill*, 1963

Long, Chester C., *The Role of Nemesis in the Structure of Selected Plays by Eugene O'Neill*, 1968.

Mickle, Alan D., *Six Plays of Eugene O'Neill*, 1929

Miller, Jordan Y., *Eugene O'Neill and the American Critic: A Summary and Bibliographical Checklist*, 1962

Murthy, V. Rama, *American Expressionistic Drama* (analysis of *The Hairy Ape, The Glass Menagerie* and *Death of a Salesman*), 1970

Pendleton, Ralph, *The Theatre of Robert Edmond Jones*, 1958

Raleigh, John H., *The Plays of Eugene O'Neill*, 1965

Reaver, Joseph Russell, *An O'Neill Concordance*, 3 vols., 1969

Samborn, Ralph and Clark, Barrett H., *A Bibliography of the Works of Eugene O'Neill*, 1931

Scheibler, Rolf, *The Late Plays of Eugene O'Neill*, 1970

Sheaffer, Louis, *O'Neill: Son and Artist*, 1974
— *O'Neill: Son and Playwright*, 1968

Shipley, Joseph T., *The Art of Eugene O'Neill*, 1928

Skinner, Richard Dana, *Eugene O'Neill: A Poet's Quest*, 1935

Tiusanen, Timo, *O'Neill's Scenic Images*, 1968

Törnqvist, Egil, *A Drama of Souls: Studies in O'Neill's Super-Naturalistic Technique*, 1968

Valgemae, Mardi, *Accelerated Grimace: Expressionism in the American Drama of the 1920s*, 1972
— 'O'Neill and German Expressionism' in *Modern Drama,* September 1967

Winther, Sophus K., *Eugene O'Neill: A Critical Study*, rev. 1961

### Elmer Rice
— *The Living Theatre*, 1960
— *Minority Report: An Autobiography*, 1963

Durham, Frank, *Elmer Rice*, 1970

### Thornton Wilder
— 'Some Thoughts on Playwriting' in Auguste Centeno, *The Intent of the Artist*, 1941

Burbank, Rex J., *Thornton Wilder*, 1961

Edelstein, Jerome M., *A Bibliographical Checklist of the Writings of Thornton Wilder*, 1959

Goldstein, Malcolm, *The Art of Thornton Wilder*, 1966

Goldstone, R. H., *Thornton Wilder: An Intimate Portrait*, 1975

Grebanier, Bernard D. N., *Thornton Wilder*, 1964

### Sean O'Casey
*See* volume I

### Erwin Piscator
— Leo Tolstoy, *War and Peace*, adapted for the stage by Alfred Neumann, Erwin Piscator and Guntram Prüfer, trans. Robert David MacDonald, 1963
— *The Political Theatre: A History, 1914–1929*, trans. Hugh Rorrison, 1978

Innes, C. D., *Erwin Piscator's Political Theatre: The Development of Modern German Drama*, 1972

Ley-Piscator, Maria, *The Epic Theatre: Rebels, Guardians and Battles*, 1966
— *The Piscator Experiment: The Political Theatre*, 1967

Willett, John, *The Theatre of Erwin Piscator: Half a Century of Politics in the Theatre*, 1978

**George Grosz**
  — ed. Herbert Bittner, 1965
  — ed. Imre Hofbauer, 1948
  — *A Post-War Museum: Caricatures*, 1931
  — *A Little Yes and a Big No: The Autobiography of George Grosz*, trans. Lola Sachs Dorin, 1946

Lewis, Beth Irwin, *George Grosz: Art and Politics in the Weimar Republic*, 1971

**The Bauhaus**
Fitch, James M., *Walter Gropius*, 1961
Franciscono, Marcel, *Walter Gropius and the Creation of the Bauhaus in Weimar: The Ideas and Artistic Theories of Its Founding Years*, 1971
Gropius, Walter, *Bauhaus, 1919–1928*, ed. Herbert Bayer, 1938
  — *The New Architecture and the Bauhaus*, trans. P. Morton Shand; *et al.*, 1935
  — ed., *The Theatre of the Bauhaus*, trans. Arthur S. Wensinger, 1961
  — and Moholy-Nagy, László, eds., *The New Bauhaus Book*, 1939
Kostelanetz, Richard, ed., *Moholy-Nagy*, 1971
Moholy-Nagy, László, *The New Vision: From Material to Architecture*, trans. Daphne M. Hoffmann, 1932
  — *Painting, Photography, Film*, trans. Janet Seligman, 1969
  — *Vision in Motion*, 1961
O'Neal, William B., *Walter Gropius: A Bibliography of Writings by and about Walter Gropius*, 1966
Wengler, Hans, *Bauhaus*, 1969

**Bertolt Brecht**
  — *Parables for the Theatre (The Good Woman of Setzuan and The Caucasian Chalk Circle)*, trans. Eric and Maja Bentley, 1948
  — *Plays*, trans. Eric Bentley, 1944–
  — *Plays*, trans. James and Tania Stern, *et al.*, 1960–
  — *Collected Plays*, trans. John Willett and Ralph Manheim, 9 vols., 1971–
  — *The Caucasian Chalk Circle*, trans. James and Tania Stern, 1963
  — *The Days of the Commune*, trans. Clive Barker and Arno Reinfrank, 1978
  — *Galileo*, trans. Charles Laughton, *et al.*, 1957
  — *The Life of Galileo*, trans. Desmond I. Vesey, 1963
  — *The Good Person of Szechwan*, trans. John Willett, 1965
  — *The Measures Taken and Other Lehrstücke*, trans. Carl R. Mueller, 1977

— *The Mother*, trans. Steve Gooch, 1978
— *Mother Courage and Her Children*, trans. Eric Bentley, 1962
— *Mr Puntila and His Man Matti*, trans. John Willett, 1977
— *The Private Life of the Master Race*, trans. Eric Bentley, 1948
— *The Resistible Rise of Arturo Ui*, trans. Ralph Manheim, 1976
— *Saint Joan of the Stockyards*, trans. Frank Jones, 1956
— *The Threepenny Opera*, trans. Desmond Vesey and Eric Bentley, 1958

— *Brecht on Theatre: The Development of an Aesthetic*, trans. John Willett, 1964
— *Couragemodell 1949*, 1952
— *Helene Weigel: Actress*, trans. John Berger and Anna Bostock, 1961
— *The Messingkauf Dialogues*, trans. John Willett, 1965
— *Poems on the Theatre*, trans. John Berger and Anna Bostock, 1961

Benjamin, Walter, *Understanding Brecht*, trans. Anna Bostock, 1973
Demetz, Peter ed., *Brecht: A Collection of Critical Essays*, 1965
Dickson, Keith Andrew, *Towards Utopia: A Study of Brecht*, 1978
*The Drama Review*, 37 and 38, 1967–8
Eckardt, Walt von, and Gilman, Sander L., *Bertolt Brecht's Berlin*, 1975
Esslin, Martin, *Brecht: A Choice of Evils: The Man and His Work*, rev. 1971
Ewen, Frederic, *Bertolt Brecht: His Life, His Art and His Times*, 1967
Fuegi, John, *The Essential Brecht*, 1972
Gray, Ronald D., *Brecht*, 1961
— *Brecht the Dramatist*, 1976
Grossvogel, David I., *Four Playwrights and a Postscript*, 1962
Haas, Willy, *Bert Brecht*, trans. Max Knight and Joseph Fabry, 1970
Hill, Claude, *Bertolt Brecht*, 1975
Kenney, W., *The Major Plays of Bertolt Brecht*, 1964
Lyon, James K., *Bertolt Brecht and Rudyard Kipling: A Marxist's Imperialist Mentor*, 1975
Lyons, Charles R., *Bertolt Brecht: The Despair and the Polemic*, 1968
McLean, Sammy K., *The Bänkelsang and the Work of Bertolt Brecht*, 1972
Mews, Siegfried and Knust, Herbert, eds., *Essays on Brecht: Theater and Politics*, 1974
Milfull, John, *From Baal to Kenner: The 'Second Optimism' of Bertolt Brecht*, 1974
Morley, Michael, *Brecht: A Study*, 1977
Pascal, Roy, *Brecht's Misgivings*, 1978
Schoeps, Karl-Heinz, *Bertolt Brecht*, 1978
Spalter, Max, *Brecht's Tradition*, 1967
Szanto, George H., *Theater and Propaganda*, 1978
*Tulane Drama Review*, VI, September 1961
Völker, Klaus, *Brecht Chronicle*, trans. Fred Wieck, 1975
Weideli, Walter, *The Art of Bertolt Brecht*, 1964

Willett, John, *The Theatre of Bertolt Brecht: A Study from Eight Aspects*, 1959

*World Theatre*, 'Brecht, 1956–1966', vol. XV, nos. 3 and 4, 1966

Wulbern, Julian H., *Brecht and Ionesco: Commitment in Context*, 1971

## POST-WAR GERMAN DRAMA

Ber.edikt, Michael, and Wellwarth, George E., eds., *Postwar German Theater*, 1968

Hammer, Carl, ed., *Studies in German Literature*, 1963

Patterson, Michael, *German Theatre Today*, 1976

Scheffaur, Herman George, *The New Vision in the German Arts*, 1971

Shaw, Leroy R., ed., *The German Theater Today*, 1963

Subiotto, Arrigo Victor, *German Documentary Theatre*, 1972

Thomas R. Hinton, and Bullivant, Keith, *Literature in Upheaval: West German Writers and the Challenge of the 1960s*, 1974

## Max Frisch

— *Three Plays (The Fire Raisers, Count Oederland, Andorra)*, trans. Michael Bullock, 1962

— *Three Plays (Don Juan, or The Love of Geometry, The Great Rage of Philip Hotz, When the War Was Over)*, trans. J. L. Rosenberg, 1967

— *Four Plays (The Great Wall of China, Don Juan, or The Love of Geometry, Philip Hotz's Fury, Biography, a Game)*, trans. Michael Bullock, 1969

— *Don Juan, or The Love of Geometry*, trans. James L. Rosenberg, 1963

— *Sketchbook, 1946–1949*, trans. Geoffrey Skelton, 1977

— *Sketchbook, 1966–1971*, trans. Geoffrey Skelton, 1974

Petersen, Carol, *Max Frisch*, trans. Charlotte La Rue, 1972

Weisstein, Ulrich, *Max Frisch*, 1967

## Friedrich Dürrenmatt

— *Four Plays, 1957–1962 (Romulus the Great, The Marriage of Mr Mississippi, An Angel Comes to Babylon, The Physicists)*, with 'Problems of the Theatre', trans. Gerhard Nellhaus, et al., 1964

— *The Meteor*, trans. James Kirkup, 1973

— *The Physicists*, trans. James Kirkup, 1973

— *Play Strindberg: The Dance of Death Choreographed by Friedrich Dürrenmatt*, trans. James Kirkup, 1972

— *The Visit*, trans. Maurice Valency, 1960, Patrick Bowles, 1962

— *Writings on Theatre and Drama*, trans. H. M. Waidson, 1976

Arnold, Armin, *Friedrich Dürrenmatt*, 1972

Collins, Elly W., *A Bibliography of Four Contemporary German-Swiss Authors*, 1967

Peppard, Murray B., *Friedrich Dürrenmatt*, 1969

Urs, Jenny, *Dürrenmatt: A Study of His Plays*, 1973

**Peter Weiss**
— *Discourse on Vietnam*, trans. Geoffrey Skelton, 1971
— *The Investigation*, trans. Alexander Gross, 1966
— The *Marat/Sade*, trans. Geoffrey Skelton and Adrian Mitchell, 1965
— *Trotsky in Exile*, trans. Geoffrey Skelton, 1971
— 'The Material and the Models: Notes towards a Definition of Documentary Theatre', trans. Heinz Bernard in *Theatre Quarterly*, January 1971
Hilton, Ian, *Peter Weiss: A Search for Affinities*, 1970

**Heinar Kipphardt**
— *In the Matter of J. Robert Oppenheimer*, trans. Ruth Spiers, 1967

**Günter Grass**
— *Four Plays* (*Flood*, *Onkel, Onkel*, *Only Ten Minutes to Buffalo*, *The Wicked Cooks*), trans. Ralph Manheim and A. Leslie Wilson, 1968
— *The Plebeians Rehearse the Uprising*, trans. Ralph Manheim, 1967
— *Speak Out!: Speeches, Open Letters, Commentaries*, trans. Ralph Manheim, 1969

Cunliffe, William G., *Günter Grass*, 1969
Mason, Ann L., *The Skeptical Muse: A Study of Günter Grass's Conception of the Artist*, 1974
Miles, K., *Günter Grass*, 1975
Tank, Kurt L., *Günter Grass*, trans. John Conway, 1969
Williams, A., Leslie, ed., *A Günter Grass Symposium*, 1971
Yates, Norris W., *Günter Grass: A Critical Essay*, 1967

**Rolf Hochhuth**
— *The Representative*, trans. Robert David MacDonald, 1968
— *The Deputy*, trans. Jerome Rothenberg, 1965
— *Soldiers: An Obituary for Geneva*, trans. Robert David MacDonald, 1968

Bentley, Eric, *The Storm over 'The Deputy': Essays and Articles about Hochhuth's Explosive Drama*, 1964
Thompson, Carlos, *The Assassination of Winston Churchill (with Special Reference to 'Soldiers', etc.)*, 1969

**Peter Handke**
— *The Goalie's Anxiety at the Penalty Kick*, trans. Michael Roloff, 1977
— *Kaspar*, trans. Michael Roloff, 1972
— *Offending the Audience* and *Self-Accusation*, trans. Michael Roloff, 1971

  — *The Ride across Lake Constance*, trans. Michael Roloff, 1973
  — *A Sorrow Beyond Dreams: A Life Story*, trans. Ralph Manheim, 1972
  — *They Are Dying Out*, trans. Michael Roloff and Karl Weber, 1975

Hern, Nicholas, *Peter Handke: Theatre and Anti-Theatre*, 1971

**John Arden**
  — *To Present the Pretence: Essays on the Theatre and Its Public*, 1977

Brown, John Russell, *Theatre Language: A Study of Arden, Osborne, Pinter and Wesker*, 1973
Hayman, Ronald, *John Arden*, 1968
Hunt, Albert, *Arden: A Study of His Plays*, 1974
Leeming, Glenda, *John Arden*, 1974

**Edward Bond**
  — *Theatre Poems and Songs*, ed. Malcolm Hay and Philip Roberts, 1978

Coult, Tony, *The Plays of Edward Bond*, 1977
Hay, Malcolm and Roberts, Philip, *The Theatre of Edward Bond*, 1979
Oppel, Horst, and Christenson, Sandra, *Edward Bond's 'Lear' and Shakespeare's 'King Lear'*, 1974

# Index